We hope you enjoy this book. Please return or renew it by the due date.You can renew it at **www.norfolk.gov.uk/libraries** or by using our free library app. Otherwise you can phone **0344 800 8020** - please have your library card and PIN ready.You can sign up for email reminders too.

14/8/18 29		

NORFOLK COUNTY COUNCIL
LIBRARY AND INFORMATION SERVICE

Why Knowledge Matters

Rescuing Our Children from
Failed Educational Theories

E. D. Hirsch, Jr.

Harvard Education Press
Cambridge, Massachusetts

Second Printing, 2017

Paperback ISBN 978-1-61250-952-5
Library Edition ISBN 978-1-61250-953-2

Library of Congress Cataloging-in-Publication Data

Names: Hirsch, E. D. (Eric Donald), 1928- author.
Title: Why knowledge matters : rescuing our children from failed educational
    theories / E. D. Hirsch, Jr.
Description: Cambridge, Massachusetts : Harvard Education Press, [2016]. |
    Includes bibliographical references and index.
Identifiers: LCCN 2016012718 | ISBN 9781612509525 (pbk.) | ISBN 9781612509532
    (library edition)
Subjects: LCSH: Education, Elementary—Curricula. | Educational change. |
    Educational accountability. | Education—Standards. | Education—Aims and
    objectives. | Educational innovations.
Classification: LCC LB1570 .H57 2016 | DDC 372—dc23 LC record available at
    https://lccn.loc.gov/2016012718

Published by Harvard Education Press,
an imprint of the Harvard Education Publishing Group

Harvard Education Press
8 Story Street
Cambridge, MA 02138

Cover Design: Wilcox Design
Cover Image: iStock.com/jamesjames2541
The typefaces used in this book are Adobe Garamond Pro and Futura.

To Polly
In Memoriam

The new education created a kind of church that paralyzed pedagogical research. It produced curious aberrations like "spontaneity," which supposed that the child's brain is like a ball of string that the teacher should help to unwind. In reality, each generation educates and forms each new generation. Education opposes the elemental biological instincts of nature; it is a struggle against nature, to dominate it and produce the "up-to-date" person of the new era.

—Antonio Gramsci, *Prison Notebook 1* (1929)

We have prided ourselves in the past on being "child centered," on dealing with "the whole child," when, as a matter of fact, we have persistently slighted the kind of wholeness which is necessary in order to live intelligently and effectively in our present complex social order.

—Boyd H. Bode, *Progressive Education at the Crossroads* (1938)

One sees immediately that this kind of system will diminish acquisition of specific knowledge by taking refuge in vague evocations of vague general skills.

—Marc Le Bris, *Et vos enfants ne sauront pas lire . . . ni compter* (2004)

A major factor is the development of the proper mental representations . . . they are very "domain specific," that is, they apply only to the skill for which they were developed . . . This explains a key fact about expert performance in general: there is no such thing as developing a general skill.

—Anders Ericsson and Robert Pool,
Peak: Secrets from the New Science of Expertise (2016)

CONTENTS

The Tyranny of Three Ideas

THE FRENCH CONNECTION

These chapters are organized around six well-recognized educational frustrations in the United States: the over-testing of students, the fade-out of preschool gains, the narrowing of the elementary curriculum, the low verbal scores of high school graduates, the lack of progress in closing achievement gaps between social groups, and the tribulations of the Common Core initiative. These problems have defied solution—but not primarily from lack of will or money, or from poverty or the shortcomings of teachers. They resist solution because they cannot be solved under the reign of the faulty ideas that caused them to arise. My longstanding view is that idea change will be the most effective educational reform of all.

Those who know my past work may wryly object: *you* haven't changed *your* ideas for thirty years.[1] That's both true and false. The basic themes are largely unchanged. The hedgehog knows one big thing.[2] I am still chiefly motivated by the social injustice of our dominant theories and their unwitting destruction of the American dream. On that topic, I say with Matthew Arnold: "Charge once more then, and be dumb."[3] The reader will find the theme of equalizing opportunity a leitmotif of the book in all of its chapters. Against the tide of sociological and genetic explanations of achievement gaps, the path-breaking work of researchers like John Guthrie, Betty Hart, and Todd Risley should have made it unnecessary to assert once more at this late date that the achievement gap is chiefly a knowledge gap and a language gap. It can be greatly ameliorated by knowledge-based schooling.

Once the centrality of knowledge (not general "skills") is fully grasped by educators and the wider public, the right to parity of knowledge among young pupils will come to be understood as a civil right. This book continues my earlier theme that only by systematically imparting to *all* children the knowledge that is commonly possessed by successful citizens can all children gain the possibility of success—"success" understood as becoming a person with autonomy, who commands respect, has a communal voice that can write and speak effectively to strangers, can earn a good living, and can contribute to the wider community.

But this book is far more than a rehash of former ideas about what is needed for equality of educational opportunity. New findings in cognitive science have helped me gain greater clarity and depth. The book has benefited from my clearer understanding that the key task facing our elementary schools is to shift our emphasis from the goal of self-realization to the goal of community—from child-centeredness to community-centeredness. No sensible person would disparage either goal. But the emphasis must shift decisively for the sake of the community *and* the individual child.

With this book, I hope to reach readers who had barely come into the world when my *Cultural Literacy* was published in 1987. We live in an era of new possibility. We have witnessed the failures of recent educational theories, but at the same time we have also witnessed marvelous new modes of spreading knowledge—should better theories be adopted. The great physicist Max Planck, the progenitor of quantum physics, despaired of ever convincing his fellow professors to change their views. He looked to the young. He complained that professors never change their minds; they die off, and the younger generations take their places.[4] And indeed some young scholars have recently begun to invoke my name in the blogosphere as a kind of superannuated mascot. The context and the national mood have changed. Heterodox ideas that were rejected a few years ago might now be granted a new hearing after the frustrations of current reform efforts.

The most immediate impetus for this book is my discovery of shocking new evidence on these issues from France. There is a radical streak in French thinking that encourages sudden and complete national transformations—the French Revolution being only the most famous instance. For many decades the French elementary school had been the pride and the terror of the young, with every child, rich or poor, having to undergo the very same rigors under the same national curriculum. The egalitarian impulse of this uniformity was expressed early in the Revolution by Condorcet in his 1790 pamphlet *A Common Education for Children*, and re-expressed in the nineteenth century by Jules Ferry, the founder of modern education in France. In his 1883 letter to teachers, Ferry urged them to teach "that knowledge which is common to all and indispensable to all." Those sentiments were reconfirmed in 1977 by the centrist president of France, Giscard d'Estaing, who stated, "The defining and acquiring of the very same knowledge by all French children, who from now on will all go to the same primary school, and the same middle school, will be an essential element in the unity of French society, and in the reduction of inequalities of opportunity."[5] But in 1989, the bicentenary of the French Revolution, France passed a radical new education law—the *loi Jospin*—requiring all elementary schools to cease teaching the national curriculum and begin teaching locally determined curriculums, individualized further by a special emphasis in each school, called its *projet*. This drastic change had been silently prepared for during two decades of teacher indoctrination within French education schools into American-style progressive education. The new law reflected those ideas: more attention was to be paid to the individuality of each student, to his or her native abilities, interests, and home culture. To compensate for all this novel heterogeneity, the unifying emphasis was to be on general skills such as "critical thinking" and "learning to learn." In other words, in 1989 the French decided to completely Americanize their school system overnight.[6]

The sudden organizational change introduced by the new *loi Jospin* instituted a vast natural experiment. Which mode of schooling would work better and more fairly: the community-centered and knowledge-centered mode of the past, or the child-centered and skills-centered mode of the future? The broad new law enabled the Ministry of Education to conduct longitudinal studies comparing the effects of the communal elementary curriculum before 1989 with those of the individualized, skill-centered curriculums that followed.[7] It was a natural experiment because many key elements of French education, other than curriculum, stayed constant over time. Teacher quality stayed the same by objective measures. School buildings and budgets did not change significantly. The superb French preschools were not covered by the new law, and stayed essentially the same. The most decisive change was in the curriculum and pedagogy of the elementary school.[8]

Ministry researchers have now analyzed the results over twenty years among various demographic groups. Their data was gathered from ten-year-olds at the end of primary school. They reported an astonishingly steep decline in achievement in each demographic group—children from the homes of wealthy executives and professionals, children from the middle classes, children from various other well-defined demographic groups including the unemployed, with their ever-higher percentages of immigrants from North Africa. Each group was academically harmed by the new system, and the harm became ever greater as one went down the economic scale. The children of the unemployed declined most of all. Achievement decreased. Inequality increased dramatically.

The massive declines that occurred at the very top among children of white-collar workers and high-level professionals and executives cannot be blamed on the influx of North African immigrants, as some American experts are inclined to say.[9] Why are American education experts inclined to blame immigrants for the French decline? They know little about the details. This book contains the first extensive discussion in English.[10] It would certainly be reasonable to blame a big influx of immigrants for a decline in the *average* of French test scores. But a fair-minded person would hardly blame the children of immigrants (who suffered most of all from the new regime) for a big decline among the children of native-born executives and professionals.

An entire educational theory has been put to the test in France, with incontrovertible results that everyone in France now calls "the crisis of the school." The American-style, individualistic theory yielded far worse results for every demographic group. As a tenacious theory holder myself, I can't blame educational experts for seeking an alternative explanation. But I'd like to believe that I'd be willing to give up my theory rather than resist such decisive evidence. Compare this French research with our own best research—for example, our longitudinal analyses conducted by the National Assessment of Educational Progress (NAEP). That research is based on a sample size of eighty-seven hundred students from an age cohort of six million. The French longitudinal studies are based on a sample size of forty-two hundred students from an age cohort of one million. By those numbers alone, even without the refinements introduced by French and American experts, the two samplings yield very similar levels of confidence.[11] I will use the details of the French results throughout this book, and devote chapter 7 to an analysis of the French experience.

THE SILVER AGE

Underlying these chapters is a historical narrative—the story of a decline in American schooling to be followed by a renewal, if we are wise.[12] The practical policy changes that I will advocate are founded on ever-stronger scientific evidence and an ever-clearer picture of that historical narrative. It is folly to pretend that our historical mistakes are irrelevant to the problems we currently confront and the policies we need to put in place. There were past causes of our educational decline, and there are still-current reasons why we have not recovered from it. The verbal scores of our seventeen-year-olds have stayed low and largely unchanged ever since NAEP began recording them in 1971. But by that year, the decline was already in full swing. The ideas that caused the decline still remain in full force today. These historical facts, coupled with recent cognitive research, will add credibility to the view that our educational fate is largely controlled by ideas rather than by irresistible social forces.

The decline in our student test scores in the 1970s was caused by the dominance of conceptions that had begun to take over American public schools starting in the 1920s. The ideas did not complete their conquest right away. As late as the 1940s and 1950s the public education of the United States, for all its racial and social shortcomings, scored near the top among nations in both achievement and equality.[13] Moreover, as John Bishop has long pointed out, the education gap between blacks and whites had narrowed steadily until recent decades.[14] But between 1960 and 1980 American academic scores fell rapidly *at all grade levels*—more than 25 percent of a standard deviation, a big drop for large populations.[15] The verbal scores on the SAT fell 50 percent of a standard deviation! Those puzzling disasters caused the Reagan administration to convene a national commission that produced the famous alarmist report *A Nation at Risk* (1983). When the French later adopted those same ideas they suffered a decline of similar massive proportions. Our *"Nation at Risk"* of 1983 became their *"Crise de l'école"* of 2007.

The belief that there was once a golden age of American education is scorned by educational historians. They are of course right. But they concede that there was indeed a large test score decline—over a quarter of a standard deviation—in grade school and high school test scores between 1960 and 1980.[16] As this book shows, the decline occurred at all grade levels among all demographic groups.[17] Thereafter, in our own times, test scores have remained low and stable within a tenth of a standard deviation.[18] So let's call the higher-scoring era before the decline— the 1940s and 1950s—a "silver age." The subsequent test-score decline and its causes are important to know about, acknowledge, and rectify.

The chief cause of the decline was the nationwide adoption of a set of inadequate ideas.[19] Though the ideas were partly true and beneficial, they were also partly incorrect and harmful because they neglected the communal dimension of education in favor of individualistic child-centered development. The French have now repeated our experiment in educational individualism in a more concentrated and better-documented form.

Here are the three basic ideas that depressed education in both nations:

- Early education should be appropriate to the child's age and nature, as part of a natural developmental process.
- Early education should be individualized as far as possible—to follow the learning styles and interests of each developing student.
- The unifying aim of education is to develop critical thinking and other general skills.

The new policies that I (and others) recommend are based on a different set of ideas and emphases that are more consistent with current cognitive science, developmental psychology, and social science:[20]

- Early education should be chiefly communal—focused on gaining proficiency in the language and the conventions of the public sphere.
- Every child in each locality should study basically the same early curriculum.[21]
- The unifying aim of early schooling is autonomy and equality of opportunity: to impart to every child the enabling knowledge that is possessed by the most successful adults in the wider society.

No doubt our current principles—natural development, individuality, and critical thinking—will continue to be regarded with favor by many people. The ideas are attractive. They counsel empathy with the individual child, and they claim to comport with the child's natural development. Naturalists will of course concede that communal knowledge is important, while communalists will concede that nature cannot be thwarted.[22] That agreement sounds very promising. But emphasis is critical, and foes of inequality like me caution that if an advantaged child at age seven knows certain things without harm, then it *cannot* be inherently harmful or "developmentally inappropriate" for a disadvantaged child also to know those very same things at the same age.

And the communalist will further caution that there is a big distinction between accommodating shared curriculum topics for each child as the best schools do in the community-centered schools of Finland and Japan, and devising different curriculum topics for different children as we and the French now do in the child-centered school. Elementary school is a time for building socialization as the only means through which individuality can ultimately express itself. Children need to master the shared conventions of the standard language and of social interaction.[23] They need to learn the shared knowledge and vocabulary of the nation, the shared spelling, pronunciation, and other conventions in the public sphere of the grown-up world. Only full membership in the tribe leads to individuality, as G. H. Mead profoundly observed.[24]

Caricatures of the communal view dismiss it as "lock-step education," "indoctrination," "one size fits all," "the factory model of schooling." But I will show in chapter 1 that, paradoxically, it is the naturalistic and individualistic view that has turned schools into soulless test-prep factories, with endless practice of strategies and skills, as they desperately attempt to overcome children's lack of enabling knowledge—a lack partly induced by an individualized rather than a communal curriculum. I hope that my recommendation of a shift in emphasis from individual to community will not be misunderstood as lack of affection and solicitude for the individual child. On the contrary, our assumptions about how children learn have led to instruction that is far from child centered, and that perpetuates inequality among children from different backgrounds.

Old-timers in education reform might suppose that when I use the phrase *communal curriculum* I am implicitly promoting the Core Knowledge Sequence for the early grades—a coherent, cumulative, and content-specific curriculum guide offered for free on the Core Knowledge website.[25] New readers need to be aware that I started the Core Knowledge Foundation back in 1986. After four years of labor and consultation the Foundation produced the Core Knowledge Sequence for preschool through grade eight in 1990. How it was created is described in the introduction to the Sequence.[26] That Sequence proposes to teach everyone the enabling knowledge (including up-to-date, multicultural knowledge) shared by the most successful adults in America today.

But the promotion of any single curriculum guide has been far from my mind, and is not a motivation for this book. Rather, this book's aim is to promote the general communal principle. The Core Knowledge Sequence has always been offered as just one exemplification of the more general idea that there exists a de facto public commons that enables our national language to be deployed effectively, and that every child in a democracy should have access to that shared, enabling knowledge and language. No matter what the home culture might be, every child deserves to become proficient in the taken-for-granted knowledge of the standard language. The main mission of the Foundation is to serve that general communal idea, which can be realized by different curricula that vary in interesting ways.[27]

I have recently begun to name that general principle "communal knowledge." Whole nations have successfully followed communal knowledge in the form of national curriculums that have a similar communal purpose. No large nation has done so more successfully than France did from 1975 to 1985, when it had the highest achieving, most egalitarian school system of any large country in Europe. After 1989, the French in effect duplicated the American decline of the 1960s and 1970s by means of the same basic change in guiding ideas. The Americans, of course, never had a national curriculum like the French, but the schools of most American districts did in earlier days have a strong communal purposiveness.[28]

Education without an explicit communal purpose is unlikely to achieve a communal result that offers every child economic competence and entrée into the public sphere. The adoption of more communal ideas than those that now prevail in the United States and France could offer both nations a new birth of fairness and excellence.

TWO CHEERS FOR THE THREE PREVAILING IDEAS

Any idea such as developmental appropriateness and child-centeredness that keeps earning the adherence of teachers all over the world must have a strong tincture of truth. That's surely the case with two out of the three guiding ideas of current American elementary education: naturalism and individualism. But the third guiding idea, which one could call *skill-centrism*—the aim of imparting critical-thinking skills and similar general skills like problem solving—is altogether problematic.

Naturalism and individualism go together.[29] They arose from a belief that nature, as the earthly manifestation of a beneficent God, is unerring and benign. Hence the natural growth of a child is an instance of God unfolding His purposes in the world. (The root meaning of *development* is "unfolding.") So nature cannot betray. It is the true guide that will lead to physical and spiritual health. And since each child's nature is special and different, following nature will mean adjusting education to the naturally developing interests and abilities of each child. I have adopted the phrase *providential individualism* to capture this point of view. I have found it useful in describing the widely held faith that if we let affairs take their natural course we are in the hands of a benign Providence, so all will be well, even optimal, in education. The source of this faith is the unspoken assumption that a benevolent purpose is present in Nature, and will assure a beneficent result.[30]

This naturalism plus individualism is emotionally compelling. It is reinforced by our love and solicitude for young children. It leads to empathetic teaching, since love and concern for the individual child is a more sustaining and agreeable mode of instruction than fear. Of course, naturalism and individualism have no monopoly on a loving and empathetic teaching, which is in all cases the best pedagogy for young children.

But an implication has been drawn from providential individualism that has created a serious problem for American education. Naturalism and individualism, beyond implying a loving pedagogy, have also been taken to imply—and this is a fatal weakness—a *curriculum* that arises from the child's individual abilities and temperament: "different strokes for different folks," "multiple learning styles," "multiple intelligences." American school mission statements usually proclaim that the school will provide an education tailored to the individuality of each child.

But I will argue, with support from developmental psychology, that equating early education with the metaphor of individual "development" is misleading; that so-called "unnatural" social impositions are the most natural things in the world; that school systems with so-called "lockstep" curricula in the early grades (Finland, Japan) have very child-happy effective schools that score near the top in international studies.[31] Indeed, international studies have shown that a differentiated curriculum is harmful to achievement and equity.[32] To make the emphases and content of the child's early schooling largely dependent upon the child's uniqueness is an idea unsupported by developmental psychology.[33] The evidence for individual learning styles is weak to nonexistent.[34] And in practice the individualizing of the elementary-school classroom has led to fragmentation of the curriculum.

This fragmentation is defended and supposedly turned to benefit by a third doctrine: that the goal of education is the imparting of general skills like critical thinking, creative thinking, problem solving, and cooperative thinking. But reality has not accepted this hopeful idea about skills, and recent cognitive science has been fatal to it.[35]

Educational individualism has always required the general-skills idea. To make thinking skill the ultimate goal renders irrelevant the fragmenting of school topics that must occur when the teacher is urged to tailor the curriculum to the uniqueness of each child.[36] Current thinking holds that the fragmenting of the early curriculum will work out in the end, because the goal is not chiefly to impart the specific content of the curriculum but rather to train the mind to critical thinking and problem solving for any content. This connection between the general-skills idea and individualism in the curriculum was the subject of a 1910 book by John Dewey called *How We Think*. He says this in his preface: "Our schools are troubled with a multiplication of studies, each in turn having its own multiplication of materials and principles. Our teachers find their tasks made heavier in that they have come to deal with pupils individually and not merely in mass. Unless these steps in advance are to end in distraction, some clue of unity, some principle that makes for simplification, must be found. This book represents the conviction that the needed steadying and centralizing factor is found in adopting as the end of endeavor that attitude of mind, that habit of thought, which we call scientific."[37]

This statement has seismic importance for understanding recent American educational history. By no means should Dewey be scapegoated for articulating this central idea in 1910. He is stating a practical necessity: if the content of the curriculum is to be scattered and diversified by "dealing with pupils individually and not in mass," then some further principle is needed to guide instruction and lend unity to the experience of the individual student. That can only be accomplished, Dewey says, by making critical thinking rather than mere facts the proper goal of child-centered education. Dewey is right about the structure of the difficulty, and he has also identified what may be the most recalcitrant political problem in American education—that few dare challenge our emphasis on individualism.

The proposal that critical thinking is an aim that unifies fragmented and individualized schooling made sense in Dewey's era, when scientists had incorrect ideas about skill development. But research on thinking skills is now a well-developed field, and its findings are fatal to this crucial refuge of current educational theory. Here's a brief summary of findings from a recent book on the subject, *The Cambridge Handbook of Expertise and Expert Performance* (2006): "Research clearly rejects the classical views on human cognition in which general abilities such as learning, reasoning, problem solving, and concept formation correspond to capacities and abilities that can be studied independently of the content domains."[38]

Modern cognitive psychology holds that the skills that are to be imparted to a child by the school are intrinsically tied to particular content domains. This is called the *domain specificity* of skills. Thinking skills cannot readily be separated from one subject matter and applied to other subject matters. The domain specificity of skills is one of the firmest and most important determinations of current cognitive science. The Cambridge compendium from which the passage is taken is *not* called *A Handbook of Skills*, which could imply all-purpose skills. It's called a *Handbook of Expertise*, implying that the basis of skills is specific domain knowledge. Think of how significantly our view of schooling might change if suddenly policy makers, instead of using the term *skill*, had to use the more accurate, knowledge-drenched term *expertise*.[39]

Dewey's worry was well founded. The principle of unity was devised to support child-centered education and keep it from ending in fragmentation. Yet that single, overarching skill doesn't exist. Believing in that mirage has actually resulted in the "distraction" Dewey feared. It has induced an ever-more-desperate effort to gain nonexistent skills through soul-deadening drills. A benign child-centeredness coupled with a faulty theory about general skills has led us to a child purgatory of skill drills. These have produced neither good skills nor good scores on the ever-looming tests.[40] Those distracting tests will be the subject of my first chapter.

CHAPTER ONE

The Invalid Testing of Students

THE STORY OF ASTERISKS

This chapter will be critical of our current reading tests. The public agrees: a furious outbreak of antitesting sentiment has broken out over the nation, with parents and students boycotting required tests. This kind of activism seems misguided. Tests have always been necessary in education. A better solution is to make tests fewer and better. There's just one way to do that—to base them on well-defined, knowledge-based curriculums. There is no other way of making tests fair and productive. It's also the only way to make schools excellent and fair. That will be the long and short of this chapter.

If one had to choose a single measure of the academic quality of a school system, the average reading score of its graduating seventeen-year-olds would serve. Verbal scores at that age predict students' college and career readiness and their later economic success.[1] A technically valid reading test that accurately predicts a student's ability to comprehend diverse texts will also, self-evidently, predict that student's ability to comprehend both oral and written language. A reading test is a test of general knowledge and vocabulary; it gauges a student's ability to operate effectively within the public sphere. Since a valid reading test probes a student's degree of initiation into the public sphere—a fundamental aim of education—any policy that lowers or neglects to improve test scores in reading is a failed educational policy.

In math, in contrast to reading, American scores for seventeen-year-olds have been stable for many years. While it's disappointing that math scores at age seventeen haven't improved markedly, at least they haven't gone down, as reading has. For, in 2012, a decade after the test-intensive No Child Left Behind Act (NCLB) went into effect, the reading scores of seventeen-year-olds came in significantly lower than they had been in 1988 before NCLB was enacted. Figure 1.1 is taken from the 2012 long-term trend report of the National Assessment of Educational Progress (NAEP)—the latest nationwide analysis we have for long-term reading trends among seventeen-year-olds. It shows a statistically significant drop of three points in the reading abilities of seventeen-year-olds, as compared with scores in 1988, 1990, and 1992.

Notice the asterisks in the chart—a valuable feature of the long-term reports. They denote a statistically significant difference (lower or higher) between earlier results and those of 2012. Whether a prior score gets an asterisk is the result of data analysis that goes deeper than the surface averages.

This 2012 result for seventeen-year-olds seems particularly anomalous, because that same cohort four years earlier, at age thirteen, had attained the topmost score that NAEP had ever recorded—higher than any prior cohort except 1992, with which it was tied. We see such anomalies across the years. Thirteen-year-olds have made steady progress in reading, but the scores of seventeen-year-olds have remained flat. No college, or employer, or nation much cares how well students did at age thirteen if by age seventeen their verbal abilities are worse than they were before the new reforms were instituted.

Could our recent high-stakes testing regimens have contributed to this disappointment? Students who were seven in 2002 would have been old NCLB hands in 2012. They would have experienced almost ten years of high-stakes testing in reading under NCLB. Those testing regimens will have deeply affected what schools and teachers taught them in their early grades. Yet all that intensive test prep did not, in the end, help their mature reading. Since their age group scored significantly better before

FIGURE 1.1 Trend in National Assessment of Education Process reading average scores for nine-, thirteen-, and seventeen-year-old students

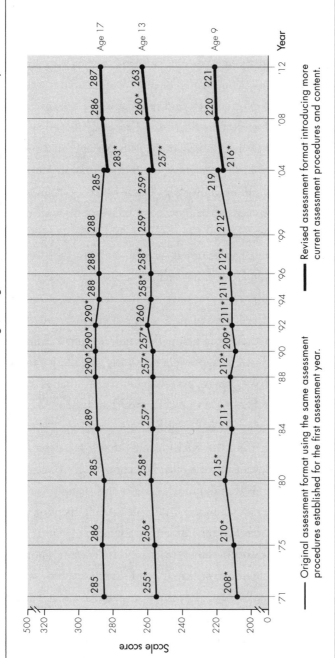

Source: US Department of Education, Institute of Education Sciences, National Center for Education Statistics, NAEP, various years, 1971–2012 Long Term Trend Reading and Mathematics Assessments

*Significantly different (p < .05) from 2012

the reign of NCLB, we might ask: Could the well-meant tests have actually promoted long-range educational harm?

That's a troubling thought to me, since the testing regimens have clearly helped improve the mechanics of early reading (that is, the ability to sound out fast and effortlessly)—an important gain. Younger students can now decode texts with more fluency and accuracy than they did before NCLB. Because of that the reading gaps between ethnic and racial groups have narrowed in those years, when fluency is an important part of the score. But, alas, those equity gaps begin widening again between ages thirteen and seventeen, when knowledge and vocabulary are decisive.

One might first be inclined to blame the high schools for undoing what the grade schools had achieved in reading. But as a specialist in reading comprehension I know that such an accusation is incorrect. The vocabulary size of seventeen-year-olds is not determined at age seventeen, or sixteen, or fifteen. It's a plant of slow growth that is determined by the knowledge that has been gradually acquired from a child's overall experience from birth to age seventeen. Early schooling can play a major role in vocabulary growth, especially for disadvantaged children, and some forms of schooling do much better than others. While current schooling in early grades has improved the sounding-out aspects of reading, we can infer from the NAEP results that it has depressed the vocabulary sizes of seventeen-year-olds. My conclusion, which sets the stage for this chapter, is that too much time is now being spent on test preparation in early grades, and too little time is being spent on gaining the wide knowledge required for a broad vocabulary.

To summarize the story of the asterisks: high-stakes tests, upon which the lives of students, teachers, principals, and superintendents now anxiously depend, became by slow degrees a feature of American education in the decades after *A Nation at Risk* of 1983. That report showed that American public schooling had declined in quality during the 1960s and 1970s. After the governors' education summits of 1989 and 1996, all but one state (Iowa) developed grade-by-grade reading standards on which schooling in the state would be based. Then the No Child Left Behind

Act, which was signed into law in 2002, mandated standards and yearly high-stakes testing in reading and math based on the state standards.

I mentioned one consequence of these reforms: an improvement in the teaching of decoding (i.e., turning written marks into sounds and words). That in turn should also have produced an improvement in reading comprehension, and it did so for undemanding texts on everyday topics in the early grades. But it has not produced improvement in the reading comprehension of more demanding texts on more demanding topics. I was mentally prepared to look for this anomaly because a number of schools told me, after high-stakes reading tests came into effect under NCLB, that they could no longer teach history and the arts. They now were being made to teach "reading" instead, with a strong emphasis on test preparation. Their higher-ups were under the impression that intense classes devoted to "making inferences" and "finding the main idea" would improve reading scores more effectively than learning about ancient Egypt or the solar system or the reasons why Nevada has just as many senators as New York.

By an iron law of unintended consequences, the low scores of seventeen-year olds were probably caused by misguided, time-consuming efforts to raise scores. This chapter will predict that the high-stakes reading tests that accompany the new Common Core State Standards are going to have a similar nugatory or depressing effect on the reading competence of our seventeen-year-olds of the future—unless we take strong steps to make knowledge acquisition a chief goal of schooling starting in the earliest grades.

HOW CURRENT HIGH-STAKES READING TESTS AFFECT SCHOOLING

Till that which suits a part infects the whole,
And now is almost grown the habit of my soul.[2]

As I write now, the too-frequent testing of students in American schools has at last become a subject of concern and even self-criticism by the US Secretary of Education and the President of the United States.[3] An

October 2015 report from the US Department of education states: "Done poorly, in excess, or without clear purpose, [tests] take valuable time away from teaching and learning, draining creative approaches from our classrooms. In the vital effort to ensure that all students in America are achieving at high levels, it is essential to ensure that tests are fair, are of high quality, [and] take up the minimum necessary time."[4]

Secretary Duncan and President Obama had probably been prompted by an alarming study recently produced by the Council of Great City Schools reporting that each student in the large cities now takes about eight standardized tests in a year. Just sitting for the tests takes over 4 percent of school time.[5] But that's only the tip of the iceberg. The school time usurped by sitting for the tests has not been the most disabling consequence of over-testing.

In language arts, for instance, schooling has been bent out of shape and made boring and ineffective by test-prep exercises in skills like "summarizing" and "questioning the author." Yearly focusing on these exercises is supposed to improve students' comprehension of any text. And indeed students do show an *initial* positive effect from practicing finding the main idea. But their progress quickly reaches a limit and then halts. We know this from various metastudies as well as from the stagnant NAEP data.[6] Drills in formal comprehension skills have not raised mature reading scores; rather, they have taken up a lot of class time that could have been devoted to knowledge building.

Nervous superintendents and principals have insisted on these test-prep programs, acting on the theory that strategies are the keys to reading comprehension. Teachers have been told that subject matter is secondary, that they can teach strategies just as well with *Tyler Makes Pancakes!* or *Stupendous Sports Stadiums* as with a biography of Abraham Lincoln. This emphasis on technique at the expense of building subject-matter knowledge in early grades produces students who at age seventeen lack the knowledge and vocabulary to understand the mature language of newspapers, textbooks, and political speeches.

They can read *Stupendous Sports Stadiums*, but not *The Economic Consequences of the Peace*.

How can a teacher know whether too much time is being spent on practicing formal skills like summarizing? The basic principle is straightforward. We know that the skill of reading comprehension in any given case depends more on relevant knowledge than on formal strategies.[7] Once briefly learned, the strategies will take care of themselves.[8] When a school follows a coherent and specific knowledge-based curriculum, and makes that knowledge the chief object of tests, then we can make sure that students are advancing in the substantive knowledge set forth in that unit. The basic principle for schools to keep in mind is that, once decoding has been mastered, the "skill set" that most reliably determines reading comprehension is relevant knowledge. The wise teacher and school will therefore create better summarizers and main-idea finders automatically if they focus on knowledge building—a happier, more productive, and far less boring focus for schooling.

TECHNICALLY VALID, EDUCATIONALLY INVALID READING TESTS

There is no way of predicting the topics that will appear in passages on current reading tests. That is an expected, even obvious, characteristic of an all-purpose sort of reading test, which is, of course, the only sort that could possibly be fair when the topics of the school curriculum are unknown. That structure automatically forces schools to focus on strategies and skill drills, rather than on systematic knowledge acquisition. The unpredictability of the test topics forces the schools to stress the externalities of test taking and of meaning guessing.

Despite their indifference to the school curriculum, the better reading tests are technically reliable and valid. The Gates-MacGinitie reading test, the Iowa Test of Basic Skills, and the National Assessment of Educational Progress are good measures of the average reading abilities of large groups of students. Gates and Iowa each show strong internal correlations between different forms of the same test (about .9 on a scale in which 1 is perfect). That means that the tests are reliable and that the same person will score about the same on different forms of the test. Well-established tests like Gates, Iowa, and NAEP are also technically valid. They really do roughly test a student's average reading ability. They show a fairly high correlation with other reliable tests (about .7 to .8).[9] All these well-calibrated tests are probing the average level of a person's reading fluency and vocabulary size. Such well-established tests are the means by which we confidently know about the average reading abilities of our students. That's how we know that our nine- and thirteen-year-olds have improved, and our seventeen-year-olds have not.

But these tests as currently used by the schools have hindered, not raised, mature reading skills. That is to say, they are technically valid but educationally invalid, a distinction brought into prominence by the important testing theorist Samuel Messick.[10] His phrase was "consequential validity." His key insight was that the technical validity of a test is of little value by itself. The point of educational testing is to help education. If a test actually hurts education, then it is ultimately *invalid* for schooling. Current reading tests, by giving the misleading appearance that they are testing generalized how-to skills that don't exist, cause schools to engage in self-defeating practices. They are consequentially invalid.

That defect lies less in the tests themselves than in the scientific shortcomings of the empty state standards on which they are based. The standards have misled the schools regarding the nature of reading skill. By focusing on main-idea finding, the standards promote the myth that there is a generalized main-idea-finding skill, which if practiced and developed will enhance reading ability. But if that were so for mature reading ability, the current generation of students would be performing better on the tests, for they have all been well schooled in main-idea finding.[11]

The test questions about main ideas and inference making imply the misleading message that they are probing all-purpose strategies and skills of predicting, summarizing, and "inferencing." But they are doing no such thing. The tests are probing knowledge and vocabulary. To the credit of the No Child Left Behind Act, the new focus on decoding has been highly productive for the mechanics of early reading. But once decoding has been mastered and fluency attained, relevant knowledge becomes the chief component of reading skill. Every cognitive scientist specializing in the subject would agree with that statement.[12] No doubt unintentionally, and with inadequate knowledge of psycholinguistics, the test makers are implying a lie. By the form of their questions they suggest that they are probing formal skills. But, no matter how well trained students become in main-idea finding, the student with the smaller relevant vocabulary and knowledge is the one who will fare worse on the test.

That parents and teachers alike are demonstrating against the new tests, and opting out of them, is a pretty good indication that they have correctly concluded that something has gone wrong. The opt-out protest against excessive testing and test preparation has spread to significant numbers of districts.[13] Teachers have complained that test preparation has narrowed elementary schooling—pushing out social studies, science, and the arts. Parents have complained of the neglect of history and the arts, adding that constant testing has placed unfruitful stress upon their children. This from a recent story in the *New York Times*:

> Parents railed at a system that they said was overrun by new tests coming from all levels—district, state and federal. Some wept as they described teenagers who take Xanax to cope with test stress, children who refuse to go to school and teachers who retire rather than promote a culture that seems to value testing over learning.
>
> "My third grader loves school, but I can't get her out of the car this year," Dawn LaBorde, who has three children in Palm Beach County schools, told the gathering, through tears. Her son, a junior, is so shaken, she said, "I have had to take him to his doctor." She added: "He can't sleep, but he's tired. He can't eat, but he's hungry." One father broke down as he said he planned to pull his second grader from school. "Teaching to a test is destroying our society," he said.[14]

Such protests need to be channeled into productive directions. They can be.

DEFECTIVE READING STANDARDS

State tests in math have been based on specific content standards, but the situation is vastly different in reading, where test makers in their own defense can rightly say: "How is it possible to create a test that encourages the imparting of concrete knowledge when the *standards* on which the tests must be based are content free and encourage the teaching and testing of general skills?"

The makers of standards have decided that while it is politically feasible to create a definite content guide in math, fierce controversy would follow if they created a definite content guide in reading. So, American makers of standards have felt themselves forced into content cop-outs in reading. Current math standards are much better guides for teachers and test makers than are current standards in reading.

I'll illustrate this with a few examples comparing the two kinds of standards. Here are some current Texas math standards concerning fractions. They are clear and content-specific, and build on one another from year to year.[15]

> **Grade 3:** "Explain that two fractions are equivalent if and only if they are both represented by the same point on the number line or represent the same portion of a same size whole for an area model."
> **Grade 4:** "Represent a fraction a/b as a sum of fractions 1/b, where a and b are whole numbers and b > 0, including when a > b."
> **Grade 5:** "Represent and solve addition and subtraction of fractions with unequal denominators referring to the same whole using objects and pictorial models and properties of operations."

Here are some Texas reading standards concerning informational texts. They are neither specific nor progressive. Wary of *specifying* either topics or texts, the standards makers focus on the skill of finding the main idea.

Grade 3: "(A) identify the details or facts that support the main idea."
Grade 4: "(A) summarize the main idea and supporting details in text in ways that maintain meaning."
Grade 5: "(A) summarize the main ideas and supporting details in a text in ways that maintain meaning and logical order."
Grade 6: "(A) summarize the main ideas and supporting details in text, demonstrating an understanding that a summary does not include opinions."
Grade 7: "(A) evaluate a summary of the original text for accuracy of the main ideas, supporting details, and overall meaning."
Grade 8: "(A) summarize the main ideas, supporting details, and relationships among ideas in text succinctly in ways that maintain meaning and logical order."

My own state of Virginia is more forthright about the inherent repetitiousness and content emptiness of its reading standards:

Grade 2: "g) Identify the main idea."
Grade 3: "g) Identify the main idea."
Grade 4: "d) Identify the main idea."
Grade 5: "g) Identify the main idea."
Grade 6: "g) Identify the main idea."
Grade 7: "g) Identify the main idea."
Grade 8: "h) Identify the main idea."

Nor are the new Common Core State Standards in English language arts exempt from this same lack of real progression or content:

Grade 3: "Determine the main idea of a text; recount the key details and explain how they support the main idea."
Grade 4: "Determine the main idea of a text and explain how it is supported by key details; summarize the text."
Grade 5: "Determine two or more main ideas of a text and explain how they are supported by key details; summarize the text."
Grade 6: "Determine a central idea of a text and how it is conveyed through particular details; provide a summary of the text distinct from personal opinions or judgments."

Grade 7: "Determine two or more central ideas in a text and analyze their development over the course of the text; provide an objective summary of the text."

Grade 8: "Determine a central idea of a text and analyze its development over the course of the text, including its relationship to supporting ideas; provide an objective summary of the text."

Such standards are not just empty; they are deeply flawed. The notion that skill in finding the main idea can take the place of content is worse than empty; it's actively misleading. There is *no* reliable main-idea-finding skill. If readers understand a passage, they will reliably answer the test question about the main idea. If they don't understand the passage, they won't. Moreover, in good, complex writing there isn't usually a single main idea. What's the main idea of the Pledge of Allegiance? Aren't there at least three?

These empty standards were created out of political expediency. The makers of standards and tests have built up an artificial construct, politically painless for the makers of standards and of tests, but based on a faulty and unproductive picture of reading comprehension.

EMPTY SKILL STANDARDS CAUSE TESTS TO PRETEND TO PROBE EMPTY SKILLS

Test makers have dutifully followed the standards makers, presenting reading comprehension as an all-purpose skill like decoding. Since it isn't, the current standards and tests have created a fictional alternative universe in our classrooms. In the real world, an ability to comprehend a piece of writing depends on one's having the knowledge and vocabulary relevant to that passage. If the school does not teach students the knowledge and vocabulary they need to understand the passages on the test, then the test is unfair as a measure of what the school has successfully taught. (Yes, that means that the current tests *are* unfair, a subject I take up in more detail in the next chapter.) The test simply reflects the knowledge and vocabulary that students have picked up from *all* sources. A school test that does not accurately measure the matter that a student has been taught in school is an unfair test of schooling. Such tests cannot measure whether students have mastered the knowledge and vocabulary that the school *has* taught. Test makers cannot know what knowledge and vocabulary schools have taught. The standards do not state them. Nor do the schools know what knowledge they are supposed to teach. The language arts standards do not specify content.

Under these circumstances, a method has had to be devised that *seems* to make these inherently unfair tests fair. That method has been to define reading ability as a set of strategies, and then to create test items that appear to probe those strategies. The external forms of the test questions are constructed to give the impression that they are testing the various skills that were being practiced so endlessly in test-prep classes. Here are some "stems" taken from released items on the Texas tests. Their form indicates misleadingly that strategy expertise rather than specific knowledge is being probed.

> The main purpose of paragraphs 7 and 8 is to [main idea]
> The author wrote this selection most likely to tell the reader that [main idea]
> Which sentence expresses the main idea of paragraph 2?
> The reader can infer that Chu is concerned about Dusty's habit because she ["inferencing skills"]—
> Which of these best summarizes the selection? [main idea]
> The reader can infer that the author's attitude toward Dusty is one of [inferencing skills]
> The reader can infer that the long life span of bristlecone pines is mainly a result of
> What is the main idea about bristlecone pine trees presented in the selection?
> The organization of paragraphs 2 through 4 contributes to the author's main idea by[16]

Answering such items is easy for students who understand the passages, but not for those who don't—no matter how many drills in comprehension strategies the students had before the test. A child who has the relevant domain-specific background knowledge will understand the passage and get the right answer fast, without conscious strategizing. A child who does not have enough relevant knowledge will have to use special glosses in the test and consciously apply strategies; that child won't finish the test and will get many answers wrong.

In sum, to mask the inherent unfairness of these tests, a fictitious alternative world has been devised in which metaskills look as important as knowledge and vocabulary. The substance of the reading curriculum had been described in the content-evading state standards as consisting of all-purpose techniques like inference making, predicting, and main-idea finding.[17] With such standards, all-purpose techniques *became* the curriculum, and reading tests that asked main-idea questions seemed to be "standards-based" and "curriculum-based." Despite their unfairness (especially to disadvantaged students), they have thus been made to appear to be fair.

But aren't there in fact such all-purpose strategies? And won't learning them improve reading? The evidence is summarized in a recent review article by Willingham and Lovette, "Can Reading Comprehension Be Taught?"[18] They answer: "Not really." Lessons in reading strategies offer an initial score boost for test taking, but are quickly learned; they plateau fast, and they don't have to be practiced. Their utility ceases after about ten lessons. Two weeks on comprehension strategies is optimal. There is no practical utility after that. Huge amounts of time are being wasted. Worse, making young students become highly self-conscious about applying strategies distracts their attention and degrades their performance.[19]

The "accountability" principles based on this misconceived scheme have not induced real progress in higher-level reading competence. If progress is to be made, an alternative structure of teaching and testing reading will have to be instituted. The structure will need to become more like that of math, with specific content in the standards and the curriculum, and with tests based on that content. Perhaps the Common Core State Standards will ultimately move in that direction.

THE NEW COMMON CORE READING TESTS

I will devote a later chapter to the Common Core initiative. The responses of many schools to the new Common Core tests can already be seen. Many school administrators are responding to them as unproductively as they did to prior high-stakes tests under No Child Left Behind. Schools are intensively practicing techniques like making inferences and finding the main idea, and now they are also practicing close reading and complexity managing in preparation for the new versions of high-stakes reading tests that, as before, pretend to test the general skills of close reading, complexity managing, and main-idea finding—general skills that do not exist.[20]

It's with some reluctance that I end this chapter with a criticism of the reading tests being designed by the test consortia for the Common Core State Standards. The Common Core Standards themselves are in some respects superior to most standards for individual states. They contain the welcome admonition that the standards can only be properly implemented through a "curriculum intentionally and coherently structured to develop rich content knowledge within and across grades."

Those precious words are to my mind the most important ones in the new standards. But there is little sign that districts or states are paying much attention to them, for that general admonition is not a standard that can readily be coordinated with the items on a reading test. In the absence of specific grade-by-grade content guidance, the makers of the Common Core tests are placed in the same position as the makers of the previous tests that were based on state standards. The new test items will need to probe main-idea-finding skills and inference-making skills, as before, and now they will probe close-reading skills as well.

So, despite the expense and computerized novelty of the new reading tests, it will be hard for them to be any more educationally productive than the tests they are displacing. The new reading tests, like the old ones, will need to be based upon main ideas and inference making. The new kind of inference is to be connected with an additional inference strategy called "close reading," according to the standard: "Read closely to determine what the text says explicitly and to make logical inferences from it."[21]

The sample items made public by the new test consortia for the Common Core amply fulfill my prediction that the tests will stress both main-idea finding and close reading. Those are the Common Core standards that are the most content-free, strategy-like elements. Thus PARCC, one of the two test consortia, has developed two-part questions, the first part gauging comprehension of a passage, the second part demanding a close reading and "logical inference" to justify the student's answer. Here's a multiple-choice example from PARCC for grade 3:

> **Part A:** What is the meaning of the word "avenge" as it is used in the story?
> **Part B:** Which detail from the story best supports the answer to Part A?

This structure is perfectly reasonable, so long as schools can be brought to realize that the secret to answering such questions will not be hours of practice of "inferencing skills" and "close-reading skills," but can only be answered through the student's prior relevant knowledge of the words and the topics.

The "Smarter Balanced" consortium puts the two-part structure into a single question, such as this one for grade 4:

> Read the sentence from the text. Then answer the question.
>
> > "Nanodiamonds are stardust, created when ancient stars exploded long ago, disgorging their remaining elements into space."
>
> Based on the context of the sentence, what is the most precise meaning of disgorging?
>
> > scattering randomly
> > throwing out quickly

spreading out widely
casting forth violently

No doubt, the student is meant to answer the question in the following way after close reading: "Let's see. The stars exploded—a violent event. *Disgorge* must mean that the bits were cast forth violently. So 'casting forth violently' must be right."

But this very example illustrates the inadequacy of the suggestion that close reading consists in "making logical inferences." Readers who already know the word *disgorge* know that the sense of the word can make *all* the proffered meanings correct—that the nanodiamonds were "thrown out quickly" or "spreading out widely" or "scattering randomly," in addition to the supposedly correct answer. The right answer depends on what we decide the passage is meant to emphasize: whether the result of the action or the action itself. I'd guess that the author meant to imply something not all that violent, since *disgorge* is usually not used to describe violent, explosive action. Anyway, logical acumen will not decide that particular issue. Either full credit should be given to *all* the nanodiamond answers, or the question should simply be nullified. It's based on a wrong theory of inference and reading comprehension.[22]

Much more interesting is the phrase "remaining elements" in the passage. The phrase is ignored in the question, and is far less susceptible to close reading and logical analysis. One could close-read "remaining elements" all day long and come up empty or wrong. Its meaning requires specific background knowledge of a highly sophisticated kind (probably already provided earlier in the source), which most fifth graders will normally lack. It's conveniently ignored in the test item, but well illustrates how knowledge trumps "skill" every time. Knowledge is by far the most promising avenue to carry us out of the reading slump we are in. It is by far the most promising way to advance reading skill for all, and narrow the reading gap between demographic groups.

I recently did a *Huffington Post* piece with the following subtitle: "The Common Core Tests in Language Arts Will Soon Be Coming to

Your Child's School. Tell Your Local Superintendent: 'Don't Worry. Students Will Ace Those Tests If They Learn History, Civics, Literature, Science, and the Fine Arts.'"[23] The comments by teachers on my piece were sobering. They carried this message: "Well, Mr. Hirsch, that's all very well, but if you were in my shoes you'd realize that your job would be at stake if you did not do test preparation as instructed."

Quite right.

Parents and teachers need to get vigorously involved in the testing issue, not just to complain about stress, but to change the character of reading tests and reading instruction. Those wasted hours ought to be spent on far more interesting and rewarding subject matters that will build up knowledge and vocabulary, and therefore induce greater reading competence. A positive aim of parents should be to demand knowledge-building substance in their child's language arts classroom, to replace exercises that are knowledge-displacing, soul-deadening, and essentially useless after ten lessons. When a student gains a real advance in substantive knowledge, it's the best long-range comprehension strategy.

Yes, we do need tests. Yes, students, teachers, and schools should be accountable. But accountable for what? The standards have not told them with adequate specificity or adequate insight into the actual nature of reading. Only standards that are guides to curricular content can be foundations for fair and productive tests. Policy makers who stress accountability are right to do so. But they must come to understand that without definite content standards, there can be no fair and productive accountability in reading. The authorities can't just wave their hands and imperiously demand better reading without stating what children need to learn and schools need to teach in a given grade in order to gradually reach that long-range goal.

Accountability hawks need to show more grit in creating state and local curriculum standards. They should join with parents and teachers to help define the grade-by-grade knowledge that all the children in their local purview should gain. A more responsible view of accountability would recognize that providing definite content standards is the only policy that can possibly lead to productive and fair reading tests.

Meanwhile, a positive intermediate step would be to remove the punitive threats to teachers attached to our educationally invalid reading tests—the subject of the next chapter. If the high stakes were removed, sensible teachers and principals would be willing to pay more attention to the long arc of knowledge acquisition, which is the route to producing good readers and competent high school graduates. To sum up: This chapter has shown that recent, technically valid reading tests make fraudulent claims if they are used to gauge what the schools have taught. And they have had a disastrously narrowing effect on schooling. They are "consequentially invalid." They do more harm than good. Their defects could be repaired if the tests were to be based on good, knowledge-based standards. Such reconstituted standards and tests would do far more good than harm—an outcome that will require greater courage and scientific insight than has been shown in the recent past.

CHAPTER TWO

The Scapegoating of Teachers

TEACHER QUALITY OR THEORY QUALITY?

People who emphasize teaching quality and the central importance of teachers are right to do so. Where some go wrong is in thinking that teacher quality is an innate characteristic. The effectiveness of a teacher is not some inherent competence, as the phrase *teacher quality* suggests. Teacher effectiveness is contextual. I have witnessed over and over that in a coherent school most teachers can become highly effective. My defense of teachers in this short chapter is not a defense of irresponsible, lazy, or nonperforming teachers. Like most people I am opposed to any policy that would impede the dismissal of demonstrably nonperforming teachers. Children and the community come first. Most teachers agree.[1]

Why has the topic of teacher quality suddenly reached such a crescendo? Education reform has been on the national agenda since 1983, the year of *A Nation at Risk*. Only in the last few years has the teacher quality issue risen to the top. I think it may be reform fatigue, possibly desperation. We are blaming teachers because of our disappointments with the results of our reforms.

The "back-to-basics" and "whole-school reform" strategies disappointed. The state standards movement and the No Child Left Behind law have left high school students just about as far behind as they were before the law was instituted. Charter schools, despite their laudable triumphs, are highly uneven in quality.[2] Their overall results are not much better than those of regular schools.[3] When favored educational ideas do not pan out as hoped, reformers understandably think: "The flaw is not in my theory; it must lie in poor implementation (i.e., it must be the fault of the teachers)."

But the most likely cause of disappointing results from the various reforms is that they have been primarily structural in character. They have not systematically grappled with the grade-by-grade specifics and coherence of the elementary school curriculum. Educational success is defined by what students learn—the received curriculum. Not to focus on the particulars of the very thing itself has been an evasion that is not of the teachers' doing. The underlying theory of the reforms (reflected in state reading standards) has been that schools are teaching skills that can be developed by any suitable content. That mistaken theory has allowed the problem of grade-by-grade content to be evaded. It was that fundamental mistake about skills that has allowed teachers to be blamed for fundamental failures—the failures of guiding ideas, not of teachers.

Elementary school teachers are people who for the most part love children, who want to devote their lives to children's education, but find themselves stymied and frustrated in the classroom. They apply the notions received in their training, and do what they are told to do by their administrators, under the ever-present threat of reading tests that do not actually test the content that is being taught. Under these extremely unfavorable conditions of work, it's no wonder that teacher unions have focused on bread-and-butter concessions—and have pushed back against punitive but unproductive reforms. When the classroom, which should be a daily reward, becomes a purgatory, one turns to contract stipulations.

It's true that in the United States, there has been a deep problem with teacher preparation for more than half a century. We have a system that, according to teachers themselves, does not prepare them adequately for classroom management or the substance of what they must teach.[4] Yet, as I will illustrate with the example of France, even with a staff of well-trained, highly qualified, and well-educated teachers, the schools can suddenly decline when a substantive curriculum is abandoned, and fallacious ideas about skills begin to dominate. Therefore my counterthesis to the blame-the-teachers theme is blame the ideas—and improve them.

When an early Core Knowledge school was started in Fort Myers, Florida, in 1990—the Three Oaks School—I visited the school and its upbeat, excited teachers. They were intimidated that first year by having to teach things they did not know themselves. The next year when I visited, they were enthusiastically explaining that they were learning these things along with the children. They started having a signal success in improved morale of students and teachers, and improved test outcomes. If "teacher quality" is to be judged by outcomes, their quality had suddenly risen.

The "quality" of a teacher is not a permanent given. Within the content-incoherent American primary school, it is impossible for a superb teacher to be as effective as a merely average teacher is in the content-cumulative Japanese elementary school. For one thing, the American teacher has to deal with big discrepancies in student academic preparation, while the Japanese teacher does not. In a system with a specific and coherent curriculum, the work of each teacher builds on the work of teachers who came before. The three Cs—cooperation, coherence, and cumulativeness—yield a bigger boost than the most brilliant efforts of teachers working individually against the odds within a topic-incoherent system. A more coherent system makes teachers better individually and hugely better collectively.

American teachers (along with their students) are, in short, the tragic victims of inadequate theories. They are being blamed for intellectual failings that permeate the system within which they must work. The real problem is idea quality, not teacher quality. The difficulty lies not with the inherent abilities of teachers but with the theories that have watered down their training, and created an intellectually chaotic school environment based on developmentalism, individualism, and the skills delusion. The complaint that teachers do not know their subject matter would change almost overnight with a more specific curriculum and with less evasion about what the subject matter of the curriculum ought to be. Then teachers could prepare themselves more effectively, and teacher training could ensure that teacher candidates have mastered the content they will be responsible for teaching.

Those who hope to find amelioration of the "teacher quality problem" through the use of computers and "blended learning" may be fostering yet another skills delusion. Technological fixes haven't worked in the past. Computers seem to work best in helping older students learn specific routines. No doubt well-thought-out computer programs can help teachers do their work, especially for teachers in their first years. But there are *inherent* limitations. For example, after decades of work and billions spent, computers cannot accurately translate from one language to another. Probably they can't even in theory.[5]

Such current limitations do not lend confidence that they can transform primary education. Young students rely on an empathetic personal connection that not even our most advanced computer-adaptive programs can deliver. This is not to say that computers have no important place; it is to say that their place is supplemental, not transformative. They need to be used in support of teachers under a coherent cumulative curriculum. Computers cannot magically replace the hard thinking and political courage needed to create one.

A FATAL FLAW IN VALUE-ADDED TEACHER EVALUATION

In the face of unfair scapegoating, teachers have understandably become demoralized by being constantly blamed for failures not their own. Here is the new conventional wisdom about teachers taken from the nonpartisan policy magazine *Governing* of June 13, 2013:

> The research is clear: Teacher quality affects student learning more than any other school-based variable (issues such as income and parental education levels are external). And the impact of student achievement on economic competitiveness is equally clear. That's why

it's so disturbing that in 2010, the SAT scores of students intending to pursue undergraduate education degrees ranked 25th out of 29 majors generally associated with four-year degree programs. The test scores of students seeking to enter graduate education programs are similarly low and, on average, undergraduate education majors score even lower than the graduate education applicant pool as a whole. Education schools long have accepted under-qualified students, then offered them programs heavy on pedagogy and child development and light on subject-matter content.

This scientific-sounding comment is incorrect from the start. The assertion that "Teacher quality affects student learning more than any other school-based variable" is not footnoted. According to two summaries of research by Dr. Russ Whitehurst, a better curriculum can range from being slightly to dramatically more effective than a better teacher.[6] That's not surprising when you consider that the curriculum is what teachers teach and what students are supposed to learn. Teachers are not to blame for ideas and curricula that are inherently inadequate.

Some policy makers have recently decided that the way to improve teacher effectiveness is to institute value-added teacher evaluations as part of a system of incentives, rewards, and sanctions, potentially including dismissal. The theory is that such a system will energize teachers, boost their performance, and bring highly qualified people into the profession. Some jurisdictions, including Chicago, Washington, DC, and New York City, have instituted value-added measures (VAMs) of teacher effectiveness, based on formulas like:

$$Ag = \theta\, Ag\text{-}1 + \tau j + S\phi + X\,\gamma + \varepsilon$$

where Ag is the achievement of student i in grade g (the subscript i is suppressed throughout); $Ag\text{-}1$ is the prior year student achievement in grade $g-1$; S is a vector of school and peer factors; X is a vector of family and neighborhood inputs; θ, ϕ, and γ are unknown parameters; ε is a stochastic term representing unmeasured influences; and τj is a teacher fixed effect that provides a measure of teacher value added for teacher j.[7]

Statistical analysis is indispensable, but can be very misleading unless supported by a valid theory of the underlying causes of the results. But, in fact, the results themselves cry out that something is amiss, since the value-added principle has exhibited far more uncertainty and variability for language arts than for math. That's not surprising. In math, as I showed in chapter 1, there is a high correlation between what is supposed to be taught and what is actually tested, whereas that's not true for the language arts curriculum and current reading tests.

Two false assumptions underlie applying VAMs to reading tests. The first mistake is the assumption that reading comprehension is a general skill. The second is the assumption that existing reading tests can accurately gauge the value that has been added by the teacher to reading comprehension from one year to the next. Our current reading tests cannot in fact reliably and validly gauge the value the teacher has added.

Here's why. Scores on reading tests reflect knowledge and vocabulary gained from all sources. Advantaged students are constantly building up academic knowledge from both inside and outside the school. Disadvantaged students gain their academic knowledge mainly inside school, so they are gaining less academic knowledge overall during the year, even when the teacher is conveying the curriculum effectively. This lack of gain outside the school reduces the chance of low-socio-economic-status (SES) students showing a match between the knowledge they gained in school during the year and the knowledge required to understand the individual test passages.[8] The tests are fairly accurate means of gauging a student's general knowledge, but they have no way of indicating the sources of students' general knowledge. Not being curriculum based, they cannot be an accurate means of testing how well the particular knowledge in the school curriculum has been imparted. The implicit assumption that "general reading skill" is itself the content of the curriculum is a technical mistake and an incorrect assumption. Once that mistake has been exposed, the validity of the VAM projects in language arts collapses. Any judge in a lawsuit, properly alerted to the falsity of their assumptions, should rule against the fairness of value-added measures for rating language arts teachers. These reading tests may be roughly accurate measures of a student's average reading abilities, but, not being curriculum based, they *cannot* be accurate measures of school-driven gains in a given year.

In short, there's no valid or reliable way of determining what test-relevant verbal knowledge is school based and what is not. How could it be determined? *Tests that are curriculum-blind cannot gauge how well a curriculum has been imparted.* VAMs in reading are thus inherently unfair both to low-SES students and to their teachers. Reading tests at best are 70 percent accurate at the individual level.[9] The inherent uncertainty of the school-based contribution to a student's reading scores between one year and another must reduce the validity of test inferences even more. Statistical manipulations cannot make a test reveal what it cannot reveal in principle. The whole VAM effort in reading will need to meet this objection head-on in order to establish the effort's validity. It's hard to see how it could do so. It has not done so thus far.

Another evil consequence of test-based evaluations of language arts teachers has been the demoralization of millions of public school teachers.[10] But merely avoiding unfairness to teachers does not solve the underlying problem, which is rooted in incorrect ideas that teachers themselves have often not cast aside. Like their administrators, they have been indoctrinated in individualistic, child-centered education. My plea to teachers—for the sake of their students, and themselves—is to rebel against the skills delusion; to insist on coherent and cumulative multiyear content; then cooperate and consult.

That teachers cannot be replaced by computers doesn't mean that individual teachers should not be replaced. The problems with teacher evaluations that I have discussed in this chapter concern the unreliability of the value-added measures of teacher performance in language arts, but do not apply to estimates of poor teaching based on clear evidence. There is no reason that teachers should enjoy special job protections at the expense of children. Tenure protections at universities were instituted to avoid censorship of opinion. But even in universities there is no tenure protection for "failure to meet a specified norm of performance or productivity"; nor should there be for schoolteachers.[11]

If I were a principal in a primary school I'd spend my money on teachers, on their ongoing development, and on creating conditions in which the work of teachers in one grade supports the work of teachers in the next, and in which teachers would have time to consult and collaboratively plan. One especially vivid story about collaboration in the Japanese elementary school was told to me directly by the late Professor Harold Stevenson, who studied Asian schools. He had observed the event in a fourth-grade math class. A student was having grave difficulty with a math problem and its concepts. After allowing the student to work on it for a short time, the teacher quietly made a surprising analogy with the student's daily experience as a way of dealing with the problem. The student's face brightened, and he instantly began to solve the problem.

After the class, Stevenson went to the teacher to congratulate her (in perfect Japanese) on the most remarkable bit of teaching he'd ever witnessed. The teacher shook her head: no, it wasn't her brilliance that produced the result, and from her desk drawer she took out a handbook that teachers had cooperatively compiled. "Here it is," she said. "It's suggested as a good tack to try when you run into that situation." The incident illustrated how good teaching can often depend more reliably on the coherence of the wider system, and the cooperation it brings, than on virtuoso performances. Schooling takes twelve years. Its success depends on slow but sure progress, not bursts of brilliance— welcome as those are when talented teachers inspire a whole class.

CHAPTER THREE

Preschool and the Persistence of Fadeout

THE PUZZLE OF FADEOUT

Amana is a bright four-year-old African American daughter of a single mother. She is attending a good Head Start program. By June, she is scoring higher on an IQ test than Candice, who is an equally bright girl in similar circumstances who had scored the same as Amana last October, but didn't attend Head Start. Preschool has given Amana a head start.

The IQ test they took has a large vocabulary component. Amana now knows more things and more words than Candice, and that's one reason Amana scores better on the IQ test.[1] Amana is off to a better start in kindergarten and first grade. But fast-forward now to second grade. The two girls are now making the same low score on the test batteries. Amana's academic advantage has disappeared. We know that it did not inevitably disappear, because preschool in other nations and other circumstances has a permanently positive effect. Yet that good result occurs rarely in the United States. Here, fadeout is a usual frustration. A puzzle.

Federal reports going back several decades show that in the United States preschool academic benefits for disadvantaged children fade out after two years of primary school. After first or second grade there is no detectable difference in IQ, vocabulary size, or academic achievement between disadvantaged children who attended Head Start and disadvantaged children who did not.[2] Similar null results were recently reported in Georgia and Oklahoma.[3] Fadeout is usually explained by the observation that out-of-school life experiences of disadvantaged children have drowned out their in-school experiences—a self-evident truth.

But that explanation does not tell us why some American elementary schools and some whole nations have been able to overcome preschool fadeout. In them, Amana keeps her initial head start and extends it. One finds in the United States happy exceptions to fadeout.[4] Add to them the vast natural experiment recorded in detail in France between 1987 and 2012. In the 1980s, research proved that French preschools had not only avoided fadeout but by age ten had greatly narrowed the achievement gap.[5] But after the radical *loi Jospin* ("Jospin law," described in chapter 7) went into effect in 1990, the excellent French preschools suddenly ceased narrowing the achievement gap. Preschool fadeout had come to France.[6] The excellent preschools had not changed; only the elementary schools had. That is a crucial piece of evidence in the preschool fadeout puzzle.

Another piece of evidence about the critical importance of the primary grades for disadvantaged students is a second fadeout phenomenon that occurs in later grades as students approach high school. Chapter 1 showed that in recent years, the whole cohort of students who have improved their verbal scores at age thirteen show no advance over prior years by the time they reach age seventeen. The progress they made as thirteen-year-olds has disappeared. So there is fadeout after middle school as well as after preschool. Moreover, there's another form of late fadeout: the achievement gap between groups at age thirteen has widened at age seventeen. There is an equity fadeout too, with gaps widening after middle school.[7]

We now have good evidence that all of these versions of fadeout can be blamed on the incoherence of an elementary curriculum that fails to build upon the gains of preschool and also fails to lay further groundwork for future success. After elementary school, the test results that appear at age thirteen, after students have experienced a knowledge-diluted curriculum, did not fully reflect progress in knowledge and language. Children's scores on a reading test in elementary school don't capture all of the verbal progress children may or may not have made in the primary grades. Test makers deliberately limit the range of knowledge and vocabulary tested. Students' reading and writing abilities lag behind actual speaking and listening abilities until about grade 7.[8] Elementary school test scores in reading cannot reveal the true extent of knowledge and vocabulary differences among students—and are thus inadequate predictors of test scores at age seventeen.

Recent work on vocabulary growth in relation to test scores has shown what has always been inferred by specialists: there is a latency period in a child's knowledge of a word.[9] His or her past experiences of the word have formed associations and narrowed possibilities, paving the way to more confident word knowledge later on. Many of these latencies are not reflected in the results of standard reading and vocabulary tests.[10] The verbal tests that we use in school to gauge student progress are not highly detailed. Elaborate procedures are required to test a person's latent knowledge of new words.[11] This means that the foundation for future verbal growth by students in grades K–4 is not readily apparent from test scores during those early grades. But the soil is tilled, and the seeds are planted for later growth; they just aren't yet visible. The lack of readily available evidence about latent knowledge and incipient vocabulary in grades K–4 yields an incomplete picture of the critical importance of those grades. Latent knowledge may be invisible to tests at ages nine and thirteen, but it is critical—and becomes potent—in the years that follow.

A thesis of this chapter, along with important policy implications, is that while good preschools and high schools are extremely important, the practical nub of the fadeout problem at *all* ages is the elementary curriculum. This finding should influence the debate over whether it makes sense to spend a lot of public money on preschools. It does make sense—but only if a good preschool is followed by a good primary school that consolidates and extends the early boost. The substance of what is learned in grades K–5 will determine whether disadvantaged students will start catching up to their peers, whether middle school students will be ready for high school, and whether high school students will be ready for colleges or careers. A communal-knowledge-based preschool should be followed by a communal-knowledge-based elementary school. All three forms of fadeout could then be forestalled, as this chapter will show.

FADEOUT WITH "DIRECT INSTRUCTION" AND "SUCCESS FOR ALL"

Among programs designed to overcome disadvantage in the early grades, two stand out as the most fully studied and successful: Direct Instruction and Success for All (SFA). Both programs are highly scripted modes of teaching early literacy. No educational programs in the United States have likely been more fully documented as being effective early reading programs. Both Direct Instruction (which had its origins in the 1960s and 1970s) and Success for All (which took hold in the 1980s) were scripted programs; that is, they defined rather closely what the teacher was to do and say in order to bring elementary school children to competence in reading. They both succeeded better than more naturalistic approaches in bringing children to elementary competence in sounding out printed text.

In the case of Direct Instruction, the chief evidence came from one of the most ambitious longitudinal studies we ever carried out: Project Follow Through. That huge study, reported on in the 1970s and 1980s, tried to ascertain which kind of instruction in preschool and the earliest grades would have the strongest positive effects on disadvantaged students.[12]

In Project Follow Through, several early literacy methods were put to the test. Developmental, natural-growth, Reggio Emilia–style preschools had the least effect; deliberate, step-by-step skill instruction had the greater positive effect on both attainment and on the attitude of the young students. And, among the step-by-step approaches, leading all the rest on all measures was Direct Instruction. Few schools paid attention to these results, however, since step-by-step skill instruction was felt to be childhood-killing and developmentally inappropriate—an early illustration of the invincibility of developmental ideas about early childhood.

But then in 1982 a study appeared that confused the whole picture. It was clear from Project Follow Through that natural-development approaches had not succeeded with disadvantaged students. But now it became clear that the intensive-skills approach of Direct Instruction had not succeeded either. Project Follow Through evaluations had stopped at grade 3. What happened to Direct Instruction students in grades 5 and 6? They still decoded a bit better than disadvantaged students. But they could not understand what the texts were saying any better than students who had not had Direct Instruction—a null effect in the end. The phenomenon of fadeout had struck even Direct Instruction.[13]

Fast-forward to September 2015. The evaluative results have now begun to come in for the model programs funded under President Obama's Investing in Innovation program. Success for All, after many years of proving its high effectiveness, had given us every reason to hope that such a well-thought-out and well-tested reading-skills program would show its high value in overcoming disadvantage. Not so. When scaled up so that credible real-world evaluations can now be made, it has been found that Success for All does not avoid fadeout. The 2015 report says: "Students in the average SFA school did not outperform their counterparts in the average control group school on tests of reading fluency or comprehension."[14] It appears from an over-hasty inference from these results that neither a natural-development approach nor an intensive-skills program can overcome verbal disadvantage.

But perhaps a different sort of conclusion should be drawn. Natural-development programs and intensive-skills programs share a common feature: they both offer a fragmented curriculum from the standpoint of knowledge building. The natural-development approaches consider the content of the curriculum mainly to be a vehicle for gaining general reading skills. That same view—that content is basically a vehicle for skills—also characterizes scripted programs like Direct Instruction and Success for All. They are superior to natural-development approaches in teaching the mechanics of reading. But we now know that this superiority fades out over time, once the mechanics are gained. Both natural-development programs like "balanced literacy" and intensive-skills programs like Direct Instruction and Success for All end up very much the same by grades 5 or 6. They are alike in aiming to teach general comprehension skills. They are alike in taking a fragmented approach to knowledge building. Neither naturalistic nor scripted programs have been able in the long run to overcome disadvantage or avoid fadeout.

In retrospect, these disappointing long-term results in reading could have been predicted simply from consideration of the topic of vocabulary size. That subject will be a recurring theme in this book, because vocabulary size is a convenient index to a person's breadth of knowledge. Vocabulary size is the single most reliable correlate to reading ability.[15] The best route to vocabulary gain is firmly established by the work of Richard Anderson, George A. Miller, Keith Stanovich, John Guthrie, and others, who have shown that systematically contextualized verbal experiences are the most efficient means for gaining big vocabularies.[16] In schools, the most effective route to highly contextualized verbal experiences is a highly coherent, well-planned-out communal school curriculum centered on subject matters. In this chapter I'll consider fadeout in connection with how well early grades systematically impart the communal knowledge of the public sphere.

NATURALISTIC PRESCHOOLS AND PRIMARY SCHOOLS

In preschools the stars are the children, and the children are learning no matter what theories are being followed. All preschools are sensible enough to use play as a primary mode of learning in those early years. Over time, though, there is excellent evidence that a communal preschool can best overcome disadvantages of language and knowledge. There is far less evidence that an individualized, go-at-your-own-pace naturalistic preschool can help disadvantaged children nearly as well. Project Follow Through established that.

These two types of preschool—communal and naturalistic—are represented respectively by the preschools in France, which are deliberately communal, and by those in Reggio Emilia, Italy, which follow the individualized, natural-development principle. When American policy makers were researching the two kinds of preschool in 2001, Alessandra Stanley of the *New York Times* went along. She shrewdly observed, as others have, that the children in Reggio Emilia are nearly all from middle-class homes, so much of the work into the communal standard language has already been fostered by parents. That permits a naturalistic approach:

> The word "no" rarely passes a grownup's lips. There are no wrong answers, or written report cards. Children, sprawled on thick carpets, work in small, quiet groups on complex art projects in sunlit classrooms . . . There are no alphabet charts, blackboards or cut outs of Mickey Mouse. "We don't believe in formal instruction," said Angela Barozzi, a preschool teacher at La Villetta. "We try to nurture each child's innate desire to communicate and develop their joy of learning."[17]

Stanley observed that Reggio Emilia has declined to study the relative effectiveness of its methods. The French, in contrast, have conducted elaborate studies, and have refined their methods over decades. Before I discuss what happens in the French kind of preschool, it will be useful to consider what happens to the education of a disadvantaged child when a preschool of the Reggio Emilia type is succeeded by a primary school that continues its naturalistic principles.

The naturalistic *primary* school was an object of Diane Ravitch's criticism in her classic essay "Tot Sociology."[18] It memorably described how the elementary curriculum began to be less knowledge-rich in the United States during the first half of the twentieth century.

In 1982 I began to research the condition of history instruction in the public schools. The more closely I examined the social studies curriculum, the more my attention was drawn to the curious nature of the early grades, which is virtually content-free. The social studies curriculum for the K–3 grades is organized around the study of the relationships within the home, school, neighborhood, and local community. This curriculum of "me, my family, my school, my community" now dominates the early grades in American public education. It contains no mythology, legends, biographies, hero tales, or great events in the life of this nation or any other. It is tot sociology.

Ravitch explains that this nullity in the social studies classroom was the result of a much broader decline in substantive content in the schools, resulting from the naturalism and individualism that began to take over American elementary classrooms in the 1920s and 1930s.

The present K–3 curriculum was introduced in the 1930s, as part of a new approach to the teaching of social studies. At the same time, historical literature and imaginative historical activities were ousted from the curriculum of the early grades. During the 1920s and 1930s, progressive educators led a national curriculum movement; at least 37 states and hundreds of cities revised their school curricula in accordance with progressive principles. The common goal of progressive educators, whatever their political orientation, was to make the curriculum less academic, more utilitarian, less "subject-centered," and more closely related to the students' interests and experiences.[19]

Professor Ravitch expressed puzzlement that the "my neighborhood" approach to social studies should be so confidently supported by "years of research" when there was so little scientific support for it.

In the course of my research, I was told by many educators that the present K–3 curriculum was based on years of educational research . . . Leading scholars in the fields of cognitive psychology, child development, and curriculum theory know of no research justifying the expanding environments approach. In fact, they make repeated references to the "vacuousness" and the "sterility" of the content offered to young children in their social studies classes. Imagine the plight of the typical first graders: They have seen television programs about space flight, wars, terrorism, foreign countries, and national elections, but their social studies textbook is about neighborhood helpers and family roles.

Here we see the Reggio Emilia, natural-development theory of the early curriculum applied to the primary school. The expanding-environments curriculum is confidently followed because it is conceived to be natural. Since the natural way is always best, the situations that would occur naturally outside the school must be replicated inside the school. For example, the project method of instruction replicates hands-on, real-world experiences. That lends confidence under the providential point of view. It is the natural way, so it must be the best way. This idea of creating "natural" experiences *inside* the school became the hallmark of the new primary curriculum in the 1930s. The "project method" and other imitations of the natural, like "expanding environments," became the favored techniques, whether or not they taught communal knowledge to all children effectively. They did not. They did not consolidate the gains that Amana had made in Head Start, which faded and disappeared.

COMMUNAL PRESCHOOLS

More than a century ago, the French instituted free preschools to help equalize opportunity. They have universal preschools now, of universally high quality, with well-trained teachers and an effective curriculum:

> Preschool teachers in France have the same training, civil service status, and salaries as primary school teachers. The popular full-day programs emphasize academic activities . . . The impetus for the expansion of the *école maternelle* system during the 1970s and 1980s was concern over the large number of children who had to repeat first grade or who otherwise fell behind in primary education. To discover whether participating in preschool influenced retention in first grade, the government launched a survey of a national sample of 20,000 students who were sixth graders in 1980, comparing those who had attended pre-

school for one, two, or three years before entering school. The survey findings indicated that every year of preschool attended reduced the likelihood of school failure, especially for children from the most disadvantaged homes.[20]

The French preschool is knowledge based. It has a definite curriculum at each age—two, three, and four ("the littles," "the middles," and "the bigs"). Despite this supposedly "developmentally inappropriate" approach, it is a joyful, paradisal institution. On the surface, happy preschools are all alike. French preschools look much like happy American preschools. But there is a subtle difference that explains why attendance at a French preschool can have a big and lasting effect on the later academic performance and the life chances of students. That critical difference is in the nature of the preschool curriculum.

When I was researching French preschools in the late 1980s, I was once seated at lunch next to a two-year-old boy. Lunch is provided and table manners taught, as well as general politeness. This two-year-old was eating very neatly, even while conversing with me all the while—the result of social training in the *écoles maternelles* ("nursery schools"). He complained that his newborn sister made a lot of big messes at home. I was charmed. This was not a middle-class preschool. It was in a low-income district on the outskirts of town, or *banlieues*. Many of the children I met were not born of French parents. They included new arrivals from North Africa, China, Turkey, and elsewhere.

I was prepared to be charmed because that morning I had listened to an expert teacher read a story to a group of four-year-olds. The story was about a bear and a rabbit. The teacher read expressively, and explained no words until she came to "carnivore." That was worth discussing. Then she resumed the story for her rapt audience. Not only were the children polite, they were having a wonderful time. Their day was very clearly mapped out, leaving plenty of time for play and physical exercise. Provisions were made for a lot of semi-gymnastics indoors for bad weather, with children tumbling vigorously over padded towers and mattresses. The French have been doing preschool for a long time, and they have learned how to do it well.

The first thing I noticed was that no child seemed left out. Essentially *all* the children understand all the activities in a French preschool and are engaged by them. That's because the sequence of experiences has been planned with great care. The French do not assume that the spontaneous interests of the child determine the best course for schooling. Rather, they think that the well-trained teacher and the Ministry of Education know better than the child what sequence of experiences will work best.

Thanks to YouTube it's not necessary to take my word for the universal joy and sense of participation every French preschooler experiences regardless of race or social class. A Google search for "youtube ecole maternelle" yields several videos. One, lasting seventy minutes, shows the activities of a typical full day. Do they have play stations? Yes. Are all the children enabled to participate? Yes. Do the children appear to be bored or wishing they were somewhere else? Emphatically not. The main difference you will see between the free, universal French preschool and the most expensive, play-oriented private American preschool is simply that everyone is speaking French. But it's still easy to see what is going on. You will notice that every child is participating. How did they accomplish that universal participation? The activities—including a lot of physical activity and individual creativity—are occurring after a well-planned sequence of prior contexts that are orderly and inclusive. After such a carefully prepared sequence, no child is disadvantaged for the current activity. The activities that have led up to it ensure that each child can happily and intensively participate. But that hardly leads to uniformity of personality, as will be obvious from YouTube.

In the guides for parents published by the Ministry of Education you find statements like this:[21]

> Each day, in the different activity domains, and through the stories which the instructor narrates or reads, the children understand new words. But simple exposition does not suffice for them to learn the

words. The acquisition of vocabulary requires specific sequences of classification and learning of words and re-utilization of the words learned, and the interpretation of unknown words within their context. In connection with activities and readings the instructor habitually introduces new words each week, growing in number in the course of the year and from year to year.

"Specific sequence." "Year to year." The implicit academic curriculum is planned out not just for next week or month, but over a multiyear span. Vocabulary growth is enhanced by being integrated with the sequence of knowledge domains that are carefully mapped from week to week in the preschool curriculum—arithmetic, history, the natural world, and the arts—in addition to physical and social development.

That's the subtle but essential characteristic of a communal preschool. Each child is engaged and makes progress because of this well-mapped-out hidden curriculum, clothed in the same garb of joyful activities that you will find in the jolliest and most expensive naturalistic preschool. But in France, underneath that happy activity lies a conscious, careful sequence—meticulously planned day-to-day, week-to-week, year-to-year, then delivered at a leisurely, child-friendly pace. Because of that deliberately slow pace, there's plenty of room for spontaneous play within the plan. Of course it helps immensely to carry this out over a two- or three-year period—and to start very young.

Although poor children are behind in preschool, the vocabulary gap in the early years can be numbered in hundreds of words, not thousands. So, while there are many kinds of skills, conventions, and habits that children should usefully learn in preschool, a chief aim of preschool from the standpoint of equal opportunity is to enhance the knowledge and vocabularies of children.

What is the surest way to do that in preschool? It's the strategy of "domain immersion," a principle followed in the *écoles maternelles*, and also later in good primary schools. It is a key characteristic of an effective curriculum that I will emphasize in this book. It works this way: We know that advantaged children are ahead in vocabulary because they have heard many more total words, and many more different words, than disadvantaged children. We need a program, then, that enables them to catch up little by little, but at the same time is interesting and appropriate for their more advantaged peers.

An effective preschool or primary teacher will introduce a subject— let's say "plants and farms"—and tells stories about plants and farms, and asks questions about them, not just on one day, but over several. Of course it's not all verbal; there will be hands-on planting of some quick-germinating seeds. I choose this example, because many American preschools already do plants! At first, there will be a big difference between children who already know something about plants and food and associated words, and those who do not. Gradually, though, over several days, the subject becomes familiar to all. The most verbally impoverished child will begin to answer questions about plants and farms, and will know implicitly what *soil* is, what the main parts of a plant are, how many of our foods come from plants, what is needed to make plants grow—to take a simple example—with plenty of stories about the countryside.

Because all of the children are gradually coming to understand the stories and their sentences, they will also be learning general words like *moreover*, *however*, and *nonetheless*. When they learn about kings and queens, they will learn *evil* and *generous* and *secure*. Some of those words were already known by advantaged children, but in the course of a few days they will also begin to be known by disadvantaged ones. The coherent series of stories about kings and queens will have enabled the disadvantaged children to catch up a bit. They will have learned words that were already familiar to advantaged children. They will learn relatively more words because they began far behind. That key aspect of a good, coherent curriculum is discussed more fully in chapter 5 on the subject of achievement gaps between social groups.

When this principle of domain immersion is applied consistently over a careful sequence of domains—over a full school year and then, ideally, over the next year and the one after that—with independent readings directed to the purpose, vocabulary catch-up occurs by a natural process of implicit word learning.[22] Years of data (prior to 1989) from French academic preschools and primary schools show that such an academic early education is consistent with developmental and cognitive psychology. We have large-scale, reliable evidence that it works.

Preschool has been part of French egalitarian educational policy since the mid-nineteenth century. By the late twentieth century, French research showed that starting preschool as early as age two had beneficial equity effects. Today, about one-quarter of all French children attend preschool at age two. The French research that led to adding an age-two cohort to preschool was some of the most significant in the field of early education (see figure 3.1). The longitudinal research

FIGURE 3.1 Effects of preschool in France in the 1980s at the end of fifth grade

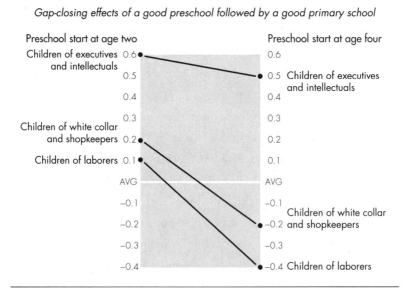

Gap-closing effects of a good preschool followed by a good primary school

Note: Labels show "head of household" demographic; vertical scale = z scores for fifth grade combined reading and mathematics 1987. Z scores are percentages of the standard deviation of a distribution. They allow results to be compared in different eras, even when the underlying tests use different scales.

traced some two thousand children from their earliest years up to age ten, comparing age-ten outcomes of students who started preschool at different ages: four, three, or two. The results showed that if a disadvantaged child started at age two, that same child by age ten will be ahead of a middle-class child who started at age three, and will have almost caught up with a highly advantaged child who had started at age four![23] Note how in the 1980s the gap between the top and bottom group has been cut almost in half by starting early.

These big equity results are not being recorded at the end of preschool, but at the end of grade 5 (age ten), and show the cumulative effects of preschool *after several years of knowledge-based primary school have consolidated and amplified the preschool gains.* Note that starting at age two brings shopkeepers' children above the average, whereas they are below the average if they start at the usual age of four—a remarkable result, the opposite of fadeout.

THE NATURALISTIC *PRIMARY* SCHOOL IS THE CAUSE OF FADEOUT

France has proved the positive case for preschool. But France is also now a model for the null effects of preschool. After the French primary schools suddenly adopted individualistic and naturalistic principles in 1989, France began to exhibit post-preschool fadeout. And this fadeout occurred despite the fact that the superb preschools, with their near-optimal content and expert teachers, had not changed with the 1989 law. (It would have been difficult politically to change an institution that is universally regarded in France with pride and affection.) But disappointments and puzzlements have now begun to set in. Early preschool starting at any age is now reported to have minimal effects on later academic outcomes.[24]

This change in policy offers precious data. It is an unintended twenty-seven-year longitudinal study with millions of young subjects in one group in France from 1980 to 1987, and millions in the experimental group from 1987 to 2007.[25] French preschools used to have a large equity effect before the *loi Jospin* of 1989. But after 1990, when an unchanged preschool was followed by elementary grades that had become unsystematic and diluted in their content, the achievement gaps reopened. Today, a communal French preschool is now followed by a naturalistic primary school that allows the gaps to widen. Researchers now pronounce the preschool effect to be *mince*—"meager."[26]

This is exactly the result that psycholinguistic research would predict. The gap in knowledge and vocabulary that had started to close in preschool years has reopened because the primary curriculum no longer capitalizes upon the slender early improvements. Without a systematic follow-up in primary school, the verbally impoverished environment of low-socioeconomic-status children *outside* of school becomes the dominant factor in word learning.

This lack of sustained follow-up is also the explanation for the middle-school fadeout recorded in the long-term National Assessment of Educational Progress scores. The underlying causes of preschool fadeout in the United States and France are also the causes of the puzzling way in which the apparent verbal gains of thirteen-year-olds in middle school fade out in high school at age seventeen. The earlier verbal tests for thirteen-year-olds in the United States have failed to capture the knowledge and latent vocabulary that will show up as manifested knowledge and vocabulary four years later, when seventeen-year-olds are tested with more demanding reading passages. The big differences in latent verbal knowledge between advantaged and disadvantaged students, which are hidden from the earlier, simpler tests, become manifest in the later ones. Clearly the way to actualize these latencies is to expose all students to the enabling knowledge systematically by a coherent elementary curriculum. That big change appears to be the key to the whole educational system early and late, as the French data show so emphatically. The French experience has shown that only a knowledge-based preschool followed by a knowledge-based kindergarten and elementary school can achieve excellence and equity.

To sum up: We have learned from France that preschool gains do not persist even from a communal preschool unless they are consolidated by systematic, knowledge-based schooling in the primary school. Vocabulary gain is a very slow, incremental process requiring multiple exposures to a word in multiple contexts. Without such reinforcement over time, a sense of the word will not get fixed in the mind.[27] Advantaged children whose parents read aloud to them will encounter academic words outside of school, and word meanings will become established whether or not the school supplies meaningful exposure. Disadvantaged students will learn unusual words only if the meaningful context is created and sustained in the classroom by a coherent curriculum and a carefully selected choice of materials for a child's independent reading. What we have learned from the virtues of French education of the 1980s is that a knowledge-based preschool followed by a knowledge-based elementary school is the school policy that, in all the world, has best achieved the double goal of high achievement coupled with equality. If we do not learn from massive early success in France followed by massive later failure, it will be a reproach unto us and our generation.

CHAPTER FOUR

The Dilution of the Elementary Curriculum

WIDE RECOGNITION OF THE CURRICULUM CRISIS

It is widely conceded that the high-stakes testing introduced by No Child Left Behind (NCLB) in 2002 caused a reduction in the knowledge students have gained in history, civics, music, visual art, literature, and science. In 2014, the journal of the National Education Association published an article called "The Testing Obsession and the Disappearing Curriculum." The data were appalling. In one study, the researcher noted that there had been a 47 percent reduction in class time devoted to subjects beyond math and reading.[1] The *NEA Today* article went on to say: "The law is uniformly blamed for stripping curriculum opportunities, including art, music, physical education and more, and imposing a brutal testing regime that has forced educators to focus their time and energy on preparing for tests in a narrow range of subjects: namely, English/language arts and math. For students in low-income communities, the impact has been devastating."[2]

In chapter 1 I agreed with that view. Testing arrangements have contributed to low reading scores by narrowing the school curriculum. But that is only part of the curriculum-narrowing story. In this chapter I will probe more deeply into the causes of curricular dilution in the elementary school. These go beyond the influence of high-stakes tests, and pertain to fundamental guiding ideas—including an unproductive emphasis on skills rather than on knowledge. My positive, corrective thesis will be that imparting a well-rounded, knowledge-based curriculum will be the solution to many recalcitrant problems of our schooling, including preschool fadeout, unacceptable achievement gaps, and the tribulations of the Common Core State Standards. All of these problems are largely attributable to a diluted and aimless elementary curriculum, emphasizing hands-on natural development and the child's uniqueness. These curriculum principles were introduced in the 1930s, and consolidated throughout the land by the 1950s.[3]

The emphasis on individual uniqueness arose from the idea that the natural development of each child should be our guide in early education. Because nature has made each of us unique, so the theory goes, education must be child-centered, so that each child's uniqueness is honored and allowed to develop providentially according to its nature. Proponents of this curriculum were confident that the content diversity of child-centered education and a de-emphasis of book learning would *not* lead to fragmentation and incoherence. Why not? Because the diversity of individual child-centered topics was to be unified by the attainment of general skills. The content through which those skills were to be imparted was deemed secondary. In the twentieth century these general skills were called "twentieth-century skills" and included critical thinking, problem solving, creativity, teamwork, and communication. These are now termed "twenty-first-century skills," or "information age skills."

That is the thumbnail structure of the history that has brought us to the present moment. It is the story of the victory of incorrect ideas, and of the disappointments that are bound to arise when reality is thwarted. The root ideas were that natural development is providential, and that nature and the child's interests are therefore the best guides to the sequence of studies in the early grades. The more immediate causes of our currently incoherent and diluted primary curriculum are the two pedagogical principles that arose from the natural-development idea: individualism and skill-centrism.

The result has been a fragmented elementary curriculum with unpredictable topics being studied in different classrooms at the same grade level within the same school. Knowledge is not built up systematically. In the absence of a specific curriculum, tests cannot be devised that are based on specific curricular content, so they must be based on skills. The current focus on test preparation has therefore led to a hyperemphasis on general skills. Skills and tests have now become the main subject matters of our elementary schools.

Viewed in retrospect, the progression of the scenario seems inevitable: from education as natural development, to education according to each child's unique nature, to education as teaching all children the general skills of reading, critical thinking, problem solving, and test taking. The history of the dilution of the curriculum is the history of the triumph of developmentalism, individualism, and skill-centrism. In this chapter I'll discuss the flaws in each of those curriculum-diluting ideas.

DEVELOPMENTALISM AND CONTENT DELAY

In appendix I, I provide a brief history of how developmentalism triumphed with quasi-religious sentiments about the God-infused progress of the human race. (Young Horace Mann's valedictorian address at Brown University in 1819 was entitled "The Gradual Advancement of the Human Species in Dignity and Happiness.") Today, education-as-natural-development is said to be sanctioned by the work of the eminent scientist Jean Piaget (1896–1980) and his disciples. Educators assert, for example, that Piaget has shown that some topics are "developmentally inappropriate" for children in a particular age group.

Piaget was a great scientist and a brilliant, charming man. He observed the growth of his own children from infancy, taking careful notes. He detected four stages in their mental development: the "sensorimotor stage" from infancy to age two, the "preoperational stage" from ages two to seven, the "concrete operational stage" from seven to eleven, and the "formal operational stage" in adolescence and maturity.[4]

Piaget's theory has had to be modified in detail. But his description of the first three stages has held up, with the main qualification being that the stages are not discrete. They are very subject-matter dependent, just as with adults. Children (like adults) will be at a more advanced operational stage with more familiar topics. And young children have their ups and downs. One day they will be preoperational and the next day sensorimotor.[5] But on the whole the first three stages have proved to be universal across cultures.

Piaget's theory of the fourth stage—formal operations—may not be universal. Upon reaching that final stage, a mature child or an adult should be able to solve the following problem: If A is bigger than B, and B is bigger than C, is A bigger or smaller than C or the same? "Who knows?" say highly able adults in some cultures, where the mark of maturity is not the manipulation of formal operations but the understanding of human motivations, personalities, and power relationships. The anthropological field researchers who report this finding conclude that the fourth stage in Piaget's theory may be culturally determined, not universal.[6]

Piaget came to agree that his stages were not simply a mark of physiological maturation and brain development, but were highly co-determined by schooling and culture. The following is from a talk he gave in 1964:

> The ordering of these stages is constant and has been found in all the societies studied. It has been found in various countries where psychologists in universities have redone the experiments but it has also been found in African peoples for example, in the children of the Bushmen, and in Iran, both in the villages and in the cities. However, although the order of succession is constant, the chronological ages of these stages vary a great deal. For instance, the ages which we have found in Geneva are not necessarily the ages which you would find in the United States. In Iran, furthermore, in the city of Teheran, they found approximately the same ages as we found in Geneva, but there is a systematic delay of two years in the children in the country. Canadian psychologists who redid our experiments, Monique Laurendeau and Father Adrien Pinard, found once again about the same ages in

Montreal. But when they redid the experiments in Martinique, they found a delay of four years in all the experiments and this in spite of the fact that the children in Martinique go to a school set up according to the French system and the French curriculum and attain at the end of this elementary school a certificate of higher primary education. There is then a delay of four years; that is, there are the same stages, but systematically delayed. So you see that these age variations show that maturation does not explain everything.[7]

Instead of confirming the principle that natural development determines readiness, Piaget here outlines why that cannot be so. "Maturation," he says, "does not explain everything." The stage of development—of readiness—is not entirely a natural unfolding. Using the same curriculum, the French-speaking children in Montreal unfolded four years earlier than the French-speaking children in Martinique. Why?

Was it the climate? That would have favored Martinique. Was it genes and race? There are multiple genetic types in both places. Was it diet? The World Health Organization does not report child malnutrition in Martinique: "There have been no reports of disorders associated with protein or vitamin deficiencies."[8] The most likely factor is the knowledge base of the children as determined by their learning environments at home, and in their schooling.

The same kinds of cultural factors that speeded children in Montreal or delayed them in Martinique are those that place children ahead or behind in the United States, and cause scores on reading tests to be associated with zip codes. The experiences and language of the home and the curricular effectiveness of the school together explain the difference between Martinique and Montreal. Educational factors, not maturational factors, were the chief causes of the age when children reached the "concrete operational stage." It was external education, not internal unfolding, that explained why some children were ahead, and some behind.

Parents and teachers who are reading this book will have been exposed to an expert-sounding phrase: "developmentally appropriate practice."

To label a topic "developmentally inappropriate" implies that it is being taught prematurely, like feeding small children oysters Rockefeller when they should be eating oatmeal. But as the eminent research psychologist Jerome Bruner once memorably observed, the idea that there are ages for which particular topics are appropriate has no scientific support.[9] Moreover, recent advances within developmental psychology have ascertained that the universal pathways of mental development *inherently* owe as much to culture as to nature. The idea of letting the child develop on his or her own is decidedly unnatural for human beings.[10]

Certainly the level and the mode in which a topic is broached for a child can be appropriate or inappropriate. That is a reasonable use of the term "age-appropriate practice." There have been several news stories about the inappropriate use of "drill-and-kill" work sheets in kindergarten classrooms.[11] Effective teaching is an empathetic activity that always depends on where the student is with respect to the teaching goal. Such variability makes all the more important the tolerant Bruner principle that any topic can be taught appropriately, and provides a further reason to stop using the term "developmentally inappropriate" as a reason for delaying substantive content. Some would delay, for example, the teaching of Mesopotamia in first grade and offer instead "my neighborhood" as being more age appropriate. But to delay Mesopotamia is simply to put disadvantaged students at a further disadvantage compared to those first graders who for decades have been happily learning about Mesopotamia while their parents have read aloud to them from *What Your First Grader Needs to Know.*[12]

Piaget himself became persuaded that readiness depends upon factors other than physical maturation. Appropriate topics are determined less by the child's age than by what the child has already learned.[13] And that knowledge tends to vary with social class, and the degree to which children have been read aloud to. By kindergarten, what makes a topic inappropriate for children is not their stage of development but the state of their relevant knowledge. Natural unfolding from within is not the critical factor for the cognitive appropriateness of topics in the school curriculum. What the child has already learned in school and at home is the critical factor.

In light of the Bruner principle, teachers might consider abandoning the phrase "developmentally inappropriate" as a club to shame other teachers who are successfully teaching high-level topics to eager young students. Parents should be aware that "developmentally inappropriate" is a scientifically suspect phrase whose only possible efficacy is to keep interesting knowledge from a child. To pretend that harm would somehow result is altogether baseless.[14] First graders haven't been harmed by being exposed to the Pledge of Allegiance just because they don't yet quite understand it. The only important real-world effect of such sanctimonious bullying is to withhold from disadvantaged students high-level material that is widely known to advantaged ones.

The entire idea of natural development as it is conceived by the postromantic tradition in education is incorrect, and must be vigorously rejected.[15] It has been a cause of disadvantaged children not receiving a coherent, challenging curriculum. It has also been the cause of the unfortunate anti-verbalism and anti-intellectualism of post-1940 American education. Somehow the idea became accepted among theorists, again without scientific support, that the tactile and visual are more natural than the abstract and verbal.

Even Dewey got caught up with what he considered the priority of the image for the child.[16] He was wrong. Just as high a priority for the child, and for humans in general, is the word. By undervaluing what is verbal (in books and lectures, and whole-class discussions), recent early education has scorned the assimilation of mere facts, and the "artificial stuffing of children's heads" with accumulated wisdom. This has held back disadvantaged children differentially, because advantaged children are being read aloud to and are hearing plenty of words, facts, and abstractions at home.

Transmission (introducing your child to what successful people in the society know and convey to their own children at home) is especially scorned by theorists today as being culturally imperialistic, conservative, and illiberal.[17] Transmission of traditional knowledge is said to be conformist and suppressive of individuality. This anti-transmission doctrine is probably the most astonishingly misguided principle yet devised under the natural-development conception. Transmission, far from being in conflict with human development, is essential to it. And in a democracy, where each meets each on an equal footing, initiation into the shared knowledge of the standard language alone can make the ideal of equal opportunity a reality.

By not properly taking communal knowledge into full account, the developmental tradition in schooling commits a basic developmental error. Human mental development does not slavishly follow physiological development.[18] In all societies, shared knowledge is the elephant in the room. In modern societies many citizens must be at home in at least two traditions. The universality of initiation into the group is the decisive refutation of education as "natural" development. Or to put the matter more precisely: romantic educators have misunderstood the principle of natural development. Nothing is more universal and natural than the explicit transmission of communal knowledge.

To read the writings of developmental educators of the recent past and present is to be transported into a world where everything can be made new through education. But human development absolutely requires social inculcation as part of a child's natural development. It's totally unnatural for a child to grow up without a community. Language and communal knowledge are human universals. In a modern democracy, whatever the home culture, the duty of the schools is to transmit the shared knowledge of the standard language—to transmit the cultural commons of the nation, its public sphere. The transmission of communal knowledge is as natural as mother's milk.[19] More particularly the transmission of the nationally shared knowledge of the public sphere is essential to equality of opportunity. It is foundational to democratic education. An uncritical and incorrect version of child development led to narrow hyper-individualism in education. Transmission and socialization are universal. A communal education is the most natural form of human development. It is also the most equitable.

CURRICULUM DILUTION THROUGH HYPER-INDIVIDUALISM

The gradual dominance of the everyone-is-unique idea of education has resulted in curricular fragmentation. When many children in a classroom are learning different, uncoordinated subject matters from different texts in the language arts class, there is no practical way of ensuring that all children will gain the knowledge they need to master the public sphere. Language arts classes occupy the most classroom time in the earliest grades. Content fragmentation is tolerated because the particular content is felt to be somewhat irrelevant. The larger purpose is thought to be that of developing general reading skill while accommodating topics to students' individual interests and abilities.

The attempt to implement such individualism in the primary school has been just as hard on teachers as on students. When individualism took over the language arts curriculum, it left an impossible task for teachers, and little long-term basis for cooperation among colleagues in building a cumulative curriculum over the years. Language arts teachers were formerly key figures in the Americanization project.[20] Now they teach the helter-skelter content of the different books that their children are reading under the imperative to adjust the curriculum to the nature and interests of each child. But no teacher can successfully individualize the content of a language arts class of twenty, or even twelve, without neglecting other students while doing so.

The assumption that the educator must never go against nature originally led developmentalists to the idea of forming the curriculum around the young child's interests, strengths, and impulses. In recent years that view sanctioned an enthusiastic embrace of quasi-scientific theories about different kinds of intelligence and learning styles. But the theories have not passed scientific muster. Neither "multiple learning styles" nor "multiple intelligences" is accepted by experts in the relevant fields. One meta-analysis concludes as follows: "In the absence of adequate validating empirical support, and in the absence of concord with neuroscience findings, [such theories] should not be applied in education."[21] Paradoxically, our assumptions about the learning styles and types of "intelligence" of individual children have led to instruction that is far from child centered, and has perpetuated inequality among children from different backgrounds.

One defect of multiple-intelligences theories is that they are far too nativist; that is, they overstress the innate, genetic component of learning and understress the importance of relevant shared knowledge in a child's ability to reach a high level of achievement. Inside the developmental conception of education has always lurked the danger of genetic determinism. In the naturalistic and individualistic character of child-centered education there has always been an implicit overemphasis on inborn ability as well as inborn interest—as Antonio Gramsci so wittily observed when he said that the new education conceived "the child's brain as a ball of string that the teacher should help to unwind."[22]

Those recent multiple-intelligences theories did not cause the problem, however. The emphasis on the individuality of the child was a key feature of the child-centered approach from its beginnings—going back to the nineteenth century. Early in his "Pedagogic Creed" of 1897, John Dewey says: "Education, therefore, must begin with a psychological insight into the child's capacities, interests, and habits. It must be controlled at every point by reference to these same considerations." Current American education has not deviated from that individualistic principle. The recent theories of "learning styles" and "multiple intelligences" fulfilled that established need for a constantly updated version of the individualistic principle. That preexisting market accounts for their instant popularity. But as George A. Miller observed in his review of the multiple-intelligences idea, it is not only underevidenced scientifically, it is also unhelpful educationally.[23] It does not determine whether educators should conform their teaching to the existing interests and strengths of students, or rather focus on overcoming those weaknesses and points of ignorance—or a bit of both. For any of these educational decisions one does not need the sanction of a questionable psychological theory. One needs a firm conception of what the child needs to master under this year's defined curriculum.

The decision about what a student should learn does not in any case depend on the rightness or wrongness of theories about innate intelligence or innate learning styles. The main value of those notions has been the virtue of saying democratically (and perhaps with unconscious condescension) that everybody is innately smart in his or her own way. But such self-gratulatory right-thinking becomes unnecessary if a school focuses less on innate gifts and more on what students need to learn, whatever their gifts.[24] One already perceives a common-sense reaction setting in against nativism with a new research emphasis on hard work, grit, persistence, and delayed gratification—work popularized by Paul Tough.[25] Similarly, Carol Dweck's work on "mindset" has shown that taking a fixed view of intelligence discourages progress, whereas a belief that hard work will make you smarter can indeed, with hard work, make you smarter.[26] But the school has to do its part by making the hard work productive through a specific, cumulative curriculum based on the acquisition of enabling knowledge. With a change of basic ideas there can be a renewal of the promise of schooling in a democracy. With clear, sequential focus on shared content, each of our neighborhood schools across the land can become an excellent school that gives every child a good chance in life.

The incoherent classrooms and curricula supported by these scientifically challenged theories of individuality have not worked to improve either academic performance or fairness. Of course students differ in their academic abilities and rates of learning—a fact surely known to all human groups since prehistory. That is not the issue. There is a growing body of evidence that many practical differences in students' ability to learn the academic curriculum are differences in the topic-relevant knowledge that they already possess.[27] That is the conclusion of the most recent 2012 Program for International Student Assessment (PISA) study, which focused its analyses on the ways in which various nations had been able to narrow achievement gaps between rich and poor students. That goal was achieved best by systems that followed a long, multiyear arc of commonly learned subject matter in the elementary grades.[28]

In retrospect, the attempt to individualize the content of the language arts curriculum has been a quixotic idea that has put teachers under enormous pressure to achieve the impossible. This report from the field on "differentiated instruction" reflects the experience of many teachers:

> It seemed to complicate teachers' work, requiring them to procure and assemble multiple sets of materials. I saw frustrated teachers trying to provide materials that matched each student's or group's presumed ability level, interest, preferred "modality" and learning style. The attempt often devolved into a frantically assembled collection of worksheets, coloring exercises, and specious "kinesthetic" activities. And it dumbed down instruction: In English, "creative" students made things or drew pictures; "analytical" students got to read and write. In these ways, Differentiated Instruction, or DI, corrupted both curriculum and effective instruction. With so many groups to teach, instructors found it almost impossible to provide sustained, properly executed lessons for every child or group—and in a single class period. It profoundly impeded the teacher's ability to incorporate those protean, decades-old elements of a good lesson.[29]

When a teacher is attending to the individual needs of one student in a class of twenty, nineteen are *not* receiving the teacher's attention. All sorts of techniques conspire to obscure that fact—group work, isolated seatwork on boring work sheets, and "independent study" with choice of books from the leveled-reader bin.

The essence of the leveled-reader-bin system is that children will select from their assigned Lexile level (often secretly denoted by letters or labels on the bins) their own books on subjects that interest them.[30]

In some schools, time is set aside for "independent reading" during the class as well as outside of class. The policy is based on the finding that children become better readers when they spend more time reading independently.

While haphazard leveled classroom libraries have grown, regular school libraries with real books have languished.[31] Yet good school libraries with good librarians are the places where the most productive student-centered independent reading will be cultivated. Reading real books that go into a bit of depth and lodge themselves in our memories—whether in the class as a whole or in take-home books—is a far more effective way to foster individuality and student interest than brief picture-book excursions with inherent superficiality, chosen with no cumulative pattern, and few words. There's no evidence that the individualization of leveled-reader bins develops deep student interest or makes better readers.[32] On the contrary, it neglects systematic knowledge building—the key to high reading ability. In effect it's a perfect example of how solicitude for the individuality of the child leads to subject-matter incoherence and, in a larger, long-range view, to individual neglect. It must not be assumed that a different approach— whole-class instruction of real books and subject matters—means gray uniformity. On the contrary, real knowledge breeds real interest and individuality. Another of life's paradoxes.

These comments have every likelihood of upsetting the devoted teachers who are pursuing these popular methods. The thought of upsetting our much-maligned teachers is troubling to me. But I ask them to consider that right now in the United States we are not improving the reading comprehension of disadvantaged students as well as other nations that don't follow these hyper-individualistic methods. Our teachers have simply not been sufficiently informed about the knowledge basis of reading comprehension—that reading comprehension is *not* a general skill that can be developed through any appealing vehicle; that to advance comprehension abilities there needs to be systematic knowledge building with more whole-class instruction and discussion, more system, more coherence.[33]

It's been demonstrated that the very best way to ensure high reading comprehension in the long term is to ensure high *oral* comprehension in the earliest grades.[34] And the best way to do that is to make sure that our children learn a lot in the early grades through listening and talking as well as through reading. As their knowledge expands, so do their vocabularies. It's critical that language arts classes busy themselves with helping *all* children systematically expand their knowledge and their vocabularies, and their comprehension, with oral as well as visual language. Basic arithmetic says that this can only happen effectively when most of the time children are on the same page. Language arts needs to be part of a coherent knowledge-based curriculum just as much as other subjects like history, math, the arts, and science. That can be reliably accomplished only through plenty of whole-class learning, ensuring that all the children are advancing in knowledge and language, with no big gaps and boring repetitions.

A semantic slippage occurred with the term "independent reading." It is now taken to mean "reading books selected by the students themselves." But independent reading doesn't necessarily mean that; it can also mean reading books on one's own that have been assigned and are then later discussed communally in the classroom. This small semantic slippage has had big consequences. One can see how it happened. Under child-centered principles, it would seem malpractice to have all the children in a class read the very *same* title, and then discuss the contents. Under a communal view of education, such whole-class activity would seem the most natural thing in the world. It is by far the most lively and productive kind of classroom. A teacher could well object that a child cannot decode certain words; that children are not all at the same decoding level. That's true, but it's best to separate early phonics training from taxing substance.[35] That's why listening to and discussing substantial books in class is one element of a better approach.

Nowadays, with each child reading a different book, the chief curricular duty of the teacher is to set the difficulty level of the books from which the child may choose. These books at the right difficulty level are called "leveled readers." The knotty problem of choosing the subject matters of the language arts curriculum is thus partly solved by a technical difficulty–rating device that satisfies the imperative to individualize the curriculum to suit each child's interests and abilities. Grading the difficulty level of books has become a big, lucrative industry. And the technical beauty of the whole system is that the only person who has to make the final curricular decision is the child.

Teachers are being blamed for the poor results of this system. But our teachers have been misinformed about the actual nature of reading comprehension. They have been told, incorrectly, that it is an all-purpose skill. But two texts that are rated at the same difficulty level are rarely of the same difficulty for an individual student. Actual difficulty, not theoretical difficulty, is what counts. A student can be an excellent reader about dinosaurs and a terrible reader about mushrooms; the leveled-reader system is not individualistic in the one respect that it needs to be. It cannot determine the actual difficulty level of a book for an individual student, nor gauge how best to overcome the knowledge deficits that make reading difficult for that student.

To see why the computer-rated difficulty level of a text does not define its difficulty for an individual child, one need only glance inside the text-leveling machine. The formulas are mainly interested in lengths of sentences and rarity of words. The actual difficulty of a book is highly dependent on an individual student's familiarity with the topic, whereas the formulas that determine a book's difficulty level are quite indifferent to topics and meanings. Here is the old Lexile formula, similar to the one in widest use today. (The current formula is a business secret.)[36]

$$((((9.82247 \times \text{the } \log_n \text{ of the mean sentence length}) - (2.14634$$
$$\times \text{ the } \log_n \text{ of the mean word rarity})(+ 3.3)) (\times 180))) + 200$$

The five decimal places speciously imply an exactitude of one in one hundred thousand. Teachers are being lulled into premature dazzlement by this pseudo-precision, which makes all seem ripe for skill classes in main-idea finding, which in turn will supposedly raise the Lexile skill level and the student's ability to read at a higher Lexile level. Professor Tim Shanahan has shown that the whole leveled-reader edifice has no firm scientific basis and no evidence of success.[37] The arrangement conveniently preserves the hyper-individualistic orientation to the elementary classroom.

But the Lexile system should not be made to shoulder the blame for this meaning-free approach to curriculum choices. Like the theory of multiple learning styles, it is simply meeting a preexisting market demand that has been created by the compulsory idea that the elementary school must be highly individualized, whether or not students are learning very much in a coherent way.

When it comes to developing knowledge effectively, the language arts classroom is not in principle different from any other classroom. Decoding is a subject matter in its own right, and once decoding is mastered it becomes habitual through reading. What is read and discussed in language arts classes, whether plot and character in a story or the nature of light, becomes a subject matter for students, just as in any other classroom. In good primary schools over the world, students enthusiastically learn new things and have vigorous discussions about them in class, whatever the topic. Language arts need not be an inherently amorphous subject. It can contribute its part in a well-planned overall curriculum. The most efficient route to *reading* skill in early grades will include a lot of listening and talking at the expense of in-class silent reading. Being read to and talking are powerful tools for reading progress, and are more efficient for vocabulary building in the early grades than independent reading is—though independent reading is also essential, of course.

A systematic approach to content that includes *all* students in the language arts class, and prepares them for knowledge to come, is the most effective method for all students to gain new knowledge—and with it, new interests and skills. Heterogeneous leveled readers on arbitrary topics can't accomplish that. Successful whole-class instruction in which all students are deeply engaged is a way of giving *more* attention to each child. Each child is actively constructing knowledge in such a class. Expert teachers can keep everyone engaged, calling on individuals in effective ways while keeping every other child's attention. Keeping everyone's attention is accomplished readily if the students are learning the same subject matters and reading the same books. Starting in kindergarten, and continued year after year, children will gain similar background knowledge. In such high performing school systems over the world, teachers and students alike will then have a manageable task in teaching new subjects.

In sum, the effort to individualize the elementary curriculum, especially in language arts, has led to incoherence and, paradoxically, to a failure in reaching all students. It has contributed to a deterioration in the primary socializing aim of the school. It has helped sustain the gaps between advantaged and disadvantaged students by neglecting the long arc of coherent subject-matter learning and vocabulary building over the years. Such fragmentation of what children learn is supposedly overcome by the unifying principle of all-purpose skills. Let me now turn to the reasons why that attractive idea has not worked and cannot work.

CURRICULUM NARROWING THROUGH SKILL-CENTRISM

Since the current language arts curriculum is fragmented with little content coherence across the grades, the elementary school teacher in later grades cannot know what topics are already familiar to students from prior grades. So the question arises: Can schools make such a haphazard curriculum effective by developing general skills like all-purpose reading-comprehension ability and all-purpose critical-thinking ability? That has continued to be the theory set forth by school systems to justify the fragmented curriculum.

Public school systems in the United States issue mission statements phrased in terms of thinking skills. Here's a random sample:

- Milwaukee, WI: Students will "develop organizational, critical-thinking, and problem-solving skills."
- Oakland, CA: Wants its students to "read, write, speak, and think critically."
- Tucson, AZ: "Fosters creativity, critical thinking, and problem solving."
- Santa Fe, NM: Promotes "critical thinking, problem solving and creativity."
- Richmond, VA: Imparts "critical thinking, responsibility, mutual respect, citizenship, and a lifelong love of learning."
- Montgomery, AL: "Will encourage and support critical thinking, problem solving, active questioning."

While these statements are certainly believed by those making them, they are also convenient things to say to the public when it hasn't been clearly determined what students will be learning in history, literature, music, art, science, and civics. It's not just administrators who like to be free from curricular restrictions. Some teachers, especially in language arts, like to have a free hand with content. They, too, say things like: "We need to move away from strictly teaching content and move toward teaching strategies on how to find information. In a world where most information is instantly available online, the mass memorization of facts is no longer required. In order for students to be competitive in a global economy, we need to teach them thinking and logic skills to help them use information already available to them."[38]

Many educators now deplore the "memorizing" of mere facts: "Learning should not be a matter of stuffing a person's head full of facts, but rather a process of lighting a fire in people so they have the confidence to successfully learn and become motivated to take charge of their educational journey."[39]

"Stuffing one's head full of facts" is often coupled with the phrase "rote memorization." So when a new state or district superintendent of schools makes an inaugural statement in the United States, he or she often says something like: "We need less memorization of facts, and more emphasis on critical thinking skills for the twenty-first century." Here's the first hit that came up when I searched "superintendent critical thinking": "The Santa Barbara Unified School District will focus on changing its culture and teaching style in the coming year, as teachers, staff and administrators prepare for the Common Core State Standards . . . 'All of that fits into the nationwide move to new academic standards, which will embrace learning across all subjects, and have students practice critical thinking, curiosity and creativity instead of merely memorizing content,' Cash said."[40]

To this chorus of educators must be added the chorus of reformers who continue to urge schools and the public that we must improve our students' critical-thinking, problem-solving, and teamwork intelligence if the United States is to remain competitive in the new global economy. Such are the themes of popular books like *The Global Achievement Gap* by Tony Wagner. And some of that thinking has spilled over into economists who urge the need for better thinking skills—including greater critical thinking, problem solving, and teamwork.

To be fair, all of these advocates for new twenty-first-century skills include "communication skills" along with "critical thinking" and "creativity." All the participants in these discussions should therefore quickly seize upon that point about communication skills, emphasize it strongly, and then go forward to reach a productive agreement. We could start by agreeing on the need for a coherent knowledge-based elementary curriculum. For communication skill includes speaking and listening, reading and writing—not just emotional intelligence and skill in creating PowerPoint files. Verbal skills are necessary in the twenty-first century to teamwork and learning new tasks. Communication skills are essential to "looking things up." Everybody in these discussions should agree that verbal skills are central to *all* the twenty-first-century skills.

Certain things follow. Effective verbal skills depend on a big vocabulary and an effective initiation into the language community of the public sphere—something that can only be gained by a good communal education, and essential to "communication skills." That simple observation may yet someday bring together reformers of all stripes, and save the schools from content-indeterminate skill-centrism—for skill-centrism on its own, without communication skills, cannot succeed. And our low communication skills are documented by our low national scores on reading comprehension tests. Those NAEP verbal scores for seventeen-year-olds are critical indices to how well we are achieving all twenty-first-century skills.

Let me digress here to explain what I mean by the phrase *public sphere*, and why its mastery is essential to communication skills. Everybody agrees that "literacy" is a necessary aim of schooling. Only recently has it been fully understood that literacy entails much more than sounding out from print, and deriving meaning from simple texts. In a modern democracy, literacy entails the ability to communicate effectively with strangers, and to understand rather complex texts. That means mastery of the standard language of the nation in its spoken and written forms. This language mastery entails not just a big vocabulary but also a big range of irrational idioms and unspoken shared connotations. As I was writing these words, I received an e-mail that started off: "You beat me to the punch." Most Americans understand the phrase, but most of us have no idea what it means literally or where it came from. If we consciously thought it came from boxing (possibly, or to the "punch line" in a story), we might think it implied some enmity or rivalry. But that's not necessarily the case. How do I know that? Because I've become initiated into the public sphere. All fully functioning citizens are functional because they have become initiated into the common language, whether or not they were born into it. When people speak of "communication skills" they properly imply the ability to communicate effectively with strangers, which is to say, mastery of the language of the public sphere.

American educators have been pronouncing ideas about all-purpose critical-thinking skills for more than a century.[41] But we now know from cognitive science that the idea is essentially mistaken. Critical thinking does not exist as an independent skill. Cognitive scientists have known since the 1940s that human skills tend to be domain specific, and do not transfer readily from one domain to the next.[42] No matter how widely skilled people may be, as soon as they confront unfamiliar content their skill degenerates. That is true even of reading and writing skill. An unfamiliar topic will quickly degrade both reading and writing. The domain specificity of skills is one of the most important scientific findings of our era for teachers and parents to know about.

Yet this psychological truth is not widely known in the school world. Indeed, the view that information is "instantly available online," has intensified the antifact sentiments. I'll briefly summarize some of the key research on the domain specificity of skills. I've observed that once teachers know about these little-discussed findings, they begin to change their practices in constructive ways. The news needs to be spread far and wide: a well-stocked mind is the skill of skills—essential to critical thinking and to looking things up.

Some years ago I wrote a piece for *American Educator* on looking thing up.[43] It focused on work by the late George A. Miller that showed that looking things up was a completely unsatisfactory procedure compared to having a well-stocked mind. Just to make sure Miller's work was up to date in the age of Google, I checked the literature and found that indeed, still in 2015, both researchers and students themselves are "keenly aware of the limitations" and "distractions" of using online dictionaries, encyclopedias, and hand-held devices to look things up.[44] Their findings were consistent with Miller's in the pre-Internet era.

In the days of paper dictionaries, Professor Miller had conducted some research on how young children looked up words, and what the results were.[45] Children did not like looking things up. The normal child's aversion to doing so, Miller found, was amply justified. In the time it took children to find a dictionary word and construe its meanings, they usually forgot the original context and never found their way back. They mainly experienced frustration. (Those who have done research in the digital age have reported similar frustration with the distractions of hyperlinks.[46]) Looking up words with any platform is exacerbated by the inherent uncertainties and ambiguities of word definitions. That turned out to be the chief problem. Words are ambiguous; dictionaries must list multiple meanings. A young, uninformed child, faced (as Google Translate is) with ambiguous possibilities, cannot know which of the meaning possibilities are in play.[47] Their guesses are often wrong. As a consequence, children consistently produced sentences like:

"Mrs. Morrow stimulated the soup." (That is, she stirred it up.)
"Our family erodes a lot." (That is, they eat out.)
"Me and my parents correlate, because without them I wouldn't be here."
"I was meticulous about falling off the cliff."
"I relegated my pen pal's letter to her house."

Of course, Professor Miller was in favor of dictionaries and encyclopedias at appropriate moments. But those moments turn out to be rare occasions when one already possesses enough background knowledge to confidently understand nuances of meaning.

Have computers greatly diminished some of the time-consuming distractions of looking things up? Do instant hyperlinks to dictionary definitions on a screen-read text at least ameliorate the need for a big vocabulary? Everyone concedes the convenience of instant, linked access to dictionary definitions and to relevant websites while we are reading on a screen. But regardless of the platform, we already know some practical facts about dictionary use and word learning. Psychologists have found that students simply will not read at all if they have to look up too many words.[48] Moreover, we know that looking up words on either paper or screen is not a good way of learning new words. It has two defects: it is a slow, cumbersome mode of vocabulary building compared with implicit word learning, and it is a far less accurate mode of gaining the subtle connotations of words.[49]

Dictionary use is just one example of a more general principle. When looking *anything* up, there is simply no substitute for already possessing a lot of knowledge relevant to the subject. This is obvious when the looking up is being conducted in language. The language of what is being looked up is like language use anywhere else. To understand it requires a lot of relevant background knowledge. That leads to the following paradox: Because experts already know a great deal, one might suppose that they would learn very little when they look something up, whereas the novice, with so much to learn, would learn more from consulting the Internet or a dictionary or encyclopedia. But in fact it's the expert who learns more that is new, and learns it much faster. It's extremely hard for a novice to learn very much in a reasonable time by looking things up.[50] One reason is that the human mind is able to assimilate only three or four new items before further elements evaporate from working memory. So novices have to put things together fast—faster than they often can. Experts have already assimilated most of the elements being looked up, and therefore need pay attention only to one or two novel features that can easily be integrated into their prior knowledge.

The Internet thus mainly rewards people who already have wide knowledge and a big vocabulary. It makes the rich richer. Reference works, including those available on the Internet, are immensely valuable to already knowledgeable people. Google is not an equal-opportunity fact finder; it rewards those already in the know. Instead of being an agent of equality, Google rewards cognitive insiders. It consolidates educational inequality. Just as it usually takes money to make money, it takes knowledge to gain knowledge. Education is bootstrapping, governed by the "Matthew Effect," that unfair paradox in the Book of

Matthew: "For whosoever hath, to him shall be given, and he shall have more abundance: but whosoever hath not, from him shall be taken away even that he hath."[51]

Problem solving is another all-purpose skill like critical thinking proffered by our public school systems. Yet the skill of problem solving is also dependent on domain-specific knowledge. There exists no consistent all-purpose problem-solving skill, independent of domain-specific knowledge.[52] The famous Duncker radiation experiment showed that even when people are carefully shown how to solve a problem in one domain, they will tend to be baffled by that same structural problem when it is set in another domain.[53] That result has continued to be supported by current research.[54]

The study that started the whole field thinking about the domain specificity of thinking skills was Dutch chess master and psychologist Adriaan de Groot's chess experiment in the 1940s. A chess position was displayed from an actual game with twenty pieces left on the board. Participants looked at the board for twenty seconds, then went to the next booth and tried to reproduce the position. A novice could reproduce only four pieces correctly. A chess master could always reproduce the whole twenty-piece position without flaw. It seemed as if the expert had developed a piece-reproducing skill. But then the same experiment was conducted with pieces placed randomly, rather than from an actual game. Novices and masters then performed the same. All placed only four pieces correctly—a surprising result. It turned out that masters had *not* developed an all-purpose skill. Rather they had a great deal of chess knowledge in long-term memory that enabled them to reproduce the position from a few key traits when it came to actual game situations. De Groot concluded that these experts did not possess a skill but rather what he called *erudition*—deep domain knowledge.

By now, an overwhelming body of evidence has generalized the de Groot finding that thinking skills depend on domain knowledge, and are not readily transferred from one domain to another.[55] A 2011 publication by the National Academy of Sciences was devoted to the problem of thinking skills. The report stated that there's "little evidence that critical thinking exists as a domain-general construct distinct from general cognitive ability."[56] And even if such general thinking skills did exist, it continued, there would be reason to doubt that they transfer across different subject matters: "such transfer seldom occurs naturally, particularly when learners need to transfer complex cognitive strategies from one domain to another."[57]

The state of research on the subject of critical thinking was nicely summed up in an e-mail to me by an expert in skills, Nathan R. Kuncel, professor of psychology at the University of Minnesota: "'Critical thinking' as it is typically discussed is a misguided educational fad. It is often portrayed as a universal skill that is independent of domain specific knowledge. I argue that research does not support this view. Instead, what people call critical thinking is either a class of very specific reasoning skills, or the formation of expertise in a field (e.g., medicine, accounting). In all cases, domain specific knowledge is necessary to make anything more than trivial progress with most problems."[58]

In earlier days the stress on critical-thinking skills was justified when John Dewey proposed it in 1910 as a solution to the problem of curricular fragmentation. We now know why it has not worked out in practice. The general skill of critical thinking does not exist; and even if it did, the process of looking things up is far more cumbersome than having a well-stocked mind that quickly populates working memory with the necessary elements before it "forgets the original context and never finds its way back."

In the rest of this chapter I will try to make these findings about skills more concrete by focusing on the skill of reading—a chief object of our schooling and testing. Reading ability serves as a rough proxy for verbal expertise generally, including effective writing, speaking, and listening. The topic has been muddied by the ambiguity of the word *reading*, which does not discriminate between decoding and comprehension.

Decoding is now being better taught in the United States, which accounts for the rise in third-grade reading scores. Decoding is a skill that applies to all texts in standard written English, though of course it is domain specific to that language and its standard spellings. But reading *comprehension*, unlike decoding, is not a general skill for standard written English. Comprehension involves making hypotheses about what the words mean. It applies to listening as much as to reading. That's why listening ability in early grades is the key to reading ability later on. In listening the young mind does not have to be slowed down by the new chore of decoding, and so can learn new words and concepts efficiently. Reading aloud to children and classroom discussion should play a big role in the early grades.

The policy world has not adequately understood the nature of reading comprehension. Two assumptions about reading dominated the current No Child Left Behind Act, and to some extent the Common Core initiative: first, that incentives and sanctions would change teachers' behavior; and second, that reading could be taught and tested as a general skill.[59] The incentives *did* change behavior productively in one area: decoding instruction did improve. But mature reading comprehension did not improve, because the assumption that reading comprehension can be taught as a general skill is incorrect.

We all know people who are good general readers. We can sympathize with the framers of NCLB when they assumed that reading ability is a general skill—especially since strategy instruction appeared in the recommendations of the National Reading Panel of 2000. Yet if a new report from an expert panel were issued today, it would almost certainly qualify that advice. We know more about reading comprehension now than we did in 2000.

In that year, two quite different, equally compelling pictures of reading were current among specialists. One picture conceived of comprehension expertise as a general strategic skill that enables a person to navigate any and all texts. The other (more correct) picture was that an expert reader is a person who has become knowledgeable about many different topics, and for that reason chiefly can navigate texts on those and related topics. That's why a well-rounded education is the best means of attaining all-around reading skill. Actually, it's the *only* means of doing so.

This insight was slow to develop. I will outline some key research that led to that conclusion. In 1983, Teun van Dijk and Walter Kintsch published a path-breaking book on verbal comprehension that extended insights gained during the preceding twenty years in psycholinguistics.[60] They stated the key insight as follows: "One of the major contributions of psychology is the recognition that much of the information needed to understand a text is not provided by the information expressed in the text itself but must be drawn from the language user's knowledge of the person, objects, states of affairs, or events the discourse is about."

Kintsch and van Dijk developed the insight further with the concept of the "situation model" to describe how readers construct meanings as they read. Readers build up meaning from both the words of the text and the relevant topic knowledge they already possess. If students lack the unwritten, unspoken knowledge required by the topic, they cannot comprehend what is written down. Knowledge of things unwritten—beyond word meanings—alone enables the written or spoken utterance to be understood. Language is surrounded by a cloud of taken-for-granted, unsaid knowledge, without which the said cannot be understood. This penumbra of unspoken knowledge that surrounds speech, and makes it comprehensible, is the knowledge possessed by well-educated insiders in a speech community. It is the shared knowledge that creates a large language community—the public sphere.

After publication of the Kintsch and van Dijk book, which summarized work of decades, further work on the role of specific background knowledge gained momentum. Here are three representative studies from 1998 to 2011.

- 1998: The Recht-Leslie study.[61] In 1988, Recht and Leslie showed that "poor readers" outperformed "good readers" when the poor readers knew more about the subject matter—in this case, baseball.[62] The underlying situation of the experiment was amusing. One group of twelve-year-olds was academically knowledgeable and scored well on reading tests, but knew little about baseball. Another group didn't know much in the academic way, and therefore scored poorly on reading tests, but knew a lot about baseball. On this particular task, the sports fans proved to be better readers, and illustrated the general principle: when a topic is familiar, "poor" readers become "good" readers; moreover, when a topic is unfamiliar, normally better readers lose their advantage. The Kintsch/van Dijk insight into "situation models" explains why this is so. The meaning of a text is constructed from both presented information and reader-contributed information to form the needed situation model. When the topic is unfamiliar, the reader can't contribute information; the situation model is fuzzy at best and comprehension is degraded. Mere strategies cannot provide the necessary information.
- 1999: The Schneider et al. study.[63] The following year, Wolfgang Schneider and his associates confirmed the Recht-Leslie result with a new wrinkle. The knowledge variables in their experiments were soccer knowledge versus soccer ignorance, and the variables were not higher and lower reading scores, but higher and lower IQs! The IQ element brought an added dimension to this line of research, because it showed the extent to which topic-relevant knowledge trumps basic cognitive differences. The low-IQ students who knew a lot about soccer outperformed the high-IQ students who had little soccer knowledge. Moreover, when both low- and high-IQ students were soccer experts, the low-IQ students performed just as well as those with high-IQs! That is an especially interesting result from the standpoint of equity, showing that substantial domain knowledge can reduce achievement gaps even when based on IQ—clearly an

important finding for school policy. Equity is served by systematic knowledge gain both among the economically and the cognitively disadvantaged.

- **2011: The Arya et al. study.**[64] In 2011, Arya, Hiebert, and Pearson reported—against their own prior expectations—that comprehension of texts depends less on text complexity than on the reader's familiarity with the topic. With topics unfamiliar to third graders, like *tree frogs* and *soil*, text complexity slowed reading and debased understanding. But when the topics were familiar, as with *toothpaste* and *jelly beans*, the complexity of the text had little effect on accuracy or speed of comprehension. The significance of this result is that domain knowledge trumps text complexity, just as it trumps average reading ability and IQ.[65] And it does so for the same reason that domain knowledge facilitates problem solving in chess and physics: verbal comprehension is a form of problem solving. Topic familiarity makes the task of forming a situation model fast and accurate, leaving more space in working memory to figure out word relations, whether they are complex or simple. Text complexity is shrugged off and unfamiliar words are rightly guessed when the topic is familiar.

Domain knowledge facilitates problem solving in any domain—hence, the best way to teach "problem-solving skill" is to offer a broad education! When a third grader confronts a text about tree frogs, the problem to be solved is: What is the text trying to say? Rare third graders who know something about tree frogs are much more likely to solve the meaning problem than those who don't. But most don't know about tree frogs. They get stymied. But when they are given a technically harder text about jelly beans, they read with ease. They know about jelly beans, so they build a situation model. They make good fast guesses about what the words are trying to say—even though the words are rare and the sentences complex. Making such guesses is how they (and we) learned most of the new words we know. The more we already know about the topic, the more accurate will be our guesses about the text's meaning.

The mistaken conception of reading as a general skill has led to a frantic short-term, quick-fix view of education that has resulted in little long-term payoff—much like the business practice of paying attention only to earnings for this quarter, and ignoring what is needed for long-term growth. The narrowing of the elementary school curriculum that ensued through the increased focus on technique over knowledge gain has diminished knowledge and vocabularies, and thus the communication skills of older students.

A substantive and coherent elementary curriculum that builds the factual and conceptual knowledge of all students during the seven years from preschool through grade five and then beyond is the most effective way to ensure competent verbal abilities in grades six through twelve. On the basis of the evidence and the research to date in the year 2016, such a curriculum is the only means yet devised to bring nearly all students in a nation to adequate competence, and a large percentage to very high competence, in reading and writing. It is the best route to communication skills and other twenty-first-century skills, rightly understood.

CHAPTER FIVE

The Persistence of Achievement Gaps

WHEN PROGRESS STOPPED

With the help of good schools, exceptionally brilliant and resourceful students can almost completely overcome the disadvantages of poverty and a suboptimal home environment.[1] But no national school system in the world has been able to overcome disadvantages of birth completely. No school system could do so, because the schools alone are not the sole agents of education. Advantaged children enjoy a superior nonschool education with richer language, better nutrition, better health care, and wider experiences—advantages that cannot be entirely overcome by good schools. But the gaps between advantaged and disadvantaged students can be greatly narrowed; they can also be greatly widened. Some national systems have narrowed the gap better than others. The French school system is a textbook case in which the gaps had been narrowed, but were subsequently enormously widened when France abandoned a national curriculum in favor of a less communal scheme. Those details are described in chapter 7. In this chapter I will discuss the American experience of achievement gaps, and their relation to school quality, especially the quality of the school curriculum.

In 2010 the Educational Testing Service (ETS) published a report called *The Black-White Achievement Gap: When Progress Stopped*. The reason the black-white gap was chosen for analysis by ETS instead of including all low-scoring groups was that the black-white gap has been studied longer, and offers fuller opportunities for historical analysis. That long span of study revealed an intriguing pattern. The gap narrowed through the twentieth century, reaching its narrowest in 1988; then, it stalled.

A confounding element was school desegregation after *Brown v. Board of Education* in 1954. Desegregation had an initial positive effect, which then ceased.[2] Some have argued that the halt was caused by resegregation. But the ETS report demurs, summarizing a massive 1994 study by David Grissmer and his colleagues on this issue. After reviewing the various *social* causes of the gap stasis, Grissmer et al. concluded that some two-thirds of the causal effects remain unaccounted for after such social factors as economic status and school integration are taken into account. The inside-the-school causes within that unaccounted-for two-thirds could not be factored in, because changes in school factors—including school curriculums—are unknown.

But school factors can still be guessed at intelligently. Polices can be undertaken within schools to narrow the achievement gaps between demographic groups. For one thing, we can know with near certainty that the nature of the *learned* curriculum will exercise a very large school effect on the reading gaps between groups of seventeen-year-olds, according to the following logic:[3]

> Reading comprehension scores of seventeen-year-olds (where the scores count for life chances) are very highly correlated with vocabulary size.
>
> 1. Vocabulary size is the product of slow, multiyear accretion.
> 2. The school's contribution to vocabulary gain is largely determined by the breadth of the learned curriculum in the pre–high school grades.
> 3. The breadth of the learned curriculum is correlated with the breadth of the actual school curriculum—highly correlated if the school does a responsible job.

4. A broad curriculum that is effectively taught to all students inherently narrows vocabulary gaps, because the students who knew fewer words to start with are now learning more words per lesson than their advantaged peers who already knew some of the words in the lesson.[4]

5. To narrow the vocabulary gap between demographic groups narrows the reading-comprehension gap and therefore also narrows the achievement gap.

Conclusion: the school's contribution to narrowing the verbal achievement gap depends greatly on the breadth and cumulativeness of the elementary curriculum.

As the saying goes, to a man with a hammer everything looks like a nail. A social scientist looks for social causes. A school reformer like me looks for school effects. Both are important, but there has been little analysis of school effects—understandably, since the substantive content in the American school curriculum remains unstated and largely unknown.

As a social policy, busing and reintegration make sense so long as the schools attended by advantaged children continue to be far superior to those attended by disadvantaged children. What has not been successful is the policy of trying to make all neighborhood schools far better—an aim that can only be accomplished when schools offer a well-taught, well-planned, multiyear curriculum that systematically builds up knowledge. Such good schools can transform the atmosphere and sentiments of the neighborhood.[5] Interviews with parents make overwhelmingly clear that parents prefer the nearby school especially if it is a good school.[6]

That finding about parental preferences should be an important fact for advocates of "choice." Those reformers who emphasize the need for parental choice as well as those who favor renewed busing might well consider the parental voices that overwhelmingly favor improving the neighborhood school. At present, only some 30 percent of parents in inferior schools favor transporting their child to another school.[7] Until we have good schools in poor neighborhoods—a possible goal, achieved in other nations—that 30 percent of parents who desire busing should certainly have viable choices, as choice advocates insist. The other 70 percent of parents who wish to stick to their neighborhoods also deserve good schools for their children. That is what they would certainly choose—as would many of the 30 percent as well. This is the true principle of "choice." Who wouldn't prefer to send their young children in early grades to the closest school that is safe, orderly, caring, and high performing?

Support for the key importance of school effects in closing gaps comes from international comparisons of national systems in which curriculum content is well documented. Some national systems perform better than others in narrowing achievement gaps between economically disparate groups. The 2012 PISA studies of fifteen-year-olds across the globe have devoted a volume to that subject.[8] Those nations whose elementary schools perform the best overall—Finland, Canada, Japan, Korea—also rank high in narrowing the achievement gaps between economic groups. In the highest-scoring nations the year-to-year curriculum topics are known to all—students, teachers, and parents.[9] This chapter is devoted to the reasons for a correlation between curriculum quality and equality. It will explain why our own progress in narrowing the achievement gaps between groups has largely come to a halt. The "new education" caused curriculum quality to decline, stopping progress in equality, and putting a nation at risk.

UPDATING THE COLEMAN REPORT

A clue to what happened to cause the halt can be found in a famous study from the 1960s that focused on equality of schooling. In 1964, the US Civil Rights Act authorized a major study to determine whether the public schools were giving minority students a fair shake. The ensuing 1966 report was entitled *Equality of Educational Opportunity*. It is the most famous educational study ever undertaken in the United States, and probably the largest. It sampled some 650,000 students.[10] The report has continued to inform our thinking about school policy ever since it was issued.

The lead author of the American study was James S. Coleman, a distinguished and thoughtful scholar. It became known as "the Coleman Report." Its data have been pored over and reanalyzed. A recent reanalysis, published in 2010, was able, as it states, to "disentangle how schools and students' family backgrounds contribute to learning outcomes. The new methodology offers a clearer interpretation of the relative effects of school characteristics, including racial/ethnic composition, and family background, on students' academic outcomes." The 2010 reanalysis summarized its findings as follows: "Our results suggest that schools do indeed matter, in that when one examines the outcomes across the national sample of schools, fully 40% of the differences in achievement can be found between schools. Even after statistically taking into account students' family background, a large proportion of the variation among true school means is related to differences explained by school characteristics."[11]

This is a timely correction to initial reactions to the Coleman Report. After the report came out, educators highlighted the finding that family and poverty were affecting educational outcomes more than schools did. That interpretation enabled schools to keep doing in good conscience what they had been doing, without feeling open to the reproach that they were injuring poor minority children.

But, as Coleman ruefully noted, there was always a logical flaw in the "it's not the schools" interpretation of the Coleman Report. It had taken its soundings at a particular historical moment: in the 1960s after the child-centered takeover of American elementary schools. Even if that critical historical event had not occurred, a more punctilious and precise interpretation of the data could conclude only that family and poverty affected educational outcomes more than schools *as American schools were then constituted.* Coleman drew precisely that more accurate interpretation—quite different from the social determinism of apologists for the performance of the public schools, who emphasized only the finding that family then mattered more than schools.

Coleman was distressed by both the minimal equity effects of current schools and by the self-protective reaction to his report by the education community. The data actually implied, Coleman said, that schools *could* indeed matter a great deal. He was so disturbed by the social determinism of the interpreters that he pursued further studies showing that Catholic schools were doing an excellent job in reducing the impact of family and poverty on educational achievement. That buttressed his larger point: schools *can* educate all children well, and greatly ameliorate disadvantage *if* they are good orderly schools that impart a strong, coherent curriculum as the Catholic schools did.[12]

Moreover, he found a hint of potential high-equity effects in the original data itself. He pointed out that the data contained an anomaly from which one might infer that better schools *could* greatly ameliorate educational disadvantage. Here is how he described the anomaly:

> The average white student's achievement seems to be less affected by the strength or weakness of his school's facilities, curriculums, and teachers than is the average minority pupil's. To put it another way, the achievement of minority pupils depends more on the schools they attend than does the achievement of majority pupils. Thus, 20 percent of the achievement of Negroes in the South is associated with the particular schools they go to, whereas only 10 percent of the achievement of whites in the South is. Except for Oriental Americans, this general result is found for all minorities. The inference might then be made that improving the school of a minority pupil may increase his achievement more than would improving the school of a white child increase his. Similarly, the average minority pupil's achievement may suffer more in a school of low quality than might the average white pupil's. In short, whites, and to a lesser extent Oriental Americans, are less affected one way or the other by the quality of their schools than are minority pupils. This indicates that it is for the most disad-

vantaged children that improvements in school quality will make the most difference in achievement.[13]

Coleman thought this finding was probably the most important of his report. It was the one he stressed in the two-hundred-word abstract that appears in the educational clearinghouse called ERIC.[14] An inferior school widens the achievement gap, because it harms poor children *more* than it harms rich ones. A good school narrows the achievement gap, because it benefits poor children more than it benefits rich ones.

Thus, good schools *inherently* narrow the gap. While bad schools have at least twice the negative effect on poor children as on rich ones, bad schools also have a considerable negative effect on rich children. Conversely, good schools affect rich children positively, but they benefit poor children at least twice as much. By that math, gap closing will occur in any good school. The solution to the equity problem is basically to have good schools with coherent curricula, as the Catholic schools did. That policy will be inherently effective in narrowing educational gaps.

Coleman's insight that school quality affects disadvantaged students twice as much as advantaged children deserves to be memorialized as the "Coleman Differential Effect." Consider the potential implications of his discovery. If poor children get twice as much academic benefit from a good school as rich children do, then in each year of good schooling that differential causes poor children to catch up a little. But the gap gets bigger in each year of poor schooling.[15] And indeed, the National Assessment of Educational Progress (NAEP) shows that the black-white equity gap in reading consistently *increases* between age thirteen and age seventeen. If K–12 schooling had been good schooling, that could not have occurred; the gaps would have consistently narrowed as children stayed in school. The finding of the Coleman Differential Effect is thus a reproach to the American school system as it now stands. If schools become better, the gaps will narrow rather than widen between ages thirteen and seventeen. Moreover, the current gap is really greater than appears at age seventeen because NAEP does not include the thousands of low-scoring students who drop out between thirteen and seventeen.[16]

DOMAIN IMMERSION AND GAP CLOSING

Let's consider the details of how the Coleman Differential Effect works in high-achieving nations that narrow achievement gaps. Doing so will entail getting into the scientific and pedagogical weeds, which is where gap closing occurs. Let's suppose we start in a good preschool, the ideal situation. At age three or four, poor children are significantly behind linguistically, but the vocabulary gap is only several hundred words, not several thousand.[17] So, while there are many things that children should learn in preschool, the chief aim from the standpoint of social justice is to enhance their knowledge, syntax, and vocabularies. The surest way to do that in preschool is the strategy of "domain immersion," described in chapter 3. It is a principle that should continue to be followed also in later grades. It requires a definite and coherent curriculum.

When domain immersion is applied consistently with a careful sequence of domains over a full school year, and then in the next year and the year after that, with independent readings directed to the purpose, vocabulary catch-up occurs by implicit word learning. The coherence of the curriculum benefits all students. Crucially, it benefits the least prepared the most.

The domain immersion method was pioneered and evaluated systematically in the United States by John Guthrie.[18] He called it "Concept-Oriented Reading Instruction" (CORI). He could just as well have named it "Domain-Oriented Reading Instruction." "Domain immersion" is also a useful alternative description of his method, since the word *domain* fits in with the principle of "domain specificity," a key principle of cognitive science. Domain immersion is a method that works equally well for fiction and nonfiction.

What does not work nearly as effectively for vocabulary building is the isolated study of words. Such study has its place, as it comes up in context within the study of domains, but not in isolation from that larger context. The intensive study of word lists in our schools today is an inefficient, fallback position made necessary by the absence of common cumulative content in the language arts class in elementary school.

Let's take a look at the best-authenticated practice of explicit word study. It divides words into three categories: tier one, tier two, and tier three.[19] Tier-one words—like *tree, child,* and *field*—are used so often that native speakers understand their meanings without special study. Tier-two words—such as *frequency, compilation,* and *manifestation*—are used somewhat less frequently but are important to know, because they are found in all sorts of different contexts. Tier-two words, therefore, are the words that skills-curriculum experts recommend as objects of explicit word study. But these experts do not recommend devoting much time to rarer tier-three words (e.g., *halide, nullification,* or *Winston Churchill*). Such words, they say, will be gained on special occasions or in studying special subjects but, taken as a group, they're so numerous yet so rarely used that student time is better spent on more frequent, tier-two words.[20]

On the surface the argument is reasonable, but we have seen (in the case of main-idea seeking) that overdoing reasonable ideas quickly reaches a point of diminishing returns. Is there an opportunity cost to explicit word study, after which point schools will build student vocabulary faster by *not* dedicating special time segments to explicit word study? Yes, indeed. One quickly reaches the point of diminishing returns, because *implicit word learning is much faster and more accurate than explicit word learning.* That's an unexpected finding.

It was demonstrated mathematically in a series of articles by William Nagy, Patricia Herman, and Richard Anderson.[21] Implicit learning *appears* to be very gradual and slow because it takes place over months and years rather than days. We are grasping the partial meanings of dozens and dozens of words at a time. So we learn many, many more total words implicitly than we could ever learn by taking them one at a time. Experts estimate that by age sixteen, a typical young person has gained by implicit means about 15 words a day (including Saturdays, Sundays, and holidays, as well as summer vacation)—some 5,475 words a year. It's a misleading figure in some ways, though. We do not unconsciously learn 15 separate new words every day. It's a cumulative average, from an ongoing, gradual process.

Another advantage of implicit word learning is that it's more accurate than explicit study, as documented by George A. Miller and Patricia Gildea in their classic article "How Children Learn Words." Miller is one of the great path-breaking figures in cognitive psychology, and until his recent death he was the top researcher into vocabulary gain. In the 1987 study, he and Gildea showed that explicit word study with a dictionary often encourages a quite inaccurate sense of word connotations.[22] In his last major article on word knowledge, "On Knowing a Word" (1999), Miller helped us understand why isolated word study, besides taking a lot of time, doesn't produce *accurate* results.[23] An accurate sense of word connotations is built up gradually from multiple past contexts. We remember bits of those past contexts along with our memories of the word, and those remembered bits help us identify nuances of words among the range of multiple meanings each word potentially has. Explicit word study, while useful and even necessary at times, can be distortive as well as time-consuming. It should be used sparingly.

There is thus a connection between the supposedly child-friendly individualism of the new education and the stall in the narrowing of verbal achievement gaps. Encouraging children to follow their interests leaves them with big holes in their knowledge and vocabulary. These holes are supposed to be filled by word lists, and by drills in comprehension strategies. The verdict is in on these ideas and methods: they have not worked. And a more probing analysis says they cannot work. They have led to highly unnatural and unpleasant forms of schooling, which have left disadvantaged students disadvantaged. Who can blame disadvantaged students for dropping out of that kind of unpleasant, frustrating, and ineffectual schooling? Whole-class domain immersion is the better system, early and late.

A domain in the educational sense is not just some definite factual system, though that is a domain too. A domain is any larger context into which the things being studied are integrated and connected conceptually and linguistically. In vocabulary terms, the things studied occupy a "word field"—a set of words that tend to occur together and help co-determine meanings by their co-occurrence.[24] So if a student is studying a fictional text—a poem or novel—that is a domain too, just as much as Newton's three laws of motion. The value of the concept of *domain* for education is its psychological validity. In language use it represents the relevant prior knowledge that contextualizes a discourse and enables a student to form a situation model for the meaning. That is the key condition for learning new words *and* new things. *Domain* has the further advantage of representing the scientifically accepted understanding of the knowledge that is foundational to a skill. Knowledge is the key to gap closing, and it is best gained coherently by the cumulative, year-by-year study of domains—by a well-defined, cumulative curriculum. This chapter has outlined the underlying reasons why such a cumulative curriculum is the key to gap narrowing by the schools. On such technical, nitty-gritty psychological principles hang great issues of equity and equality of opportunity.

CHAPTER SIX

The Tribulations of the Common Core

TWO STRANDS IN THE COMMON CORE LANGUAGE ARTS STANDARDS

The Common Core State Standards in language arts can improve American education significantly, but only if we interpret them productively. They are superior to earlier state standards in some respects but all too similar to them in not stating the specific knowledge that students should gain. The Common Core language arts standards emphasize skills such as finding the main idea, managing complex texts, and reading closely. Yet real improvement in students' verbal abilities will not depend on practicing these skills; it will depend on how much students know and how big their vocabularies are.

In isolated paragraphs, the Common Core Standards acknowledge this fact. Those knowledge-centric statements are the ones that must predominate if progress is to be made. If the Core standards that focus on knowledge are interpreted as the dominant ones, overshadowing the statements about skills, then we can expect twelfth-grade results to be superior to those of past standards that emphasized skills. The long-range educational success of the new Common Core Standards in language arts will depend almost completely on interpreting them as requiring a coherent approach to building knowledge in the elementary school. If, as is currently happening, the schools continue to emphasize skills, the new standards will fail to enlarge students' vocabularies significantly and will therefore fail to improve verbal abilities significantly.

The prior chapters of this book have shown that for several decades, the policy of promulgating standards that don't name grade-by-grade content has ensured an emphasis on skills. That policy has failed students. Content-indeterminate standards plus content-indeterminate tests have caused schools to de-emphasize systematic knowledge gain. The secret to success will be found in devising means of thwarting this vicious cycle of test preparation to achieve nonexistent all-purpose skills, a policy that has neglected knowledge and sustained low verbal abilities.[1]

In the following statements the Common Core Standards show the way to thwart that vicious cycle:

> The Standards . . . do not—indeed, cannot—enumerate all or even most of the content that students should learn. The Standards must therefore be complemented by a well-developed, content-rich curriculum.
>
> By reading texts in history/social studies, science, and other disciplines, students build a foundation of knowledge in these fields that will also give them the background to be better readers in all content areas. Students can only gain this foundation when the curriculum is intentionally and coherently structured to develop rich content knowledge within and across grades.
>
> Building knowledge systematically in English language arts is like giving children various pieces of a puzzle in each grade that, over time, will form one big picture. At a curricular or instructional level, texts—within and across grade levels—need to be selected around topics or themes that systematically develop the knowledge base of students. Within a grade level, there should be an adequate number of titles on a single topic that would allow children to study that topic for a sustained period. The knowledge children have learned about particular topics in early grade levels should then be expanded and developed in subsequent grade levels to ensure an increasingly deeper understanding of these topics. Children in the upper elementary grades will generally be expected to read these texts independently and reflect on them in writing. However, children in the early grades (particularly K–2)

should participate in rich, structured conversations with an adult in response to the written texts that are read aloud.

These are golden words. But no district that I know of is paying much attention to them—for they are words without consequences. They have no direct operational impact on tests. Although the statements fairly shout that "rich" knowledge and vocabulary are the goals toward which schools should aim, those sentiments cannot affect the topics of test items, since test makers cannot know which topics in each grade level are the ones to which "an adequate number of titles" have been devoted in the schools. This disconnect between curriculum and test causes test makers to direct their attention away from standards that speak of coherent curricular content and toward those content-free Core standards that speak of "close reading," "complexity," and "finding the main idea."

These new criteria claim to be technically superior to those found in the state standards that preceded them. But as I showed in chapter 1, the Common Core Standards continue to demand that students "find the main idea," a boon to test makers who can continue to write items like: "The main idea of this passage is: A, B, C, or D." To this main-idea-finding skill, the new Core standards have added a "close-reading" skill requiring students to make "logical" inferences from the text: "Read closely to determine what the text says explicitly and to make logical inferences from it."[2] This allows test makers to create items like: "Which of the following statements are implied by X: A, B, C, or D?" Another supposed advance in the new standards is marked by the term *complexity*. It seeks to encourage a rise in the quality of texts in each grade by making the texts more substantial and challenging. Operationally this has meant using texts that have higher Lexile scores than schools used before, a potential step forward to the extent that it builds student knowledge and vocabulary more rapidly. There's little reason to hope that this will happen simply from raising the Lexile levels of helter-skelter texts.

The net result of the new standards so far has been to make the tests harder to pass, but not to make students better able to pass them. The test-anxiety cycle of No Child Left Behind has begun again, with understandable protests from parents, teachers, and students. I will explain in this chapter why the addition of close reading to main-idea finding will turn out in the end *not* to raise mature reading scores, and could even lower them by encouraging schools to usurp yet more class time in practicing formal close-reading skills in preparation for close-reading test items. The task of close reading in early grades has caused a big boost in the sale of highlight markers, which enable children to practice marking up their books.[3] That is not a very good way to increase knowledge and vocabulary. The practice of marking texts with highlighters is emblematic of the problem that schools face under current arrangements when content-indeterminate language standards are tested by content-indeterminate tests.

Still, the makers of the new Core standards in language arts must not be faulted for failing to specify content. They knew that including definite text titles would exclude gaining the adherence of over forty states, a remarkable achievement. The listing of titles other than the Declaration of Independence and the Gettysburg Address and a few others would have seemed entirely arbitrary. This is especially true for stories and poems. I'll come back to this problem at the end of this chapter. I mention it in passing, because I do not want my analysis to suggest that a failure to specify definite texts in the Common Core is some sort of moral or intellectual failing. We lack a universally agreed-upon literary canon in the United States. If the framers of the Common Core Standards had tried to impose some arbitrary list of literary works, the standards would simply have been rejected.

But in a wider view that is not an insuperable problem. It is not necessary for a student to master a specific literary canon to score well on a reading test, nor to be college and career ready, nor to become a competent citizen. On the other hand, there *is a canon of knowledge and vocabulary* known to all highly competent readers and writers. That is axiomatic; possessing that knowledge is what makes them competent. One can only become a competent reader and writer by sharing unspoken knowledge with other competent readers and writers in the wider public sphere. That knowledge canon must be mastered to gain proficiency in language arts.

Although the makers of state standards do not select particular topics, the makers of tests can't avoid doing so. They must reach specific content decisions about the particular passages that will appear on the tests. But since the specific content in the school curriculum is unknown, the test makers are not able to choose passages based on school content. Since that uncertainty is not their fault, the test makers are also morally blameless in this situation. They are compelled to offer texts on domains of knowledge not studied in school, since the school domains are unstated and unknown.

But *any* test passage silently assumes unstated knowledge and vocabulary that must be known in order to understand the passage. The situation model that the student must construct to grasp the meaning of the passage is not directly presented in the words of the text. The necessary reader-contributed knowledge must already be possessed by the student. "Reading tests are knowledge tests in disguise" is Daniel Willingham's elegant formulation.[4]

Test makers must not acknowledge the disguise. They have to pretend that reading tests are about skills. Lifting the disguise will require devising knowledge-based curricula and reading tests based on that known school curriculum—the only kind of reading tests that can be fair and productive. So long as a nationwide elementary content core is a political impossibility, we will have to give up the pipe dream of nationwide reading tests that are both fair and productive of sound school practice. If the test is not curriculum based, it will not be productive.

Nationwide reading tests taken by students in multiple states was a dream of policy makers who have been concerned that students in some states are measured more tolerantly than those in others. But getting a common yardstick and more accurate data is not as important an aim as making better readers.[5] And the two aims now conflict, for only curriculum-based tests can be fair and educationally productive. Since only states and localities can currently determine the knowledge domains of the curriculum, they are currently the only jurisdictions in a position to make fair and productive tests.[6] To be educationally valid, high-stakes reading tests would need to be composed of passages on domains from the local curriculum. The goal of higher national verbal abilities trumps the goal of uniform assessments so long as the two goals remain incompatible.

At the present time, setting forth and teaching a well-articulated *local* core curriculum is the only politically viable way to foster coherent knowledge buildup and curriculum-based tests, the only kinds that can be productive and fair. Productive and fair tests based on a coherent and effective curriculum are the only known routes out of the vicious cycle. The current alternative— the teaching and testing of all-purpose reading-comprehension skills—cannot work because such skills do not exist.

Hence my first task in this chapter on the Common Core is to show that the all-purpose skills advocated in the Common Core language arts standards are largely myths just like the all-purpose skills of earlier state standards. I will show that there is no general main-idea-finding skill, no complexity-managing skill, and no close-reading skill. If such all-purpose reading skills existed, our seventeen-year-olds, who have practiced such skills for years, would be performing better on NAEP and the SAT, not worse. There is much greater promise for progress in the "rich coherent curriculum" provisions of the Common Core Standards, even though test-anxious schools are not paying much attention to them.

It is hard to foresee progress until the basic test structure is changed. A new emphasis must be placed on building up student knowledge. It is not in the power of any policy maker, legislator, standards maker, or anyone else involved in educational policy to repeal the knowledge-based character of verbal skills.

MAIN-IDEA FINDING, CLOSE READING, AND READING CHALLENGING TEXTS

In chapter 1 I explained that the chief virtue of the main-idea concept is its convenience for grownups, not for students, who have not been much helped under its regime. For a reader who may have skipped to this chapter without reading chapter 1, I'll briefly recapitulate: The main-idea standard was devised to enable test makers to ask main-idea questions about reading passages so that those questions *appear* to follow the main-idea stipulations of the standards. But there *is* no significant main-idea-finding skill apart from the prior ability to comprehend a text—an ability that depends on the relevant knowledge and vocabulary already possessed by the student taking the test. Those who understand the text can answer the main-idea question without ever having been drilled in main-idea finding—an inferential oral skill developed from infancy. The initial boost gained by students spending a week or so practicing the skill is caused by teachers clueing in six- and seven-year-olds to the idea that figuring out what a text is saying is like figuring out what a person is saying.[7] The underlying inferential ability has already been developed by every student, since it was needed in infancy for the child to learn the mother tongue. It is further developed through talking and listening. Main-idea finding is thus a useful skill to study and practice for a couple of weeks in an early grade so the child can apply an already-developed ability to the novel task of parsing meaning from a text. They come to understand that a text is like a person who is trying to tell you something.

From an analytical view, the main-idea-finding skill is a circularity. You can't deduce the main idea until you have already construed what the text means. But if you already understand what the text means, you already know the main idea implicitly and can answer main-idea questions about the passage without consciously going through some main-idea algorithm. Advantaged children who understand the test passage through their wider knowledge and vocabulary will quickly and correctly answer the question. Disadvantaged children lacking requisite knowledge and vocabulary will not be able to answer the question. They would perform far better on the passage if they had studied question-relevant subject matter in school. And in that case they would not need to practice finding the main idea.

The new skill standard that has garnered the most attention is close reading: "Read closely to determine what the text says explicitly and to make logical inferences from it." When I consult the Internet to see how this standard is being implemented in the early grades, I find teachers advising each other about how to get their students to pay close attention to the words of the text. I find images of young students' books with every word highlighted; a printed page that was originally white is now mainly red or yellow. Other photographs show pages with penciled circles around phrases—about five circles to a page. Other pages are heavily annotated in the margins.

Close reading is an activity that is suitable for appreciating the finer points of literature in later grades. It is a good principle for writing papers about literary texts when defending an argument about an appropriate interpretation. For those purposes the tradition of close reading has proved its worth in later grades. But to encourage the practice as a mode of actual reading of texts or the testing of reading comprehension is a mistake unjustified by credible research.

Consider the following experiment conducted by cognitive scientist Rolf Zwaan at the University of Rotterdam. He and his colleagues contrived an arrangement so that one group of experimental subjects close-read a text. The comparison group read simply for meanings in the usual way, not close-reading the words as such. The first group could remember the words very well, but they could not remember the meanings as well as the group who read for meaning but did not close-read. Close reading had produced *inferior* comprehension and memory for meaning. This, by the way, is one of the few pieces of research on the subject to have come out in a peer-reviewed scientific journal.[8]

With most texts, paying close attention to the text itself debases comprehension by usurping limited mental resources that would be better applied to pondering the substantive implications and the validity of what the text is saying. Thus people who do *not* pay conscious attention to the vehicle of meaning tend to understand and recall textual meaning better than those who read in a more literary way. Close reading is mainly valuable as a specialized literary exercise for advanced students who have already understood the text, and wish to refine or deepen that understanding, usually for the purpose of writing about the text.

Three fundamental findings in cognitive science contributed to Professor Zwaan's negative result for close reading. The first is that human working memory is limited. When we pay attention to the vehicle of meaning, we are paying less attention to meanings and judgments that we might otherwise be attending to. The second finding is that we remember what we pay attention to. If we pay attention to words, those are what we will consider and remember rather than important unstated implications. The third reason that close reading can actually debase initial comprehension is equally fundamental, and is fatal to the notion of "logical implications" of words. Recent work on text comprehension shows that interpreted meaning is not reliably bound to the words that produce it; that is, close reading can be very misleading as a basis for "drawing logical inferences." That's because words are ambiguous—an absolutely critical feature of human language that allows it to become a hugely flexible instrument. Two identical groups of words can express different meanings. To use the current term in the psychological literature: the very same text can express different *propositions*.[9] That's why state-of-the-art translation programs such as Google Translate are so unreliable. They are very good at close reading, but poor at understanding, since the relation between close reading and meaning is inherently indeterminate.

The inferences we usually draw from a text are not logical but contextual—dependent upon the situation model that we construct, not upon the mere words on the page. Staring at a text, as our young students are being compelled to do, is not a good way to improve reading comprehension, because the text does not speak its own meaning. That meaning is a construct composed of what the text says plus the additional relevant, unspoken knowledge that the reader brings to it. When I examine what people actually do when they use close reading in order to write about texts, I find that they use the close-reading technique to support the meanings that they have already gained before they began to close-read. What Oscar Wilde said about Wordsworth holds for the meanings that people find when they close-read: "He found in stones the sermons he had already hidden there."[10]

The unfortunate consequences of the scientifically questionable close-reading strand in the Common Core is the effect it has had on the tests and the time-wasting preparation for them. The Partnership for Assessment of Readiness for College and Careers (PARCC), one of the two Common Core test consortia, has created two-part close-reading questions. One part asks about the meaning of a word, the other about the feature of the text from which one can logically infer that meaning.[11]

> **Part A.** Read the sentence from paragraph one:
>
> "Rufus sat beside me for a while, hoping I'd be up to something more than *misery*."
>
> What does the word *misery* mean as it is used in the sentence?
>
> Confusion
> Exhaustion
> Nervousness
> Unhappiness
>
> **Part B.** Which detail from the story provides the *best* clue for the meaning of the word *misery*?
>
> a. ". . . waiting for nothing, with nothing I wanted to do."

  b. ". . . tired of waiting and went off on his own . . ."
  c. "And right away, I knew what I had to do."
  d. "No plans."

Suppose the young test taker did not already know the meaning of the word *misery*. She is being asked to infer that meaning by close-reading the surrounding words. In that case, she could infer that "nothing I wanted to do" signified exhaustion. So from the test items alone she could logically say that (b) is the right answer to the first, and (a) is the right answer to the second. She'd be wrong—but not because she had failed to learn how to close-read; she's doing that all too well. No, her answer that *misery* means exhaustion is wrong because logical inference from close reading is a mirage. What she needed to know to answer the question was the usual meaning of the word *misery*. And for that, no logical inferences needed to be made by close-reading the surrounding text. The public has already started to protest these odd and sometimes unanswerable test items that have been constructed on an inadequate concept of reading comprehension.[12]

This close-reading standard in the Common Core should be recast (or excised) to conform with the scientific finding that paying attention to word features is less effective than reading for meaning, and in light of the fact that the defects of the concept induce unreliable test items and unproductive teaching activities.

The third skill standard of the Common Core is that of reading complex texts. It is an attempt to improve knowledge and reading comprehension ability through a technical approach to choosing texts at higher difficulty levels. It tries to induce a more challenging and productive curriculum under the political constraint that the actual knowledge domains and texts of the curriculum must not be prescribed.

The aim is noble, and it is hard to see how it can be harmful to ask students to read more challenging texts. One of the theories for the decline in reading abilities had been that the texts students have been asked to read are too undemanding.[13] It would follow, then, that if in the past we used readability measures like Lexiles to dumb down the elementary curriculum, we might use those same measures at a higher level to smarten up the curriculum. Instead of naming Lexiles with the old term *readability*, a term associated with making texts easier, we will now make them harder and call Lexiles *complexity*.

I have seen reports from the field that early implementation of the Common Core has indeed produced the hoped-for positive result: "At first we felt angry, thinking, *Students can't do this; this is too difficult and this is not a seventh-grade text.* I think it just comes from these deep-seated beliefs about what students should be doing at that age, or what you read at that age. But in actuality they can do more than we often think they can."[14]

But there are strict limits to the progress students can make if the text, regardless of its Lexile score, is on a topic that is unfamiliar. This is where the knowledge imperative and the skill imperative of the Common Core come into conflict. Intellectually, the skills-approach lives uncomfortably with the new, more communal approach of Common Core Standards that require a rich, coherent curriculum. Complexity and Lexiles are largely indifferent to subject matter. They can equally sponsor a coherent curriculum or a fragmented one. That is why they can be used as a technical crutch for content avoidance by those who wish to individualize the curriculum as well as by those who wish to avoid controversy.

The standards define *complexity* as composed of three elements: a Lexile score, a text-quality judgment, and a tailoring to the individual student. But that is very similar to the individualized system of text selection in the classroom libraries discussed in chapter 4. Such individualism is antithetical to the rich communal curriculum required by the standards. A camel is a horse designed by a committee: the various parts of the Core standards do not cohere. The requirement that "the curriculum is intentionally and coherently structured to develop rich content knowledge within and across grades" can only be fulfilled if students in the early grades mostly read the same texts. This self-contradiction within the Common Core Standards should be resolved in favor of commonality of texts in the classroom, since that's the only way to effectively implement a rich, coherent, and cumulative curriculum.

Such an approach to complexity would also be superior from the standpoint of student progress from week to week. As topics become familiar, student ability to master rarer words and longer sentences (the chief elements of complexity) increases.[15] Under a coherent common curriculum, texts with high Lexile scores might have been unreadable for many students at the beginning of a two-week unit on a domain like "Plants and Chlorophyll," but will become highly readable by the end of the unit. The people in the Common Core Standards committee who wrote about using a sequence of texts from the same domain understood this principle of domain immersion. It induces progress in reading complex texts not because an all-purpose complexity-managing skill has increased in two weeks, but because students' domain familiarity has increased. Getting familiar with a lot of domains is the best way to enhance ability to read complex texts, since there is no all-purpose complexity-managing skill. Domain familiarity is the chief complexity-managing skill.

In sum, the reliable way to achieve technical reading comprehension skills for all students, including the ability to read highly complex and challenging texts, is for the school to stress knowledge front and center as the chief reading comprehension skill: "Within a grade level, there should be an adequate number of titles on a single topic that would allow children to study that topic for a sustained period. The knowledge children have learned about particular topics in early grade levels should then be expanded and developed in subsequent grade levels to ensure an increasingly deeper understanding of these topics."

That's wonderful advice, but what should those topics be? I'll discuss some key principles in the next two sections.

"IMAGINATIVE LITERATURE" IS NOT PRIVILEGED IN LANGUAGE ARTS, BUT NARRATIVES AND KNOWLEDGE ARE

The most criticized element in the Common Core language arts standards is one of the best standards of all—that about half of the texts read should be "informational" texts. This immediately reduces the number of vacuous stories about picnics at the beach with the Beaver family, and it potentially enhances the curriculum with more systematic knowledge and vocabulary in multiple domains.

The standards have served themselves ill by using the technocratic-sounding term *informational*. The distinction need not be between "literary" and "informational" texts. Good works of fiction are informational. And good informational texts can be literature. The narrow sense of "literature" as fiction and poetry took hold in the later nineteenth century, leading to the received idea that "language arts" should focus on "imaginative literature" in the primary school. This narrow conception is the result of historical accidents that I have traced in appendix I.

The truth is more complex than the distinction between imaginative literature and informational text. If informational text isn't in the form of narratives, then it's not very effective or appropriate for the early grades. Narratives, fictional or nonfictional, are psychologically "privileged."[16] They are the most effective way to convey knowledge. By the same token, if fiction isn't informational, it usually isn't very good. Good fictional stories and novels aim at truth. And they depend on the reader's wide knowledge of the natural and social worlds. *To Kill a Mockingbird*, widely taught in seventh grade, depends on students' having a lot of prior knowledge about the social and historical world that should have been gained in the earlier grades.

Here's the fourth paragraph:

> Being Southerners it was a source of shame to some members of the family that we had no recorded ancestors on either side of the Battle

of Hastings. All we had was Simon Finch, a fur-trapping apothecary from Cornwall whose piety was exceeded only by his stinginess. In England, Simon was irritated by the persecution of those who called themselves Methodists at the hands of their more liberal brethren, and as Simon called himself a Methodist, he worked his way across the Atlantic to Philadelphia, thence to Jamaica, thence to Mobile, and up the Saint Stephens. Mindful of John Wesley's strictures on the use of many words in buying and selling, Simon made a pile practicing medicine, but in this pursuit he was unhappy lest he be tempted into doing what he knew was not for the glory of God, as the putting on of gold and costly apparel. So Simon, having forgotten his teacher's dictum on the possession of human chattels, bought three slaves and with their aid established a homestead on the banks of the Alabama River some forty miles above Saint Stephens. He returned to Saint Stephens only once, to find a wife, and with her established a line that ran high to daughters. Simon lived to an impressive age and died rich.[17]

Think of how much more informative a discussion of the book would become if students actually understood that paragraph. Why was the Battle of Hastings important to Southerners? What did "Southerners" imply? Why would it be shameful to a Southerner not to have an ancestor from an early date in England? What was "fur trading" all about in earlier days? Who were Methodists, and why were they being persecuted? Where on a map are all of these places mentioned—Hastings, Cornwall, Philadelphia, Jamaica, Mobile?

Fiction and poetry are not fact-free uses of language that can be readily understood after the requisite number of word study and comprehension sessions. Fictional stories are composed in historical time. They allude to history, geography, sociology, science, and technology. They are not off in some separate world of imagination free from the trammels of fact. Indeed, before the romantic movement the word *literature* embraced almost all genres of writing. It first meant the extent of one's reading—one's literature. Later it meant anything excellently written and memorable.

Good fiction and poetry aim at truth no less than do history and science. The sixteenth-century English poet and scholar Sir Philip Sidney said that the very essence of good literature is that it fixes moral truth in the mind and heart better than history and philosophy, not that it invents some new world. There is, of course, that fanciful kind of literature too—the creation of an imaginative world apart from this one. But even "a world elsewhere" (as literary critic Richard Poirier called such literature), even fairy tales and science fiction, depend on knowledge of this world in order to be realized in the imagination of the reader.

In earlier times, the readings in Noah Webster's *Blue Back Speller* and W. H. McGuffey's *Eclectic Readers* were directed to making moral and patriotic citizens. They included poetry and fiction, but also biographies of great persons, histories of the United States, science, health, and moral tales. It was accepted that interesting stories were the best vehicles for children, whether the narratives were fiction or nonfiction.

But later, under the influence of European romanticism, and the connection of the child's imagination with the divine in the human soul, the flavor of these early schoolbooks gradually changed. Moral tales were replaced with stories that supposedly developed the child's imagination. A vigorous debate ensued over whether to include fairy tales in school.[18] The moralists were against fairy tales because of their apparently null ethical or religious benefit (not so!). The fairy tale proponents won out in due course, because by the 1850s "cultivation of the imagination" had started to become an accepted educational goal.

For more than a century in the United States a dominant emphasis in early literacy classes has been placed on "imaginative literature," with a high value given to developing the child's "creativity and imagination." It's the sort of thing that makes intellectual history a fascinating subject. It explains the almost hysterical response to the Common Core's breaking up the near-monopoly of fiction and poetry in language arts. One writer went pretty far: "The complicity of our professional organizations plus the complicity of the unions has made Common Core a done deal. But if you believe in heaven and hell, you know where the Standardistos who rob children of imagination and dreams will end up."[19]

If I read this right, this objector to the informational-text requirement of the Common Core is saying that people who have questioned the monopoly of fiction and poetry in language arts classes will end up in hell, having robbed children of imagination and dreams. The view that a 50/50 balance between fiction and nonfiction should seem sacrilegious to language arts teachers is entirely owing to the influence of European romanticism on American education. It explains why we take creativity and imagination for granted as aims in early education, not pausing to consider their pantheistic origins, nor how worrisome those aims would have sounded, say, to the makers of the *New England Primer*, or even to Thomas Jefferson and Noah Webster, much less the anti-fairy-tale moralists. The Bible says that "the imagination of man's heart is evil from his youth." No positive uses of the word *imagine* are to be found in the Bible.[20] Imagination is most likely to be an evil lie, given the unsavory character of unredeemed human nature.

I am not, of course, suggesting that it would be a good idea to adopt the in-Adam's-fall-we-sinned-all point of view. Imagination can certainly be a positive virtue when directed to life-enhancing goals. But the idea that imagination is always positive and life-enhancing is an uncritical assumption that has crept into our discourse from the pantheistic effusions of the romantic period (see appendix I). The educational aim of developing the child's imagination represented a shift from the communal conception of early education to the romantic idea of natural individual development. But, from the prosaic, social justice point of view and in light of our children's critical need of general knowledge in order to flourish, teaching them substantial knowledge about the world is far more valuable to their future well-being—and to their creativity and imagination—than emphasizing fanciful and sometimes not-very-good stories whose only virtue is that they are "imaginative" and "encourage the imagination." That is hardly recommendation enough when what passes as imaginative literature in the early grades are rather thoughtless stories.

Good fictional stories (like good history and biographies) have always been the great educators of children and adults into human sympathies, high ethical ideals, and social understanding—as every great thinker on the subject has held. By the same token, good poetry and song are great lenders of meaning to our lives. They fix in the mind "what oft was thought but ne'er so well expressed." The poetry of Shakespeare and Emily Dickinson, and of Abraham Lincoln's speeches, intimately binds together our community. Song and story are at the center of what we share. But so also is our shared knowledge of history and the natural world. Not least of the virtues of the Common Core's emphasis on nonfiction—as well as on poetry and fiction—is the probability that, if it is applied in a coherent way and integrated with the other disciplines in the elementary curriculum, children will become much abler communicators. And that, according to the Longitudinal Surveys of Youth, will make them better students and wealthier, more active citizens—and abler readers of literature.

CANONICAL KNOWLEDGE AND THE COMMON CORE

In 2011, before current anti–Common Core campaigns were launched, the public strongly approved of the Common Core principle.[21] They thought it meant a core of common subject matter grade-by-grade in the elementary school, and that idea made sense to them. They did not know that the language arts standards were empty of specific grade-by-grade content. Their confusion on that score was understandable. They sensibly thought "common core standards" meant "common core curriculum" and the American public liked that idea.

The idea of commonality in early schooling is as American as cherry pie. It is seen in early writings about the Common School, recorded in *The Common School System of the State of in New York* (1851).[22] Nationwide commonality was uneasily consistent with localism in the same way that federalism is uneasily consistent with state sovereignty in American politics. The localism-federalism issue in the curriculum had been comfortably solved in the days when I went to public school in the 1930s in Tennessee. Localism in Memphis was acknowledged through the teaching of Tennessee history (which I scarcely remember). Federalism was acknowledged through the use of deliberately communal textbooks like the *Everyday Classics Series* and other, similar books that had wide currency throughout the schools of the nation.

That was in the mid-1930s. It was still the Silver Age, just before the child-centered individualism of the New Education had begun to be put into place after the curriculum reforms of the late 1930s.[23] In 2011, the public's initial favorable reaction to the idea of having common curricular elements in the public elementary schools, arrived at by the states getting together, was in the tradition that formed the common elements of shared American knowledge before radio, television, and the Internet. The elementary school is a single channel that children must listen to many hours of the day. It is still the place where all children have the possibility of learning the shared knowledge and values that make a nation operational. My view isn't based on nostalgia for the 1930s, but rather on technical grounds having to do with language competence and with equity. Here's why.

What makes an American competent—whether in Kittery, Maine, or Cleveland, Ohio, or Oakland, California—is mastery of the national dimension of our public sphere. When the modern nation state was created in the seventeenth and eighteenth centuries in Europe, each nation instituted a standardized national language to be promulgated and learned in the schools. In Spain and France the job was done in national academies—still very much in existence. In England it was done by individuals, notably Dr. Johnson, who was followed by his disciple and rival in America, Noah Webster. Today we learn and speak, read and write Johnsonian-Websterese.[24] Regional accents aside, we do not speak and write Tennessean, or New Yorkian, or Californian. Here is Webster's current dictionary definition of Standard English: "The English that, with respect to spelling, grammar, pronunciation, and vocabulary is substantially uniform though not devoid of regional differences, that is well established by usage in the formal and informal speech and writing of the educated, and that is widely recognized as acceptable wherever English is spoken and understood."[25] Before widespread literacy based on schooling, local languages were unsettled in spelling, pronunciation, and vocabulary. In Europe in the seventeenth and eighteenth centuries, the formation of the modern nation depended upon authoritative dictionary makers to stabilize pronunciation, grammar, spelling, and word meaning so people could reliably communicate over space and time. It enabled large national communities to be formed—and even transnational communities. Standard Spanish, all over the world, at least in its formal written manifestations, is still fixed and updated by the two-volume dictionary published by the Academy in Madrid, *Diccionario de la lengua española de la Real Academia Española*. Ever since Webster, American spelling and vocabulary have differed from English English; hence, our standard for spelling and pronunciation is called "Standard American English."

The term refers to much more than standardized spelling, pronunciation, and grammar. Since the 1960s a further insight has become widely accepted among socio- and psycholinguists—*that the normalization of language has entailed a normalization of the unspoken knowledge that makes the language meaningful to its users*. That enables the written word to communicate effectively across time and space, in written as well as oral language in movies and television, and the Internet. The standard language holds multiple registers and sets of conventions. One of these is the formal register used in print and the Internet. It uses slang and obscenity sparingly. It is the shared language used to communicate with strangers and large audiences. This formal register (taught in schools) is the instrument of communication in the public sphere. This formal use, which everyone needs to master to operate in the public sphere, is the chief meaning of "Standard American English."[26]

In short, a student cannot master Standard American English without mastering standard American knowledge. American education needs to be "global" today when economies are global and communications are instantaneous. But a global education must be conducted through the medium of a national language built upon shared knowledge. To claim, as some do, that such standard American knowledge doesn't exist, that the United States is a nation without any common public sphere, displays a disabling unwillingness to follow the implications of language mastery.[27] Unspoken knowledge must be silently shared in every language transaction. When schools ignore the educational imperatives of that psychological truth, they exclude disadvantaged children from language mastery.

In privileged households, children grow up hearing and learning Standard American English from birth. In disadvantaged households they do not. A big equity function of the schools is to enable them to do so, because that is the language of the American public sphere: of books, newspapers, public meetings, commerce, and legislatures. In certain districts, a politician might succeed by knowing some other dialect or language, but would also need to master American Standard English. It is a requirement for "college and career readiness." All this is obvious, of course, but still needs to be stated, because consequences follow from it that are not obvious.

In fact, the consequences are invisible. The competent use of a language requires a vast cloud of unspoken knowledge. Insiders get many elements of this knowledge from home. Outsiders must get it from school. To provide this universal linguistic competence is the foundational aim and duty of the elementary schools of a democracy.

This cloud of unspoken communal knowledge changes over time. In an epigraph to this book I quoted a passage from a 1929 prison notebook by Antonio Gramsci (jailed by Mussolini for being danger-ously brilliant). I repeat it here. Gramsci makes a key observation about why the new ideas about child development as an unfolding of the child have interfered with the chief point of early education—social-ization: "The new education created a kind of church which paralyzed pedagogical research. It produced curious aberrations like 'spontane-ity,' which supposes that the *child's brain* is like a *ball of string that* the teacher should help to unwind. In reality, each generation educates and forms each new generation. Education must oppose the elemental bio-logical instincts of nature; it is a struggle against nature, to dominate it and produce the 'up-to-date' person of the new era."[28]

The cloud of taken-for-granted knowledge in "the new era" con-stantly needs updating in the schools to ensure competence and com-munity. Helping the public to recognize that communal purpose is the practical key to making the Common Core Standards, or any standards, work. We must not be intimidated by the reproach that imparting the communal knowledge of the public sphere is "cultural imperialism." There have been in history benign empires (the Roman Empire at times) that did not force people to give up their local languages, modes, and customs, and the United States has been one of them. The United States was conceived as a mutually beneficial internal empire of quasi-sovereign states. Some of the founders used the term *empire* for the nation as an internal, not external, idea. Good empires, they thought, had protected peace and security and advanced prosperity while leaving people alone in their private affairs. Here is what George Washington had to say about education and our internal empire in his last will and testament, which left part of his large estate to education: "It has been my ardent wish to see a plan devised on a liberal scale, which would have a ten-dency to spread systematic ideas through all parts of this rising Empire, thereby to do away local attachments and State prejudices, as far as the nature of things would, or indeed ought to admit, from our National Councils."[29]

The universities could greatly help education and the public sphere by creating an inventory of the knowledge and vocabulary that makes a person college and career ready. That communal knowledge is what students need to possess to become effective citizens. A systematic approach to such knowledge in the early grades will greatly enhance the effort to instill all-purpose twenty-first-century skills. Those skills depend upon high verbal abilities, which in turn depend upon possessing the shared inventory of knowledge and words that make Standard American English useable and effective. The language arts standards of the Common Core are best interpreted as requiring an elementary curriculum that fosters such enabling knowledge.

That knowledge is multicultural. All modern national cultures are multicultural. Philosopher and social anthropologist Ernest Gellner brilliantly showed that they are artificial constructs sustained by schools and mass communication. They are constantly undergoing change. In North America in the eighteenth century the English mingled with other Europeans, Native Americans, Africans, Asians, and others to produce the Americans. Currently the Americans are mixing in all directions, continuing the Enlightenment ideal that a new artificial nation could be created "out of many one" to transcend the warring tribal instinct and offer individual liberty and social peace.

To achieve this social-political result, the traditional connection between language and tribe had to be broken. In the eighteenth century new modern nations devised a common written language as the basis for the new national political entity, artificially sustained by dictionaries and schools. In America, this common language contained all sorts of multicultural elements, with words and idioms from multiple languages, not just from Rome and Greece, but also from Native Americans (especially in place names) and from the Caribbean and African languages (e.g., *gumbo*).

The slow mixing process in America became both conscious and political in the 1980s and 1990s, as part of a leveling campaign to diminish male WASP dominance, and to elevate the status of women and nonwhite, non-Anglo minorities. The first question I was asked on the day *Cultural Literacy* was published in 1987 was whether its infamous list of power terms contained *Cinco de Mayo*. The question was asked by an Anglo reporter sympathetic to the multicultural campaign. (The word *Anglo*, by the way, is a recent "multicultural" addition to the list!) I said no, because *Cinco de Mayo* was not at that moment widely shared verbal currency among literate Americans, but I said that it might well become so. Whether it did would be up to writers, speakers, and schools. If schools taught it across the land, and if print and TV writers and now bloggers used the phrase often without defining it, then indeed it would come to appear on such a list.

For me it was a memorable exchange. It made me realize how misleading was my book's subtitle "What Every American Needs to Know." The list at the back of the book was actually a list of what literate Americans who made a good living and could communicate with other Americans in fact *did* know in 1987, but which less fortunate Americans, who did not make a good living, tended not to know. My practical suggestion was that a sense of community would be served and inequality diminished if the schools taught everyone, both the haves and have-nots, the knowledge that the haves alone currently possessed. A more accurate subtitle could have been "What the Middle Classes Know, and You Need to Know to Belong to That Income Level." I claimed, and still do, that this knowledge differential is a major cause of the income differential. (That there is a strong correlation no one denies.) Asking the schools to enable *all* Americans to join that knowledge-and-language club was what the book actually talked about. But the book itself was not much read compared to the list at the back, which circulated widely in pirated packets.

Critics argued that such inventories simply perpetuate the privileged vocabulary of the already privileged. But that is a somewhat oversimplified claim. People who have that vocabulary are privileged partly *because* they possess that vocabulary. It enables them to communicate and learn, giving them economic prowess. To change that vocabulary is a fine thing to do, so long as poor children are not disenfranchised and kept poor in the meantime by being deprived of that powerful income producer. Change must not come at the expense of those not born into the club. They, too, need to have present-day intellectual currency right now. I have every hope that this more complex view will now have its moment. The alternative—skills-based multiculturalism—has, after all, been tried over the past thirty years with little help to the groups it aimed to benefit.

The public sphere is shared knowledge, and what is shared is finite. Either most literate Americans now know *Cinco de Mayo* or they don't. If they don't, and we wish to change that fact, we should advocate teaching it to everyone in the schools. That would be an act of language politics—deliberately trying to change American shared knowledge. But note that when such language politics is successful, and the phrase catches on, it is no longer exactly "multicultural"; it has then become part of what we know in common. In that case, the word *multicultural* would no longer truly apply in a strong sense to *Cinco de Mayo*. It will have become as American as *chutzpah, gumbo, jazz, St. Patrick's Day,* and *the Fourth of July*—part of our shared knowledge and language.

The productive way to achieve inclusivity in a multicultural society is to include, not to insist on separate, militant, irreconcilable tribes. The culture of the home is not the public sphere. The public sphere deploys a common language. There, the multicultural element of schooling is a matter of vocabulary and shared unspoken knowledge. Shall the common, shared language include *Cinco de Mayo*? By now it already does! All over the nation, the day is now celebrated.[30] The vocabulary item has arrived; we all need to know it.

So-called WASP language was already multicultural in its origins. It was not inherently WASP or male. The old 1987 *Cultural Literacy* list includes the word *chutzpah* as part of that so-called WASP culture. The

American middle class (hardly pure WASP) doesn't care where a word came from as long as it's useful; we are quite happy with *Cinco de Mayo* if it brings us together and helps us make a buck. We are not cultural essentialists, as some of the multiculturalists seem to be. Cultural essentialism is tribalism—the very thing the American experiment was created to eliminate.

The multiculturalists of the 1980s and 1990s accepted a too romantic, essentialist view of language that helped fragment the school curriculum. They seemed to believe that Americans could transcend particularity, that we did not need communal knowledge shared by all but could happily exist as a universe of separate cells: out of many, many. These cells could then all function together if students achieved critical-thinking skills. But neither the critical-thinking idea nor curricular fragmentation has worked out for the social groups that these ideas were supposed to help. Gap closing has stagnated; the achievement gap persists.

The movement was animated by a noble aim and an understandable mistake. It was a protest against particularism—that is, against some narrow, tribal group taking charge, instead of equal status being open to all, including those who had been discriminated against. But as it was put into effect, a subtle truth was lost—as such truths tend to be in fierce activisms and polarizations. That truth is that multicultural societies are particularistic too. Liberal democracies are particularistic in their own special way. They each include a particular shared subset of elements that are often wildly diverse in their origins. Each national democracy has its own particular language as a communicative and unifying instrument that is changing, but at any period it is what it is. All citizens should have complete access to that shared knowledge. Equality of opportunity depends upon it.

The multiculturalists are right that all cultures are inherently equal, just as all people are. But there is also the public sphere, sustained by the vocabulary and conventions of Standard American English, and the communal knowledge that enables its effective use. It is more widespread and enabling than any other language system in the United States. Proficiency with that instrument bestows financial and communicative advantages to all who master it. Membership in the language community of the public sphere is granted to any and all who possess the knowledge needed to wield that instrument of power and opportunity. If schools do not provide that knowledge, they are denying their students equality of opportunity.

With the increased polarization of American politics and social life, the decline of the public commons now seems less and less a brave, forward-looking idea. Though well meant, romantic multiculturalism needs to be revised and transformed so it doesn't perpetuate the economic exclusion of those who have not mastered the shared knowledge required by effective reading, writing, speaking, and listening. A well-rounded, constantly updated school curriculum that transmits the shared knowledge of the public sphere has always been the primary instrument of national unity and equal opportunity.

The barriers that stand in the way of enabling the Common Core work to meet that goal are many. I have shown that its skill provisions are less than ideal, and they sometimes work against its provisions favoring a rich, coherent curriculum. Its current tests are no more productive in principle than the kinds of tests that have already failed under No Child Left Behind. The greatest virtues of the Common Core ELA Standards are their raising of the vocabulary difficulty of texts at each grade level, and their insistence that half of the texts be "informational." Districts and states can make the Common Core ELA Standards transformative, should they choose to do so, by proposing a specific and coherent curriculum that builds knowledge systematically from one grade to the next, starting in the earliest grades.

That would make the Common Core Standards transformative whether or not states continue to call that transformation "Common Core." Those who oppose the Common Core need to teach precisely the same sorts of things that those who defend it need to teach. Our state language standards and Common Core language standards are currently Rorschach blots that must be formed into a reality, whatever name we give them. It's the only feasible route to higher average achievement and a reduction of educational inequality. Specificity and courage are needed. The outcome is "not in our [standards] but in ourselves."[31]

CHAPTER SEVEN

The Educational Fall
of France

TWO NATIONS AT RISK: THE USA AND FRANCE

To speak of "The Educational Fall of France" seems at first rhetorical overkill—equating mere lower scores in French elementary schools with the military defeat of France in World War II. But it isn't just an over-the-top play on words. It was the explicit theme of an important 2007 book edited by Laurent Lafforgue and Liliane Lurçat: *La Débâcle de l'École: Une Tragédie Incomprise.*[1] *Débâcle* is the term the French apply to their country's military defeat in 1940. Lafforgue, who is a highly distinguished mathematician and a recipient of the Fields Medal—a kind of Nobel Prize in math—then developed that historical analogy in his introduction to the essays. His view, which I agree with, is that top French intellectuals made big avoidable mistakes in 1989, just as higher-ups had made serious, avoidable military mistakes in 1940. The collection of essays that follows his introduction makes a highly illuminating book on the disaster that has recently befallen the French school system. It is a "misunderstood tragedy" as the subtitle states.

I first decided to write this book after I ran across the astonishing 2007 data compiled by the French Ministry of Education, recently placed on the Web by Paola Mattei of the University of Oxford.[2] It shone bright new light on our own school system. The data showed another educational system that, like our own, had adopted skill-based, individualized, educational principles, and subsequently declined from being among the best and most equitable large school systems in the world to being one of the worst and least equitable. The United States in the 1980s had similarly dropped from the top rank of international rankings into mediocrity in those rankings.[3] The data showed that France had experienced a fully documented repetition of the US decline. Ours began showing up in the 1960s.[4] The origins of our decline can be clearly traced to our having made similar intellectual mistakes half a century before.

I reached that conclusion when I found that the decline of student verbal achievement in France closely mirrored the infamous fall of verbal scores in the United States in the 1960s and 1970s. In the United States, the changes wrought by our curriculum reforms of the 1930s had been local and gradual from the 1930s to the 1950s, by which time they had become all but universal. Already, by 1936, there were thousands of progressive public schools in the United States according to a *March of Time* newsreel of that year entitled "New Schools for Old." It can be viewed on YouTube.[5]

The massive American decline in test scores of the 1960s and 1970s called forth the famous federal report *A Nation at Risk* (1983). SAT verbal scores had plummeted half a standard deviation in the twenty years between 1960 and 1980. At the time of *A Nation at Risk* in the early 1980s verbal scores seemed to be in a kind of free fall, and no one could explain the reason for it—except maybe the baleful distractions of *Perry Mason* and other TV shows.[6]

The causes of that SAT drop are still disputed by defenders of American schools who hold the theory that the decline was owing to increased participation in the SAT by low-income students. It's not necessary to review that discussion. Scholars have now shown that there was a significant score drop on virtually *all* US school tests—not just on the SAT—by all students, rich and poor, during the period 1965–1980.[7] Glossing over the major role of the schools in causing the tragedy doesn't help reverse the trend. According to the National Assessment of Educational Progress (NAEP) the verbal scores of our seventeen-year-olds have stayed flat ever since 1971, the year we first began national sampling, a decade after our decline was well under way.[8] If we insist that the nationwide progressive "reforms" of the curriculum in the 1930s and 1940s did *not* chiefly cause that disaster, we simply protect the faulty ideas that are the key to the whole conundrum.

Here are some score drops in the United States during the single decade 1965–1975 in terms of standard deviations. The SAT dropped by one-third in that first decade.[9] (The decline ultimately reached one-half a standard deviation.) In that same decade, the ACT—a precollege test similar to the SAT—dropped by one-quarter. The Iowa Test of Educational Development, given to all Iowa juniors and seniors, dropped by almost one-third; the Minnesota College Aptitude Test, given to all seniors, dropped by one-quarter. The California Achievement Test (a national test) dropped by almost one-quarter. The Stanford Achievement Test dropped by one-third.[10] A decline of a third or a quarter of a standard deviation is a significant magnitude for large populations. Particularly persuasive are the state tests in Iowa and Minnesota, administered to virtually all high school juniors and seniors in those states at a time when their pupil demographics were stable—thus eliminating demographic change as a cause of the declines in those states.[11]

A lot of Americans do not care about what happens in France. Yet if there were some persistent illness in New York City whose cause and cure had been determined by researchers in Paris, we wouldn't hesitate to import that scientific knowledge to cure New York. Our schools have long been infected by a system of ideas that prevents improvement from taking hold. The cause of the disease has now been definitively determined in Paris—and the cure as well. We should not hesitate to import that knowledge. Like a virus, providential individualism knows no national boundary or political party. As I will indicate in this chapter, the virus has also infected Britain and Sweden, and until recently

Germany, which was the nineteenth-century nursery of progressive education, and has had a decisive influence on educational thought and policy in the United States.[12]

France, with its excellent record keeping, has in effect recently completed an unintended natural experiment with ten-year-old students over a period of twenty years. The statistical and sociological analysis is on a par with our research gold standard—the National Assessment of Educational Progress.[13] We are not so imbued with American exceptionalism as to believe that American ten-year-olds are fundamentally different from French ones with respect to math and reading proficiency. France has a diverse population as big as that of California and Texas combined. We need to take note.

FRANCE, LIKE THE UNITED STATES, USED TO BE AT THE TOP IN ACHIEVEMENT AND EQUITY

In the 1980s, France could celebrate (with Sweden) the best large school systems in Europe. The new, depressed French data, which I chart in this chapter, hit me like a body blow. I had not kept up with French schooling. The last time I had visited France was in the 1980s, at a high point in the success of the school system, which was at the top in achievement and equity. I saw it all firsthand: lively, competent preschools and effective elementary schools throughout France.

I bought a copy of the national curriculum, a modest-sized paperback of about a hundred pages of large print, with an inspiring introduction about liberty, equality, and fraternity, and about the key role of schooling in achieving those goals. The document allocated a specific number of minutes per week for the study of topics in each discipline in each grade. The topics in history, math, science, civics, literature, and music were outlined with some specificity. Primary school was tough, but fair and predictable.

I visited bookstores on the Boulevard St. Michel that offered colorful summer-study books based on the national curriculum. They were designed for classroom use, and special ones were designed for students and concerned parents who wanted to get a leg up in the summer on the next year's demanding work. There were materials for practicing the dreaded *dictée*, under which students had to write down what the teacher spoke with perfect spelling and punctuation in the standard written forms of the French language. The advantages of definite grade-by-grade topics for inducing publishers to produce excellent learning materials were clear. The publishers had no control over the basic content of schooling; they gained their competitive advantage by presenting the content attractively and effectively at a good price.

France exhibited the highest average student achievement with the greatest equity of any large, diverse country. It educated immigrants better than any other European nation. Figure 7.1 is from 1991, showing the results of the system in the 1980s.[14] The vertical axis is the average score for advantaged ninth-grade students; the horizontal, for disadvantaged ones. Note on the chart how equitable the Swedish scores are also. But note also the poor performance of Germany, still under the sway of progressive ideas. I will return to the recent experiences of those other two countries after I describe what happened to France.

I had long attributed this earlier French accomplishment in overcoming inequality to the excellent French preschool system being attended by nearly 100 percent of four- and five-year- olds, and also to the fact that after preschool, children entered a highly communal primary school with a well-developed common curriculum.

Then, after 1989, things changed radically, though, as I will later explain, the intellectual preparation for the catastrophic *loi Jospin* of 1989 had been brewing in French education schools since the 1960s. Because French schooling was centrally controlled, it decentralized itself in 1989 in a wrenching, centralized manner. The suddenness and universality of its curricular changes enable us now to make some confident inferences of the sort that are impossible in the United States, where specific curricular content over time is largely unspecified and unknown.

FIGURE 7.1 Literacy level for advantaged and disadvantaged students; ninth graders by country

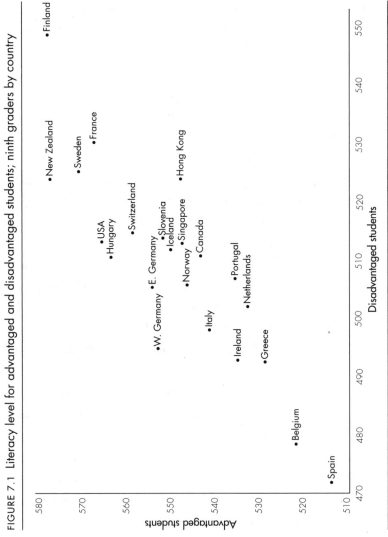

WHAT CAUSED FRANCE TO DECIDE TO CHANGE?

I mentioned in the prologue that the common curriculum of the French primary school was a recurrent theme of French education from Condorcet in 1790 to President Giscard d'Estaing in 1977, who stated the basic idea of French schooling: to enable all French children to acquire the same knowledge in order to unify society and reduce inequality. Each child would go, d'Estaing said, to the "same" primary school and middle school.[15] But just twelve years later, in 1989, France completely overthrew that tradition by passing a law saying in effect that each child would go to a *different* primary school and middle school. Instead of acquiring the same culture, each school was to respect and develop the child's home culture and conform to the individual characteristics of each locality and to the individual characteristics of each child. In addition, each school was to have its own special "project" and orientation.

To introduce this proposed new law, Lionel Jospin, the French Minister of Education, rose in France's National Assembly in June of 1989 to describe his government's plan for the total change of French education. The structure of the radical change was to be based on a new report called the Bourdieu-Gros Report.[16] Pierre Bourdieu had been chosen to head the committee (which also included Jacques Derrida) because he had been in the forefront of scholars who complained that the old-fashioned national curriculum was not as egalitarian as it claimed to be. Rather, he said, it sustained a culture that the well-off already possessed, and thus it excluded children who came from other cultures. His report advocated a more pluralistic, multicultural approach. The new epoch-making law that was passed a month later took effect the next year and became known as the *loi Jospin* ("Jospin law").

In debate, when Jospin turned to the matter of curriculum, he observed that subject matter would be determined by each district and school under its own plan. Each child would attend his or her unique school. Within the autonomous local district, the school itself was to have a measure of autonomy, with each school required to set forth its own special aims—making its plan appropriate to local values.

The ideals under which Jospin described the scheme to the National Assembly seemed inspiring: greater help for children in disadvantaged neighborhoods; insistence on more equitable academic outcomes; consideration of the individual strengths, weaknesses, and learning styles of each student; a more natural course of learning divided into cycles designed to coincide with the natural rhythms of development and growth. In 1989, the Left in the National Assembly (Socialists plus Communists) had an absolute majority; they could pass any law they wished. The vote was 280 in favor, 266 against. The conservatives were not persuaded.

Structurally, a radical feature of the new law was decentralization. Instead of having everything emanate from Paris, metropolitan France would henceforth be divided into twenty-six autonomous school districts. The Jospin law also included the institution of twenty-eight new education colleges—one in each district and two extra ones in the district of Paris to train teachers in appropriate methods for the new system. They were to codify the profession of pedagogy in a scientific and orderly way (translation: they would teach progressive theory). As outlined in the Bourdieu-Gros Report, new teachers would be trained in the new educational ideas.

When Jospin was asked in debate about the commonality of knowledge that every French child should know, he replied that the law established a national council that would produce an outline of common national standards. Now known as "the platform" (*socle*), the standards document was astonishingly short and nonspecific—nonexistent in practical terms. A telling moment in Jospin's presentation to the legislature came when he observed (following the recommendations of the Bourdieu-Gros Report) that he had instructed the national council to avoid "mere encyclopedism" and the "piling up of facts." The emphasis was to be on skills, not facts, based on the statement in the Bourdieu-

Gros Report that all-purpose skills are far more important than the piling up of knowledge.[17]

The very preamble of the new 1989 law made clear that French education was not going to be "lockstep" any longer. It was going to be child-centered. The law begins: "Education is the first national priority. It shall be designed and organized for the benefit of pupils and students . . . Everyone is guaranteed the right to an education, to develop his personality . . . Pupils and students will elaborate their own curricula according to their own aspirations and capacities."

Thenceforth each primary school was to produce its own curriculum. The schools were commanded to adopt individualism by taking "into account the plurality and diversity of aptitudes of each pupil" (an instruction the French Ministry of Education still gives to schools today, even after many years of decline). The localities were to govern the schools.

What, then, had happened in those twelve years between the pronouncement of President d'Estaing in 1977 that each child would attend the same school to the radically different pronouncements of the *loi Jospin* that each child would go to a different school?

There were two main intellectual impulses that led educators to accept and even demand a radical change in the school curriculum. The first impulse was felt by new teachers trained in the ideas of the 1960s. They had been instructed, during their training at the *écoles normales*, in a new point of view—that of *la nouvelle education*, which we call "progressive education." It had at last taken root in France. It placed the individual child at the center of concern, and encouraged the teacher to accommodate teaching to the characteristics of the child. It encouraged the naturalistic teaching of math and reading. It deemphasized memorization and grammar. This new orientation could not change the topics of instruction, since these were set forth in the national curriculum. But the new attitude did change how reading, writing, and arithmetic were taught. No longer were they to be learned by artificial impositions and rote memorization. They were to be developed naturally.

The rise of this tradition among young French teachers encouraged the teacher union to support the radical changes that were proposed in the new 1989 legislation. They felt that the time for change was ripe, and was indicated by the alarming rise in the number of primary students who could not read or reckon and who therefore had to repeat a grade.[18] This worrisome trend was blamed on the rigorous old curriculum, inappropriate for current students. This increase in grade repetition justified demands to make schooling more child-centered and up to date. It had not been understood that the rise in the number of students who were unable to read and reckon was a consequence of the new methods, not the old ones![19] For, starting in the 1960s, under the radar, traditional teaching methods of reading and arithmetic began to give way to the three disastrous pedagogical theories identified in this book: naturalism, individualism, and skill-centrism.[20] Gradually, progressive education infiltrated and then dominated teacher-training institutes in France. The new pedagogical ideas were not yet announced as government curricular policy, but they slowly took over French education schools and the ideas of the teachers who had attended them.

This silent revolution resulted in a paradox. The new naturalistic theories into which French teachers were being indoctrinated—for example, in *la méthode globale*, and *la méthode mixte* in reading—had begun to cause basic reading difficulties among the youngest pupils, even as the schools kept a common subject-matter curriculum.[21] The rise in grade retentions, caused by the *new* methods, was then deployed successfully as a further argument against the old pedagogy and the old uniformity of the topics in the national curriculum.[22] Why should today's students need to read *Le Cid*?

But there was also a second, different criticism of the old curriculum and its pedagogy that gave high intellectual respectability and urgency to the demand for radical curricular change—a demand that had continued to animate French politics ever since the alarming student revolts of May 1968.[23] These revolts criticized almost all of France's established institutions. And, with regard to the established traditions of French education, a leading critic was Pierre Bourdieu, the coauthor of a 1964 book called *The Inheritors*.

In this influential book Bourdieu and his coauthor Jean-Claude Passeron claimed that French schooling was not as egalitarian as it conceived itself to be.[24] On the contrary, they said, it perpetuated class divisions and repressions. They said that equality of opportunity was a myth. The book made a huge impression and was much cited during the great unrest of 1968. It was an analysis of the social disparities in French universities, especially in students' choice of a university major. By a clear statistical margin these decisions about a major study area were class based. Bourdieu also analyzed the different tastes in music and movies of university students, and found statistically significant correlations with class. He and his coauthor looked with indignation on these statistical disparities. They concluded that French republican education was a device for reproducing existing social stratifications. The French school system was unwittingly part of a conspiracy to keep the underclasses submerged. His radical claim: French schooling was a means of reproducing social class, not overcoming it.

To be an American reading *The Inheritors* is to be astonished at its superficiality, its indignant making of mountains out of molehills. The book embraces far too narrow a time slice in describing the social-class-based preferences of university students—merely a single generation. The French students whom Bourdieu analyzed in the book showed exactly the tastes one would expect. Children of peasants did not exhibit the tastes or the aims of children of executives. But what about the children of those peasant-students? They will come to the university from better-off, more literate homes. Will not their knowledge and tastes be more upper class than those of their parents? To imagine just one generation ahead makes the book's astonishing indignation and its equally indignant resonance with the public seem a head-shaking example of the mood of the 1960s.

What *The Inheritors* showed unwittingly was that the French republican school of the 1950s and 1960s had been doing an excellent job of bringing children of peasants to the university, thus enabling Bourdieu to study their attitudes. Bourdieu himself had grown up under disadvantage; Standard French was not his home language. No mere social reproduction there! Why dismantle a school system that had produced a Bourdieu?

The old French centralized system with a common curriculum was not, as many on the French left imagined, a product of hidebound right-wing politics, but of the old egalitarian left, starting with Condorcet's plan of 1790, *A Common Education for Children*, and Napoleon's meritocratic principle of "a career open to talents." What appeared to the young and reform-minded in France during the 1960s and 1970s as being rigid and constraining in schools had in fact been instituted to help ensure that all children were offered an equal chance in life.

Then, in the 1980s, Bourdieu was asked by the Socialist government to head a committee to issue a report about what the schools should do under the forthcoming educational law that the Socialists were intent on passing—now that the left had control of the legislature. Bourdieu was thus offered a tremendous opportunity. Yet to read the Bourdieu-Gros Report, which became the basis for new 1989 law, is to be struck by its vagueness regarding the curriculum.[25]

This defect was perhaps inevitable given Bourdieu's view that social reproduction was the chief evil of existing French education. The existing education had been following a highly specific primary-school curriculum, set forth in a thin paperback, with content and class time ordained grade by grade. Committed to changing this lockstep policy, Bourdieu's report encouraged each school to do its own thing. The new emphasis was to be on skills. It looked with disdain upon mere facts, or "encylopedism." It stated: "The growth of knowledge renders vain the ambition of encyclopedism." The report defended the hoary progressive idea of teaching critical-thinking skills, stating: "Students are to be taught 'elementary logic,' and, by the acquisition of habits of thought, the techniques and cognitive tools which are indispensable in conducting reasoning that is rigorous and thoughtful—those same general competences are required in the reading of texts." That statement, assumed to be self-evident, is not backed up by any footnotes. Its assumptions are incorrect, as this book's discussion of "critical-thinking skills" explains. In essence the Bourdieu-Gros Report recommended American-style education, and that is what the new law went on to require. Its primary principle was that the goal of education to develop general skills and the "personality" (i.e., the individuality) of the student.

Thus the intellectual origins of the French "debacle" were largely the same theories as the ones that created "a nation at risk" in the United States: the theory that schooling should be natural, and that the aim of schooling should be the development of individuality and critical-thinking skills. To this view was added a further claim about social justice. Older forms of "lockstep" education were not only outmoded but also unfair. They were said to promote continued social stratification. It was argued that a further indication of injustice was the growing percentage of students who had to repeat a grade. Only years later did it become clear that the alarming rise in grade repetitions had not been caused by the old education at all, but was a result of the new naturalistic approach to reading and math. The new methods had not reduced social stratification and inequality but instead had intensified them.[26]

FRANCE DOCUMENTS ITS DEBACLE IN DETAIL

France, with its centralized tradition and diligent record keeping, offers scholars detailed historical educational data. The French Ministry of Education takes periodic "soundings" of the public school system, recording in detail the level of student competencies, along with demographic information about the students. It is thus able to observe how educational policies affect different economic and social groups. France has thus traced its own decline in achievement and equity with remarkable precision.

The baseline data were established just before France made its sudden nationwide change. In 1987, the French Ministry had taken one of its periodic national soundings of student achievement at the end of fifth grade. Those 1987 data are the reference points for tracing the subsequent effects of the child-centered skills curriculum that began to be put in place in 1990. A second sounding, using the same test instruments, was conducted in 1997. Then another using the same test instruments was undertaken a decade later, in 2007.

In each sounding, the student sampling represented the entire student body of ten-year-olds in the schools. The last sounding totaled over four thousand fifth graders, and the total number of responses scanned for language and math was over three hundred thousand. Details are found in appendix II. The idea was to gauge school effectiveness up to age ten, after at least two years of preschool plus four and a half years of primary school. Students took identical tests in each decade. Buildings, teachers, classrooms, and budgets remained similar through the decades. The demographic categorizations of "head of household" stayed the same. The results are decisive, and constitute the most definitive comparative study of curriculum effects ever undertaken in any country. The numbers in figure 7.2, which concern literacy skills, are in standard deviations. (The math results are even worse.)

The child-centered skills curriculum had caused the average of literacy scores to fall four-tenths of a standard deviation. Because children with better-educated parents acquire academic knowledge both at home and at school, the decline was less steep among more-advantaged students. Among the neediest students, the decline was severe. This differential effect is important. It suggests the *positive* equity effects of a common grade-by-grade curriculum in the elementary school when the lines are traced backward in time—what had been lost and what could be regained.

That French chart follows precisely what theory predicts about educational inequality. If students gain the knowledge and vocabulary of

FIGURE 7.2 Curriculum effects in France 1987–2007 at the end of fifth grade

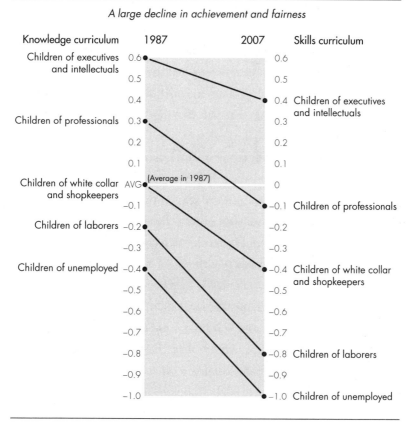

A large decline in achievement and fairness

Knowledge curriculum   1987   2007   Skills curriculum

Children of executives   0.6   0.6
and intellectuals
                          0.5   0.5

                          0.4   0.4 Children of executives
                                          and intellectuals
Children of professionals 0.3   0.3

                          0.2   0.2

                          0.1   0.1

Children of white collar AVG (Average in 1987) 0
and shopkeepers
                         −0.1   −0.1 Children of professionals

Children of laborers   −0.2   −0.2

                        −0.3   −0.3

Children of unemployed −0.4   −0.4 Children of white collar
                                          and shopkeepers
                        −0.5   −0.5

                        −0.6   −0.6

                        −0.7   −0.7

                        −0.8   −0.8 Children of laborers

                        −0.9   −0.9

                        −1.0   −1.0 Children of unemployed

Note: Vertical scale = z scores for 1987; average in 1987 = 0; average in 2007 = minus .37.
Z scores are percentages of the standard deviation of a distribution. They allow results to be
compared in different eras, even when the underlying tests use different scales.

the public sphere, they will score well on a literacy test. If accidents of
birth have excluded that knowledge from the home environment, and if
the school does not supply it, then they will score badly on a literacy test.

The hope had been held out that new, individualistic modes of
schooling would create a new, more nearly classless society.[27] The Bourdieu-Gros Report demanded a total overhaul of the system to make it
more egalitarian, and demanded nothing less than a revolution of the
system. With the left fully in power in the late 1980s, they got their

revolution. The new localizing and individualizing of the schools had been proposed as a way of overcoming the reproduction of social stratification.[28] But the educational results went the opposite way, intensifying inequalities. As the French data from 1987 to 2007 show, the new 1990 arrangements greatly intensified the social reproduction they were supposed to diminish. They systematically deprived poor children of the enabling knowledge that rich children had acquired from their home environments.[29]

The French twenty-year study of curricular effects should carry the day with most people. From a scientific standpoint, the data from France are more significant for American education than any data we have ever managed to collect from our own system. The French experiment, combined with the congruence of its results with cognitive science and international comparisons, has pretty well *proved* that a specific, cumulative common-core curriculum, such as France had before the Jospin law, is far superior to the American-style individualized curriculum that followed it in France. Logic and common sense agree with the data. And in light of the current scapegoating of teachers in the United States, I would stress that entry standards for teachers into the French school system remained extremely high both before and after *Jospin*. "Teacher quality" remained constant in France by all objective measures during the period of decline.

These findings are important for us because we lack large-scale, curriculum-related data in the United States. We don't know with precision what was being taught in our variegated local communities as our schools gradually moved toward the progressive takeover in the twentieth century. The French know precisely what used to be taught, and how it differs from the incoherent curriculums being taught now.[30] And they know in demographic detail what the consequences were. These data make it nearly certain that any district in the United States that implemented a communal, cumulative curriculum in all subjects (not just language arts and math) will show higher achievement and much higher equity than it has shown in the past under the reign of the skills delusion.

My late friend Roger Shattuck wrote a book entitled *The Forbidden Experiment* about the Wild Boy of Aveyron who grew up in the French woods without parents. The French have now conducted a bigger natural experiment, replacing commonality of knowledge with individualized curricula and an emphasis on skills. The results are quite clear. If these trials had occurred in medical research, with epidemiological data from several thousand randomly assigned experimental subjects, they would quickly be halted. It would be considered unethical to continue them.

THE FRENCH PUBLIC BECOMES ALARMED AT "THE CRISIS OF THE SCHOOL"

In 2003, a young French schoolteacher named Rachel Boutonnet published a tell-all book that informed the public about the practices that had become prevalent in French teacher-training institutes and, subsequently, in the primary schools where their graduates taught.[31] She was attending one of the new education schools in order to get her license but was so outraged by the boredom, misinformation, and ideological conformity thrust upon her that she resolved to keep a journal.

When her *Journal of a Clandestine Teacher* was published, the French public became more aware of the ideas and methods that were current in teacher training and in their primary schools. Education colleges required a teacher to be called a "resource person," a guide on the side. A class lesson was to be considered a "session," not a lecture.[32] Students were to be called "learners." Above all, those learners "were to be motivated to construct their own learnings." They were not to be "fed mere information." The chief aim was the imparting of all-purpose skills like "learning to learn."

In the earliest grades, where decoding of the written word is paramount, Rachel Boutonnet was told that students must cease to be taught by phonics. They should learn to read by the naturalistic "whole-language" approach, or (since that is so controversial) by the quasi-whole-language *méthode mixte* known in English as "balanced literacy," which occasionally mixes in some phonics instruction.[33] Though confidently asserted, these edicts made no sense to Boutonnet. After graduation, she secretly taught her students to read via the phonics method, and they performed above the norm. When she came to be evaluated by the inspector, she felt confident. But, no, she received an unfavorable report. She had not followed methods of "whole language" or "balanced literacy" in reading, nor had she used "constructivist" methods emphasizing learning-to-learn skills in her instruction. American educators and policy makers will immediately recognize the French version of ideas that prevail in our own colleges of education.

In 2004, one year after Boutonnet's book, another schoolteacher, Marc Le Bris, came out with a bestselling book called *Your Children Won't Know How to Read or Count.*[34] It carried the subtitle *The Persistent Failure of the French School.* Le Bris is older than Boutonnet. From his book's opening pages he made clear that the methods and attitudes Boutonnet described were already dominant in education schools more than twenty years before. He began his book as follows:

> For twenty years, the National Education system has prevented me from doing my job. When I left the normal school in 1977, I was a young progressive teacher, convinced of the superiority of the reading method called "natural." I believed everything. I did everything demanded: small groups, enrichment activities, functional grammar, natural reading of modern mathematics, animation, self-learning, multidisciplinary decompartmentalization, creativity, self-directed studies.
>
> Yet students of older teachers, who dared to continue to use dictations and learn reading by phonics, fared better. My students, pampered by modern methods, have suffered educational disadvantages of which I am ashamed today. Shame? Not really . . . because, like many of us, I have corrected this. I write this book to alarm parents. They will save their children only if they do the work of the school at home.

Modern education only serves to justify the abandonment of ambitions that we have for our children. We have before us a real cultural catastrophe.

The chief source of the crisis was identified eloquently by an association of French teachers and researchers called *Groupe de Recherches Interdisciplinaires sur les Programmes* ("Group for Interdisciplinary Studies of the Curriculum"), or GRIP:

> We situate the main origin of the school crisis in the disintegration of the curriculum—principally the primary school curriculum. Begun decades ago, worsened by reform after reform, with some course correction recently, this curricular disintegration has rendered more or less random the subject matters taught. It has thus compromised the possibility for the majority of students to gain the wider knowledge that is necessary to academic success. In consequence, we see the reconstruction of the primary curriculum into one that is rich, coherent, and cumulative as the necessary condition for a true democratization of education.[35]

This perceptive analysis by the teachers themselves has not been seriously heeded in France. There has been no successful movement to specify once again the content of the primary curriculum across the nation. Yet the French public is deeply concerned about the decline of the schools and students' poor results on the international PISA rankings—the most recent of which, in 2012, showed that France, of all countries in the world, has deteriorated the most in the equity of its schools. In response, French headlines announced "We Are the Champions of Academic Inequality."[36] It was a stunning reversal after being at the top in the equity of its results!

Today there continue to be debates, books, and articles on the *crise de l'école*. New adjustments to the *loi Jospin* have been enacted, which change structural elements at the edges, but do not rationalize the elementary curriculum. A new law in 2005 reconstituted the idea that there should be a more significant base, or *socle*, that all children should learn, but the resulting document did not get into specifics, and has been essentially useless. Starting in 2016, the *socle* will have more force, since a student cannot get a *brevet*—a certificate of graduation—without a paper saying that he or she has met the still-vague standards of the *socle*. There is no direct movement to return to a specific national curriculum in the primary school. That seems now as unthinkable in France as it would be in the United States.

Or is it? The young in France may still throw off the old ideas, even when the old ideas—including the outworn and failed ideas of Bourdieu—are still presenting themselves as new. In 2014, a brilliant high school teacher still in his twenties published a well-received, probing, and beautifully written little book tracing and deconstructing the underlying ideas of present-day French education. With a play on Bourdieu's *The Inheritors*, he entitled it *The Disinherited: or the Urgency of Transmission*.[37] The young teacher's name is Francois-Xavier Bellamy. If France is lucky, other young people will agree with him, and will in time begin to undo the immense damage wrought by the ideas behind the *loi Jospin* and the training of teachers like Rachel Boutonnet (that other young rebel). Toward the end of his book, Bellamy writes:

> Fifty years after *The Inheritors*, our educational system, greatly influenced by that book's condemnation of transmission, has become the most inegalitarian in Europe. Pierre Bourdieu, son of an agricultural worker in a little village of Béarn: would he today have the slightest chance of entering the école normale supérieure? Without any doubt, no. The only survivors of the shipwreck of our public education are those whose parents know the tactics for escaping the disaster—which quartiers to live in, which subjects to emphasize, which options to choose. On the other end of the spectrum are the designated victims of social selection—among them, the children of immigrant families. It is with them in mind that we renounced teaching the culture of our country and transmitting to all a common heritage. Today, those young people have twice the average risk of serious academic failure. Who can fail to see that that is the true violence; that such denial of transmission cannot fail, one day, to explode?

SWEDEN DECENTRALIZES AND INDIVIDUALIZES

Bourdieu and the political left cannot boast sole ownership of decentralization, individualism, and the skills delusion. Sweden now offers a similarly compelling example from the right. It decided in 1994 to make the same sort of educational changes as France. Behind this move lay the same kind of thinking about following the providential impulses of the individual child, to which Sweden added the further idea of following the providential workings of the free market.

In 2014, after a decade of the experiment, the Swedish government commissioned a report from Professor Leif Lewin regarding the effects of its decentralization of Swedish schools, and its offering of government financial support to any school, public or private.[38] The central right government that had favored decentralization has now been made highly uncomfortable by Lewin's 2014 analysis. He showed that decentralization had caused a severe drop in students' abilities in reading, writing, and arithmetic. It had greatly widened the achievement gaps between rich and poor students. Decentralization of the curriculum had done in Sweden exactly what it had done in France.

Before the changes occurred, Lewin showed, Swedish schools exhibited only minor gaps between rich and poor students, and Sweden boasted one of the most egalitarian systems in the world. Before 1994 there was little difference in overall school performance, no matter where the school was located. Now there had developed wide differences in school performance, and wide gaps had opened between the performances of rich and poor students. The overall performance of Swedish students in the PISA studies had declined significantly. Decentralization, Professor Lewin concluded, had not worked. Of particular interest for readers of this book is the following passage from the Lewin Report that describes how the content of the curriculum had been individualized:

> The adaptation of the 1994 curricula to the new school governance meant that the previously detailed time allocations and topics were

replaced by vague time allocations that required only a minimum guaranteed teaching time. Under the new curricula, the state largely abandoned the ambition to determine the knowledge content of the school, and transferred that determination to local schools.

Previously, efforts to create curricula and syllabi had been regarded as a technical matter for administrators and subject-matter experts. Actual classroom content had been driven by time allocations plus the teaching-materials package, which translated the core syllabus into specific teaching content. In contrast, the basic idea of 1994 law was that henceforth teachers and principals are considered to be in the best position to design the curriculum, because they best know the local conditions.[39]

The Swedish PISA scores alluded to in Lewin's report are striking. Between 2000 and 2012, Swedish PISA verbal scores fell from 516, which was 12 points above the United States, to 483, which is 15 points below the United States and 17 points below the average of developed nations. It is the largest drop ever recorded by PISA. The magnitude of the Swedish decline makes the change from a common-core curriculum throughout Sweden to an individualistic approach almost as significant for American policy as the French decline, except that precise demographic data are lacking in Sweden.

As figure 7.1 showed, Sweden in 1990 was just behind France as the top large nation in Europe for excellence and equity. And then after 1994 Sweden decided to abandon common subject matter in favor of personalized education and market competition. Programs suited to each individual were to be instituted, along with free choice of schools, paid for by the government whether public or private.[40]

Before 1994, high equity and achievement in Sweden had been no accident. It had been a chief aim of national policy. Educational equality became a national priority in the 1960s, when compulsory education from ages seven through sixteen was introduced. Every Swedish child was required to attend the neighborhood elementary school, and to study the same subjects in the same classrooms under a common national curriculum, as in France. According to Professor Tomas Englund of Örebro University, Sweden followed what he calls "equality-oriented centralism," with extra resources allocated to low achieving students. Under the Swedish system, as it evolved, "the differences in achievement between different schools were rather small."[41]

The new law of 1994 discarded those arrangements. A principle of "equivalence" was legislated to replace the common curriculum, summarized as follows by the Swedish Ministry of Education: "Education should be adapted to each pupil's circumstances and needs, based on the pupils' background, earlier experiences, language, and knowledge . . . The Education Act stipulates that the education provided within each type of school should be of equivalent value, irrespective of where in the country it is provided (Chapter 1, §2). However, equivalent education does not mean that the education should be the same everywhere. Account should also be taken of the varying circumstances and needs of pupils as well as the fact that there are a variety of ways of attaining these goals."[42]

If equivalence doesn't require everyone to learn similar content, as before in Sweden, then what would be the yardstick for it? It is the answer given by progressive education since 1910.[43] All pupils will be taught different, individually adapted topics—but all will be taught the same thinking skills: "Students should train themselves to think critically, to examine the facts and circumstances and to realize the consequences of different options. Pupils shall develop their ability to take initiative and responsibility and to work and solve problems both independently and with others. The school should develop students' communication and social skills. In this way, students acquire increasingly scientific ways of thinking and working."[44] In the primary grades, the coherence of the common curriculum disappeared. With the new emphasis on individuality and thinking skills, the elementary curriculum in Sweden became as incoherent as the curriculum had become in France and the United States.

Why did France and Sweden, which stood at the top in equity and achievement, suddenly destroy two of the most admirable and effective large school systems in the world? It was because they intended to make their good systems even better. They were unlucky enough to believe the well-meant but misguided slogans about individualization and skills. Their past successes had given them an unwarranted confidence that they could get even better results by attending more closely to individual needs. Both nations had become so accustomed to effective schools that they took success in that effort for granted. Now in the PISA studies Sweden is second only to France as the country that has deteriorated the most in social equality.

In table 7.1 I list Sweden's PISA scores from 2000 to 2012, and compare them with the more favorable pattern of PISA scores in Germany in table 7.2. Germany is an object lesson in the other direction. It has greatly improved its PISA standings in both achievement and equity. In 2000, PISA had reported quite bad scores for Germany—below the United States and below the average of developed nations. That created a scandal and a national stock taking known as *der PISA Schock*. Reacting to the *Schock*, Germany began to adopt well-defined curricula. After that it began to score above average for developed nations. Germany, with notable astuteness, had discovered the cure on its own. When Manfred Prenzel, the head of PISA studies in Germany, was asked to explain what caused German students to become so much better in reading, math, and science than they were a decade ago, he had a simple answer: the post-*Schock* curriculum guides put out by the

TABLE 7.1 Sweden PISA scores

Year	Reading	Math	Science
2000	516	510	512
2003	514	509	506
2006	507	502	503
2009	497	494	495
2012	483	478	485

TABLE 7.2 German PISA scores

Year	Reading	Math	Science
2000	484	490	487
2003	513	503	502
2006	495	504	516
2009	497	513	520
2012	508	514	524

Länder (equivalent to the states in the United States) are now much more aligned with each other, and are more specific grade by grade. "The teachers," he said, "know specifically what to teach, and the students know what they have to learn."[45]

AVOIDING IDEOLOGICAL OVERSIMPLIFICATIONS

Sweden offers dramatic proof that left-versus-right ideological simplifications regarding the declines there and in France are not warranted. In Sweden, the disastrous movement toward individualism and skills that destroyed its education came from the political right, not the left as in France.[46] The theory offered in Sweden was that individual schools and students, left on their own without state interference, would yield better results than state-imposed commonality. As the Swedish government put it: "Education should be adapted to each pupil's circumstances and needs, based on the pupils' background, earlier experiences, language, and knowledge." That statement from the right was exactly the position and almost the wording of the socialist left in France, which stated: "The school shall take into account the plurality and diversity of aptitudes of each pupil."

Nor has Great Britain been exempt from premature left-right polarization of the early curriculum. In 1967, before the Bourdieu-Gros Report of 1989, Britain had issued the Plowden Report under the auspices of a left-leaning Labor government.[47] Progressive education, long an undercurrent in teacher training in the United Kingdom, now began to be institutionalized as official left-wing doctrine. The Plowden Report encouraged schools to "develop a more informal, child-centered style of education with an emphasis on individualization and learning by discovery": in short, a "progressive" style of education, which Plowden largely endorsed. But the trend was not without its critics, and the battle over different styles of primary education would continue for many years, with traditionalists blaming Plowden for what they saw as the failings of primary education."[48] Stipulations of the Plowden

Report were very Jospin-like: the involvement of parents, children finding things out for themselves, and above all, a focus on the individual.
"Individual differences between children of the same age are so great
that any class, however homogeneous it seems, must always be treated
as a body of children needing individual and different attention," said
the report. Poet W. H. Auden, protesting, stuck his poetical oar in:
"Dare any call Permissiveness / An educational success?"[49]

Lacking detailed data in Britain, it's impossible to state with confidence the connection of individualized education with the disturbing
widening of gaps in Britain. The Bennett Report of 1976 argued that the
data showed that the new methods were exacerbating inequalities without
leading to any improvement in "creativity."[50] This led the *Times* of April
26, 1976, to issue a lead editorial entitled "Progress Is Not Progressive."

Today the conservative government in Britain supports a communal
curriculum, while Labor, following the lead of the teacher unions, argues for individuality and "personalization." But teacher unions are not
inherently of that view. Their membership has simply been indoctrinated by their teacher-training institutions, which are theological institutes for progressivism. In the United States, the independent-minded
American Federation of Teachers has long supported the highly specific
Core Knowledge Curriculum because of its socially enabling power,
and its effectiveness in narrowing achievement gaps between groups.

Ever since Condorcet and Jefferson, the left has favored universal-
ism—that is, the idea of offering each child the very same educational
opportunities in the early years. That was the position of the left in Sweden and France after World War II, and it met with great success. But
then the French left reversed itself in 1989. Current political polarization of this issue reflects now chiefly a spirit of party rather than of hard
thought about achieving higher equity and a better-educated citizenry.

Educational individualism and the skills delusion have no inherent
connection with either the left or right. That was an insight that the
great liberal George Counts announced memorably to the American

Progressive Education Association as early as 1932: "Progressive Education . . . has focused attention squarely upon the child; it has recognized the fundamental importance of the interest of the learner; it has defended the thesis that activity lies at the root of all true education . . . it has championed the rights of the child as a free personality. All of this is excellent; but in my judgment it is not enough. The great weakness of Progressive Education lies in the fact that it has elaborated no theory of social welfare, unless it be that of anarchy or extreme individualism."[51]

This critique was also that of the great leftist thinker Antonio Gramsci. With his unerring penetration, he understood that poor children needed to master the intellectual tools of power rather than implausibly trying to invent their own.[52] When I have invoked Gramsci as supporting the principle of a universal common curriculum in early grades, it has induced a heated reaction from progressive educators on the left who greatly admire Gramsci, but deny that he ever said or meant anything that contravenes child-centered education and the anti-transmission point of view. In the end, it doesn't matter what Gramsci said about this, since cognitive science clearly indicates that broad, commonly shared knowledge is essential for effective language use. But one can hope that the honored name of Gramsci should encourage the best minds on the left to think again about their support of the inequality-producing child-centered curriculum.

When I questioned the Gramsci scholar Joseph Buttigieg about Gramsci's support of a common curriculum for all young children, he wrote back as follows, giving me permission to quote him:

> The phrase "la scuola unitaria o di formazione umanistica . . . o di cultura generale" [the unitary school or the school of humanistic formation or the school of general culture] is interesting because it explains that the "common school" Gramsci was thinking of was "a school of humanistic formation." The context makes it clear that for Gramsci the "common school" is necessary for "reasons of equal opportunity," as you put it, and to remedy the tendency of modernity and

modernization to channel pupils/students into special(ized) schools meant to prepare them for technical, industrial, etc. jobs.

Gramsci envisaged an educational system in which everyone would go through the "common school" before moving on to specialized schools. I've always considered Gramsci's positions on education to be informed by a profoundly democratic spirit. His views, in my opinion, are pedagogically sound. I wish more people currently involved in educational policy adopted perspectives similar to Gramsci's.

The "common school" is, of course, the very phrase and concept that helped build American democracy.

Knowing what we now know about the knowledge conventions of language, both the left and the right will need to get together and cooperate in repudiating misplaced providential ideas that leave the content of early education to benign forces in the nature of the child—or of the market. The early curriculum requires hard, specific thought, and commonality in grades preK–5. The depoliticizing of primary education could be the most important practical theme of this book.

To fulfill the promise of eager children from ages four to eleven, everyone should forget party. Both the left and the right have been misled by the theory of providential individualism in education.[53] Individualism in the early grades disables many individuals. It is an error committed by both the left and the right. The task of correcting it transcends party. Individualism with its curricular incoherence has been a chief cause of stasis or worse in the effort to narrow the achievement gaps between racial, ethnic, and economic groups in the United States, Britain, France, and Sweden. Providential individualism is an outmoded residue, a sedimentary deposit from intellectual history. It is not a logical nor a necessary element in the aims of either left or right. If equality of opportunity remains a primary aim, both parties will need to disavow the impossible dream of an effective individualized curriculum in the early grades.

CHAPTER EIGHT

The Knowledge-Based School

CREATING A COMMUNAL KNOWLEDGE-BASED CURRICULUM

Historically, the United States invented both the modern democratic nation and the common school that sustained it.[1] The guiding motto was "out of many one." Unity was to be created not just by a system of laws but also by a system of schooling that advanced a knowledgeable citizenry and social cohesion. School-based commonality is now the foundation of modern democracies everywhere. Communication and community through the common school is the hallmark of the successful modern nation. How artificial and necessary all this was and continues to be is well described by Ernest Gellner in his brilliant book, *Nations and Nationalism.*[2]

My argument for a communal early curriculum is not, then, a novelty, nor is it an elaborate promotion of the Core Knowledge plan as being the unique way to sustain the common school in the United States. The Core Knowledge Sequence is put forward only as an example of what such a curriculum looks like in the American context. At the moment, it is the only published outline of a complete, enabling elementary curriculum for American elementary schools.[3] It is available gratis to any school. Soon the Core Knowledge Foundation hopes to create a far more ambitious embodiment of the Sequence as a fully teachable, downloadable curriculum that any teacher could put into practice for free—with all the direct materials for students supplied, and all the professional development materials needed by teachers. (The Foundation has already done this for K–4 language arts.)

That material could serve as a model for what an American communal curriculum looks like. Our hope is that others will follow suit with their own versions of an American communal elementary curriculum. For widespread progress to be made, alternative communal curriculums will need to be created, since Americans do not like the idea of imposed uniformity. They demand a choice. Any broad curriculum that successfully delivers command of Standard American English by means of the standard American knowledge that enables its use would be equally effective.

That shared knowledge must be mastered by young pupils if they are to have a good chance at success in American life. Such a communal curriculum must include a lot of material that American writers and speakers have long taken for granted in their readers and listeners. Because of an inherent and inescapable inertia in the knowledge that is shared among hundreds of millions of people, the Core Knowledge plan was necessarily traditional, and was criticized in the 1990s for being so. It appeared to perpetuate the dominance of the already dominant elements of American life, while the aim of many intellectuals in the 1990s was to reduce that dominance and privilege, and valorize neglected cultures and women. So there was quite a lot of controversy attached to the Core Knowledge plan, which, though egalitarian in purpose and result, looked elitist on the surface. The aim of giving everybody entrée to the knowledge of power ran smack up against the aim of depriviliging those who are currently privileged.

How to solve that practical and moral impasse? Only by teaching traditional knowledge in elementary school, while adding in new elements. If we tried to teach children a fully nontraditional knowledge set, they could not master the existing language of power and success.[4] Disadvantaged children currently do *not* master it in most of our schools, and that puts them at a continued severe disadvantage. That's not a responsible principle for curriculum making.

If we look at what has actually happened to the vocabularies of literate adults in contemporary America, new words and names have come into currency, and have pushed out old words and names—but at a rather slow rate, despite our sense that all is changing at a dizzying pace. Here's a description of the new 2015 *Webster's Collegiate*, replacing the edition of a little over a decade ago:

> New words added to the Merriam-Webster dictionary for 2015 are today's trendiest terms when it comes to technology. There are over 1,700 new entries in the latest edition, according to an announcement made this week. In addition to that, there are hundreds of "senses" to existing words and thousands of new contextual examples. Among the new words added to Merriam-Webster, "photobomb," "meme," "emoji," and "net neutrality." The term "net neutrality" comes after a "years-long fight over the concept at the Federal Communications Commission," *The Hill* reports. As the report states, net neutrality is defined as "the idea, principle, or requirement that Internet service providers should or must treat all Internet data as the same regardless of its kind, source, or destination." "Emoji" is defined as any small image or icon used in electronic communication, while "meme," means "any idea behavior, style or usage that spreads from person to person within a culture." Another term in the Merriam-Webster Dictionary 2015 edition is "sharing economy," referencing [businesses] like Airbnb or Uber that help sell the "temporary access to goods or services." The dictionary also has the words "click fraud" and "clickbait"—meaning fraud committed by clicking through an advertisement on a website multiple times to spuriously increase the cost to the advertiser."[5]

The whole linguistic scene in the United States and other modern nations begins to look like an amoeba that is changing its shape. Some words enter usage and memory, others depart; "the old order changeth, yielding place to new."[6] *Rosa Parks* has pushed out *John Jay* in the contemporary American mind. The addition of *Rosa Parks* to canonical knowledge has been the deliberate work of cultural activists, and more power to them.

Webster's Collegiate has introduced 1,700 new entries out of about 170,000—a change of 1 percent in a decade. (It has dropped 9 entries, including *hodad* and *frutescent*.) Despite our sense of rapidity of change in the modern world, a change of 1 percent in a decade is not dizzyingly fast. At the center of the amoeba there is a nucleus that does not readily change shape or constitution. Most of the things we need to teach in elementary schools are not among the 1,700 new items in Webster.

Nor is mere word frequency a good guide to the curriculum. We need to teach the knowledge represented by a subset of the words that persist in people's minds, and continue in active usage from year to year. Some important ones do not occur every day. Today the frequency of *Franklin Roosevelt* is rare compared to *Kim Kardashian*, but there is good reason to teach *Roosevelt*, which we estimate to have more utility and durability. Rival elementary curriculums may reflect rival values, but all responsible ones will exhibit a great deal of overlap—out of a sense of obligation to the children who will need the knowledge represented by those words in order to function well in American society.

There are many ways of imparting the needed knowledge—once the inadequacy of the individualistic principle of early education is well understood, and is replaced by the far more effective and fair principle of communal knowledge. The key differences between an effective and an ineffective elementary school reside in the effectiveness of the knowledge they impart, not in their governance structures. The difference between a helter-skelter skills curriculum and a coherent knowledge curriculum is far more significant than any differences of administrative school arrangements.

Core Knowledge schools are administered under all types of governance. They are charter schools, regular public schools, and private schools. Whatever their administrative structures, they are highly similar in spirit and effectiveness. Governance structures are not educational structures. All types of Core Knowledge schools have happy, cooperative atmospheres that characterize schools the world over that have definite well-rounded curricula. That's why parents in Finland and Japan have seen no reason to institute charter schools. The new administrative structures of the charter school movement in the United States were developed because of our dissatisfaction with the results of our regular public schools, not dissatisfaction with administrative arrangements.

The Core Knowledge schools offer proof of concept for the knowledge-based school in the United States. The content-specific type of curriculum that has worked well in the school systems of the best-performing nations also works well in the United States. In this chapter I will discuss a regular Core Knowledge public school attended by low-income students, with the understanding that a Core Knowledge charter school could serve equally well as an example, and so could *any* school with a well-thought-out communal curriculum. The administrative labels "regular" and "charter" do not get to the essence of the matter.

Visitors say that the first things they notice about Core Knowledge schools are their walls and halls. They are covered with student art. The art usually has a theme—a depiction of some topic or story that the students are learning in common. The knowledge may be shared, but there is no lack of individuality in the way it is received and portrayed. The walls declare useful refutations of the usual objections to a common curriculum: that it suppresses individuality creativity, that it is dull, "rote-learned," and merely verbal. Those accusations are defensive and imaginary. They do not describe Core Knowledge schools. The claims that a knowledge-based school is defined by "rote learning of mere facts," that it is "purely verbal, not hands-on," that it is "developmentally inappropriate"—these are all untrue caricatures of the real thing, not just of Core Knowledge schools but of knowledge-based schools everywhere. These are lively places. Children are intensely interested in grown-up knowledge. They feel empowered, and they are.

WHY THIS BOOK EMPHASIZES THE EARLY GRADES

Most problems of American schooling (above all, the problem of inequality of opportunity) can be solved if we insist upon content-coherent schooling from preschool through grade 5. We now know from data here and abroad that a naturalistic, content-delayed, and individualistic approach in those grades consigns disadvantaged students to failure and advantaged ones to underachievement. The primary school is where preschool fadeout can be prevented; it is where a knowledge and a language base can be consolidated that will determine a student's subsequent chances in life. The early grades are the fulcrum of the whole school system, especially for students who have started out with major deficits in knowledge and vocabulary.[7] It determines whether poor children can ultimately catch up. Chapter 3 showed, for example, that the substance of what children gradually learn in grades K–3 will determine, by the end of grade 4 or 5, whether preschool gains will take hold rather than fade out.

In the early grades, the finite amount of knowledge to be made up is still manageable. Key deficits can be overcome through good systematic schooling, making it a critical period for overcoming the "Matthew Effect" in learning. The Matthew Effect, touched on in chapter 4, explains concisely why the period between ages four and eleven is key. The Effect was named after the Gospel of Matthew, which states: "For unto every one that hath shall be given, and he shall have abundance: but from him that hath not shall be taken even that which he hath" (Matthew 25:29). For most students, the period of the primary school is the latest time when the Apostle can be proved wrong, when the have-nots in knowledge and vocabulary *can* still be transformed into haves.

Psychologist Keith Stanovich explained how the Matthew Effect works with early reading, as well as its more general application to growth in knowledge and vocabulary.[8] The early knowledge advantage that has been gained by fortunate students is like Velcro; it is a base to which further knowledge sticks more readily. Another analogy is that of knowledge capital: just as it takes money to make money, it takes knowledge to gain more knowledge. In a carefully conducted primary school, where all students follow a common curriculum in the early grades and are prepared for each lesson by prior lessons, the have-nots can learn even more from each unit than the haves, and they are able gradually to catch up.[9]

A well-rounded elementary school thus kills two birds with one stone: it prepares advantaged students to become well educated, and it enables disadvantaged students to continue catching up with them. In discussing recent recalculations of the Coleman Report in chapter 5, I showed how this double aim of preparing the advantaged and enabling the disadvantaged to catch up can be accomplished only by a systematic approach to knowledge. An additional benefit of such a systematic approach is that it produces a happy and satisfying school for everyone—students, teachers, and parents.

Such a primary school also determines whether high school is going to be productive. The primary school is not just a place where "basic skills" are developed. It is where knowledge and vocabulary are built up that will determine a student's long-term ability to gain further knowledge and vocabulary. Content delay in the early years is harmful to all and disastrous to the disadvantaged. Hidden in the meaning of the Matthew Effect is the secret truth that a content-coherent preschool followed by content-coherent primary school can transform the larval have-nots into butterfly haves. Momentum is gained not just by a head start but by a *sustained* start. Lacking continued momentum, a mere head start slows down and fades out. The concept of "basic skills" is an oversimplification.

Growth in vocabulary and knowledge dies out without consistent reinforcement and consolidation in the primary grades. Middle school readiness depends on such reinforcement. Then, high school readiness critically depends on whether students' knowledge and vocabulary is already broadly based in science, architecture, painting, history, civics, geography, music, astronomy, literature, and math.[10] In sum, middle school readiness at age ten or eleven, based on effective primary education, is the great key to future college and career readiness. High school is too late to start taking coherent content seriously.

VOCABULARY DEVELOPMENT

Vocabulary size is the outward and visible sign of an inward acquisition of knowledge. It is also a reliable correlate to economic class. One standard deviation in vocabulary size averages about ten thousand 2012 dollars in annual income.[11] I discussed vocabulary acquisition in chapter 5 in connection with the aim of overcoming inequality. I now revisit the subject of vocabulary in this final chapter, because it is a concrete and easily grasped point of distinction between the skills-based approach to early education and the knowledge-based approach. It is a firmly observable way of illustrating how disabling the skills approach has been, and how promising the knowledge-based approach is. The latter is much better at narrowing differences in academic achievement and later earnings.

An attractive characteristic of a primary school with a coherent knowledge-based curriculum is that the different disciplines of knowledge can be integrated so that they reinforce each other. Such planned-out coherence speeds up learning and vocabulary gain. Knowledge and vocabulary are intertwined; advantaged children start out with more of both. Under a common curriculum the children who are behind slowly but surely catch up; at the beginning of each content unit they are behind, but they get up to speed by the end of each unit. This catching-up occurs in Core Knowledge schools.[12] Although knowledge and subject matters are the focus of the curriculum, the automatic side benefit of coherence is an ever-expanding vocabulary. Vocabulary size is not the primary aim of schooling; it is the consequence of broad knowledge, and a convenient check on school quality and equity.

We owe deep thanks to researchers Betty Hart and Todd Risley for helping to spread key insights about the importance of a broad early vocabulary. They dispatched their graduate students into the houses of parents from all strata of society to record and tabulate every word being directed at toddlers. During four years of observations, a child from a professional family would hear 45 million words, a working-class child 26 million, and a welfare child 13 million. This became known as the "30-million word gap." It was not just the total quantity of words that favored the top group: the quality and variety of the words they heard were also higher, and they received much more verbal feedback.

After the work of Hart and Risley became widely known, schools began placing a renewed emphasis on language in the early grades. That is a promising intellectual change. With it has come the realization that the education of young children needs also to be freed from the exclusive trammels of the *written* word. Yes, reading and writing (decoding and encoding) should be taught efficiently, but the knowledge children gain should not be constrained or slowed down by what they are able to decode from the printed word. That would simply intensify the Matthew Effect. Advantaged children have been read to and talked to, which was largely how they became advantaged. That should also be the chief mode of learning for all children in early grades, for the Hart-Risley insight is fortified by an earlier insight from the research of Thomas Sticht and colleagues.[13] Figure 8.1 illustrates the Sticht curve.

It shows that reading comprehension typically does not catch up with listening comprehension until late middle school. The child in kindergarten, first, and second grade who is starting to decode does not always have enough bandwidth to decode printed text and also ponder and grasp its meaning. That is a distraction from the important task of practicing fluent and accurate decoding. The school should not try to combine early decoding with substantive texts. That obvious bit of practicality has big implications for early schooling. It places a special emphasis on talking and listening. The Sticht curve, coupled with the Hart and Risley research, leads to a rethinking of the primary school curriculum. Reading, seeing, and doing are important, but in

FIGURE 8.1 Differences in listening and reading comprehension by age (Sticht and James, 1984)

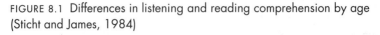
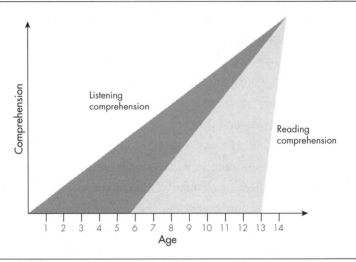

the earliest grades learning by being read aloud to and through talking and listening is fundamental to language progress and needs to receive great emphasis.

Children should hear and discuss highly interesting and demanding subject matters. They are eager to do so. The time spent on teaching decoding should be used with maximal efficiency, with a focus on practice and easily decodable texts. An hour a day on decoding has proved to be more than enough. When children see their fast progress, they take pride and pleasure in the chore.[14] As they progress through the grades, they can read for meaning in some of their independent reading.

In a carefully organized early curriculum, fiction and the various disciplines of fact are integrated and support each other. In the Core Knowledge Sequence, in fourth grade, the study of the Middle Ages in Europe is accompanied by units on the pictorial art of the Middle Ages, on the King Arthur myths in literature, on Islam in the Middle Ages, and on China in the Middle Ages. When a whole class spends two to four weeks studying stories about "Early Civilizations," all students learn words like *Christians, Muslims, Jews, mosque, temple, church, Arabia, Qu'ran, Babylon, Mesopotamia, banks, canals, reservoir, cuneiform, hieroglyphs, afterlife, sarcophagus, Aztec, Maya*, as well as *hurricane, canoe, harvest, maize, awe, legend, valley, hindrance, stationary, possessions, challenging*, and so on. Such integration of the disciplines not only reinforces the topics that are discussed and read, and written about in all subjects, but it also greatly speeds up the growth of vocabulary. By studying actual domains of knowledge, like the water cycle, students learn word meanings in context, with brief word explanations from the teacher where necessary.

In the absence of a well-integrated curriculum, reliable vocabulary gain currently depends on isolated word study, which is a method of limited effectiveness. Since the skills curriculum does not develop domain knowledge systematically, there can be no assurance that students will learn the words and knowledge they need, as indeed they do not. To compensate for that shortcoming, primary schools now set aside generous amounts of time for explicit word study—vocabulary drills, weekly lists of "new words," and so on. In the primary school, these grim exercises typically occupy twenty to thirty minutes a day in a literacy block of ninety minutes to two hours, thus taking up between 16 and 33 percent of the whole ELA curriculum.[15]

Isolated word study, well conducted, is moderately effective but has not significantly narrowed gaps between haves and have-nots. It takes too much time for too small an effect. The large amount of school time spent in direct word study is time that is not being spent on systematically becoming familiar with new knowledge domains, where word learning occurs naturally—and up to four times faster—without effort.[16] Building domain knowledge is a far more efficient, accurate, and secure way of inducing word learning than word study on its own, which can yield at best some acquaintance with four hundred words in a school year.[17] That is not a good way to arrive at the tens of thousands of words a seventeen-year-old needs to know to be college and career ready.[18] The best data we have in education—the verbal scores of whole nations, including the United States, France, and Sweden, which have massively tried the two different kinds of curriculum—show that the knowledge curriculum develops vocabulary far better than the skills curriculum does.

One type of knowledge-based curriculum develops knowledge and vocabulary in an optimal way. It is a curriculum with topics that are carefully sequenced over several years, and also integrated across disciplines within the same year—the arrangement of the best national curriculums like those of Japan and Korea, whose efficacy is manifest in the PISA scores.[19] Such an integrated approach is the optimal method for increasing the knowledge and vocabulary size of students, because topic familiarity (the secret to both comprehension and word learning) is optimal. It's true that knowledge and vocabulary are not perfectly correlated with each other; they are not the same, and I would not wish to be misunderstood on that score. But they are highly correlated, and an optimal knowledge-based curriculum will employ the optimal method for increasing the vocabulary size of students.

The most efficient and secure way to learn new words has been much studied in the field of second-language learning, and its results have been shown to apply equally well to native-language learning.[20] It is the method of incidental word learning (i.e., unconscious word acquisition) through topic familiarity. One learns new words automatically with the least time and effort when encountering them in a context that has become familiar. This means that the best vocabulary-building curriculum is one with a careful sequence of units that build up familiar contexts. It's the technique of domain immersion, advocated throughout this book. Those who teach English as a second language will quickly notice that the technique of domain immersion will be especially helpful for building the vocabularies of non-native speakers. Systematically building topic familiarity helps most those who are most behind. It is probably the most effective tool of gap closing yet devised, and it does not hold back more advanced students.[21]

If the teacher and student stay on topic, then, words more easily yield their meaning from context, because the larger meaning is being understood through familiarity.[22] The teacher pauses briefly to explain the sense of critical tier-three words like *seismic*. It's those critical tier-three words in the knowledge curriculum that demand brief explicit comment. In a rich textual environment tier-two words will take care of themselves, just as they almost certainly did for the readers of this book when they were growing up.

When students are not thinking about learning words, they are learning words most effectively. Thinking referentially about what words mean is the way we all came to know as many words as we do. Competence in language is gained by knowledge of things. The best way to learn lots of words is to systematically and coherently learn lots of things. The only enduring way to raise achievement and narrow gaps between groups of students is by closing the knowledge and vocabulary gap. That takes time and coherence. Cramming is short-lived. The most egalitarian school is one that follows a cumulative, multiyear plan of knowledge building.[23] With a well-integrated curriculum, like the one children experienced at PS 124, described next, word learning occurs automatically for all students. Such a school is also the most deeply satisfying and joyful for students and teachers alike.

WHAT HAPPENED AT PS 124

At the Core Knowledge Foundation we hear a weekly stream of enthusiasm from principals, teachers, parents, and, most gratifyingly, the young students themselves, who are proud of their knowledge and growing abilities.[24] Test scores gradually rise, and gaps gradually narrow. Over time, this inevitably happens when a knowledge sequence is followed faithfully, because the ultimate basis of test scores is knowledge. If the

word/knowledge gap is narrowed, so will be the gap in test scores between rich and poor.

If PS 124 in Queens, New York, composed of immigrant, poor, and
racially diverse students, can consistently post scores that are equal to
reading scores in more affluent zip codes, then *any* primary school can
do the same—over a period of years. Stories of quick fixes are not to
be believed.

The odds were against PS 124, located in a low-income neighborhood near a homeless shelter from which it drew some of its one thousand students, 80 percent of whom qualified for free lunch.[25] In 1998
PS 124 was not doing well, according to the New York test scores. But
Principal Elain Thompson and Assistant Principal Valarie Lewis were
devoted to giving these impoverished students a chance in life. They
were also savvy in dealing with the big New York system. They knew
how to work around the educationally wrong-headed regulations that
emanated from the New York City Department of Education. Instead
of behaving themselves like good, safe bureaucrats, these two brave
women decided that what their students needed was not more skill
drills but more knowledge. The students in Queens, they concluded,
needed to learn the same things that children in Scarsdale knew. In
1999 they decided to persuade their staff to follow the Core Knowledge
Sequence. I'll quote a page or two from Valarie's unpublished report,
which she has kindly given me permission to use. It will offer interested
teachers and parents a sense of how powerfully a coherent knowledge-
based curriculum affects students and their teachers.

> At PS/MS 124 in Queens, a K–8 neighborhood school where I was
> principal until I retired in 2014, we got real results. We even won a
> Dispelling the Myth Award from the Education Trust in 2007 for
> closing the achievement gap in all sub-group populations. Our test
> results show that we closed the achievement gap under No Child
> Left Behind; in our universal free-lunch school, our students—ev-
> ery subgroup—always made AYP (adequate yearly progress). In 2014,

on New York's tough new Common Core–aligned tests, we outperformed the New York City average. For economically disadvantaged
students (which is all of PS 124), we outperformed the city by eight
percentage points in ELA and eight percentage points in math.

The first step in our journey was to develop a new, content-rich
curriculum—just like what's now called for by the Common Core
State Standards—based on the Core Knowledge Sequence. Using the
new curriculum as a foundation, we increased teacher collaboration
and student engagement.

With a homeless shelter two blocks away, student mobility used to
be high, but after Core Knowledge was introduced in 1999–2000, parents went to great lengths to keep their children in PS/MS 124. Many
parents told me they felt their children were getting a "private school"
education. So they found ways for their children to travel to our school
even if they had been transferred to a shelter in another New York City
borough. Ever since we adopted Core Knowledge, teacher mobility
also dropped—and remains low to this day.

At first we feared that the content would be too rigorous—both for
us as educators and for our students. We soon discovered that all of us
loved being challenged. Major historical events, scientific discoveries,
and works of art are inherently interesting; with our new curriculum,
teachers and children loved learning. As our implementation of Core
Knowledge deepened, our fifth graders' achievement soared. The results indicated that the background knowledge they gleaned through
Core Knowledge in the elementary grades was sustained and extended.
Our science results for grades 4 and 8 are just as impressive as our social
studies results.

The journey to Core Knowledge started in 1998. I was struck by
student's rote approach to learning. I sought out my colleagues across
all grades: Was my experience typical? Was anyone really reaching these
students, seeing them grasp new knowledge? It became apparent that
while the teachers were planning well and adhering to state and district
instructional mandates, the students were not being inspired to learn.
After extensive perusal of the Core Knowledge Sequence, we decided
it would be the best tool for us to transform both teacher practices and
the content we asked our students to master.

. . .

Soon, all of the teachers were honestly discussing their strengths and weaknesses in content knowledge—and then they were able to support each other. For example, six teachers who had strong backgrounds in science were selected to become the lead science teachers—one per grade. This approach ensured great instruction for the students, and relieved the regular classroom teachers from having to quickly master an array of new science topics that they hadn't taught before.

Each teacher was able to master their specific subject matter from the Sequence, and develop comprehensive lesson plans. By sharing their instructional plans with each other, they expanded each other's knowledge base in all subjects. This embedded professional development was powerful. So powerful that pretty soon, the teachers no longer felt the need to departmentalize. By January, they were far more comfortable with the new content.

. . .

In reflecting on those first three years, there were important signs that we were on the right track. One of the most important was that the entire school became connected. The teachers began to communicate with each other on a daily basis, conferring on a professional level, supporting each other as they learned the content, and collaboratively planning lessons. They became risk takers, honing their craft. Many expressed, "This is why I became a teacher—to provide students with instruction that prepares them for citizenship, college, and all sorts of careers."

The most remarkable confirmation that building our content-rich curriculum was worth the effort was the students' reactions to the new learning climate. We were finally awakening their desire to learn. Very early on, students began asking more questions and even discussing the content among themselves. Academic debates happened on the playground.

. . .

PS/MS 124 went on a fifteen-year journey of seeking knowledge. When working with students daily, it is hard to know the long-term impact. Yet when they return for a visit, which many have done over the years, the stories they share demonstrate that their broad knowledge and strong skills have become an integral part of the tapestry of their lives. One of the most revealing statements I have heard countless times from the returning students is, "When I went to high school my teachers wanted to know where I previously went to school because they couldn't believe I knew so much. I loved always knowing the answers and leading the discussions."

THE SPIRIT OF COMMUNITY IN THE WELL-ROUNDED SCHOOL

Valarie's account confirms that, when the school enterprise is focused on clear knowledge goals with inherently fascinating subjects, a spirit of excitement and cooperation infects students and teachers alike. The usual atmosphere of our inner-city primary schools is far from happy or cohesive among either teachers or students. A spirit of community built upon a common purpose is often lacking. The reality of a haphazard skills curriculum adjusted to the individual child is not as happy as its individualistic theory proposes.

There's an overlooked paradox in emphasizing individuality in early years; it defeats itself. It fails to deliver the shared knowledge of the community. That cramps children's competence and thus their freedom to develop their individual tastes and abilities. Individualism in the primary curriculum thwarts individuality. The great G. H. Mead put it this way: "The individual is not initially there, at birth, but arises in the process of social experience and activity, that is, develops in the given individual as a result of his relations to that process as a whole and to other individuals within that process."[26] It's in relation to the community that individuality develops. Only by mastering the shared knowledge and norms of the community can one diverge from those norms effectively. Language mastery is a clear example. The basis of language is commonality. Individuality comes from mastery of its shared conventions; that mastery is the foundation of an individual style. Ignorance of group conventions doesn't foster individuality but ineptitude and inequality.

Common subject matter sponsors a sense of common purpose in which students and teachers feel they are a part. Core Knowledge schools are happy schools. There is no sense of the alienation so pervasive in our public schools, and so productive of misbehavior. The entire school shares a sense of common purpose, because there *is* a common purpose. There is collegiality and cooperation, because teachers know that the work of one year builds upon the work that came before in a predictable and cumulative way. There is pride in success.

THE BEST KIND OF CURRICULUM IN THE WORLD

Studies have uniformly shown that schools that faithfully implement Core Knowledge–style principles have raised achievement and narrowed gaps far more effectively than comparison schools.[27] Those principles are followed by the best-performing current charter schools—in New York City in the Icahn charter schools (led by the heroic Core Knowledge early pioneer Jeffrey Litt) and in the Success Academies, and others.[28] Some regular public schools have taught Core Knowledge for more than a decade—schools like Three Oaks in Florida, and PS 124 in Queens. The long-range effect on students' lives has been compelling, as Valarie Lewis and the researcher Karin Chenoweth report. But these longitudinal effects remain relatively unstudied in large-scale research projects on Core Knowledge schools.[29]

Successful Core Knowledge schools deliver the Core Knowledge Sequence in different ways and with different emphases. Their widespread success is best viewed not as evidence for a program but for a principle—that of a specific, communal, grade-by-grade curriculum. I call the general principle "lowercase core knowledge." So understood, the scientific validation of core knowledge does not depend on the willingness of the educational research community to authenticate its effectiveness with large-scale random-assignment studies. Educational research over the globe has already established that its curricular principle is the best grounded and most successful in the world. Any school or district using a curriculum that follows the core knowledge principle, then, is following the best-validated curricular principle known to research.

The precise contents of the Core Knowledge Sequence are not the Tables of the Law. Core Knowledge is not a scripted program. Schools adjust the specifics. This distinction between scripted programs and curricular principles offers the correct research approach to the effectiveness of a coherent curriculum. Those principles are far better grounded in science and in practical results than are the individualized skills approaches with uncertain subject matters current in American schools, which continue to yield poor results.

Lowercase core knowledge is powerfully supported both by the basic science as outlined in prior chapters and by PISA studies of achievement among fifteen-year-olds across the globe. The PISA studies consistently place Japan, Finland, and other nations that follow lowercase core knowledge at the top of the PISA rankings in both achievement and equity. PISA analysts have stated explicitly that the best results in achievement and equity are found in national school systems in which all parties—parents, teachers, and students—are made aware of the *specific* content and level of expertise that each student is expected to attain at each grade level.[30] Both PISA and common sense affirm that a systematic approach to knowledge building is more productive than an arbitrary skills approach with unspecified topics.[31]

The lack of massive, randomly assigned research into Core Knowledge has enabled educational experts to state skeptically that there isn't any massive, randomly assigned, large-scale proof that the Core Knowledge Sequence works brilliantly. That's very true. But that lack of a compelling large-scale study is an oddity from a purely scientific standpoint. The Core Knowledge Sequence is of long standing; it is fairly widespread (some 1,200 schools in 47 states), and it is unique in the American context. No other reform effort has followed for decades the principle of systematically teaching disadvantaged students the entire range of enabling knowledge possessed by highly advantaged students. Yet scientific curiosity has not induced the much-needed large study.[32]

Small studies, all favorable, have been ignored or dismissed. In 2011, New York City ordered a moderately sized comparative study of Core Knowledge language arts for the earliest grades (ten experimental and ten control schools). It showed overwhelmingly superior results for Core Knowledge. When the new chancellor in New York City arrived on the scene, she dismissed the study as being "too small," but did not propose a bigger one, despite the clear superiority of the Core Knowledge results.[33]

In sum, educational specialists in the United States (those who accept the three disabling ideas traced in the prologue) should not continue to state that Core Knowledge is an "unproved" program, on the grounds that they have declined to prove it.[34] It is not a program but a curricular principle for which there is an immense body of international evidence and research. The small-scale studies of Core Knowledge, all positive, simply confirm the large-scale conclusions of the PISA reports.

The curricular sequences of the most successful PISA nations share six key characteristics with Core Knowledge. For example, the Japanese elementary curriculum, which consistently scores at the top in all subjects, exhibits all those virtues.[35] (For a more detailed description of the Japanese elementary curriculum, see appendix III.) These sequences are all:

- **Field-tested.** The need for field testing is obvious, since only actual experience can determine how well topics interact and reinforce each other, and how much time should be allocated to each subject at a grade level.
- **Topic-specific.** Absent in American ELA standards, topic specificity is probably the most important characteristic to insist upon in the United States, since it makes everyone—teachers, students, and parents—aware of the level of expertise that students will have gained at each point, and what will need to be learned in the future.

- **Well rounded.** Those high-performing curricula are also well rounded, with art, literature music, geography, and even "morality," set forth in definite curricular topics along with math and science. The arts and the humanities, including literature, history, and civics, are important both to the life of the individual and the quality of the national community. Such well roundedness is important also in a purely practical view, since breadth of knowledge and vocabulary (including proper nouns!) is critical to high reading skill and other communicative skills. Broad knowledge is also critical for ameliorating class distinctions, and placing all citizens on a more equal footing. That was the reason Gramsci insisted that the unitary "common school" should be a "school of humanistic formation or a school of general culture." Japan does a superb job under this criterion, and so did France in former times.

- **Coherent.** Topic coherence within a grade level is particularly important in the language arts class, where topics in the United States are currently individualized, fragmentary, and disconnected. Such incoherence hinders substantive learning and vocabulary acquisition. Sustained topics requiring the same "word fields" need to last two weeks or more to be effective.[36]

- **Cumulative.** Designing a multiyear cumulative sequence of topics is important technically to make sure that students are ready for each subject over the sequence of grade levels, assuring commonality across all classes within a grade level. No student is denied critical knowledge, and everyone in the group is prepared to learn upcoming lessons.

- **Selective.** Finally, selectivity is critical in setting topics that make the curriculum successfully communal. Since communality and equality of opportunity are primary aims of early schooling, the topics of the curriculum should convey the most enabling knowledge within the national context. The idea that any sensible topic will serve to inculcate general skills has been a fundamental empirical mistake that guarantees failure. Some curricular topics are essential to the subject matter itself, such as photosynthesis and the four operations of arithmetic. Other topics, like the Civil War, are essential to shared cultural identity. Still others, like *Romeo and Juliet*, are essential to equality, because to be ignorant of them is to be ignorant of what others know, and thus to be scorned and excluded from comprehension and from the esteem of others.

Those are the curricular principles of lowercase core knowledge. They are fulfilled in all good national curriculums. They ensure universal competence and high equity. They enhance a sense of community because everyone, not just the favored few, possesses the shared knowledge of the elementary curriculum: the great nourisher of the public sphere.

CAN WE ACHIEVE A CHANGE IN IDEAS AND PRACTICES?

In Rochester, Minnesota, on Friday afternoons, there's a local radio discussion about the affairs of the city and nation called *Rochester Today*. In June 2014, I received an e-mail with a web link to the show. The subject was to be a Core Knowledge school in the city.[37] The school, the Washington School, was to be featured because it had been posting the best scores in the city, and also narrowed the achievement gap between advantaged and disadvantaged pupils better than any other local school. It had received a Blue Ribbon award from the US Department of Education. Parents from all over the city were trying to get their children enrolled there. With a total capacity of 351 students in grades K–5, the school had a waiting list of over 1,000.

The topic of the radio program was to be this: Given the unfilled popular demand for the Core Knowledge Sequence, why doesn't Rochester make that cost-free Sequence the basis for the elementary curriculum in all the schools of the city? Wouldn't all the children benefit, and the parents be less frustrated?

It was a pleasure to hear the civility and friendliness of tone between the two participants, Andy Brownell and Tom Ostrom, two civic-minded citizens of Rochester who conducted the radio program every Friday. Ostrom had no problem recounting the objections he had heard throughout the city against the idea of adopting such a curriculum sequence citywide:

- "Education is political."
- "It's about control, and budget, and ideological clashes."
- "Core Knowledge is elitist."
- "The results didn't come from the curriculum but from the excellent teachers."
- "Many of the town's teachers are opposed to those ideas."
- "Some parents and teachers don't believe in the accuracy of the test results."
- "Core Knowledge is not multicultural enough."
- "There's too much rote learning."
- "It's not child centered enough."

Finally, Ostrom suggested that the subject be changed because he had worn himself out repeating the objections he had heard.

This is a pretty good example of how difficult it currently is to change basic educational ideas in the United States, even with a sizeable number of parents eager to see a shift toward a more enabling, content-based curriculum. The effective changes in ideas that I have seen over the years have come from within—from brave principals like Valarie Lewis and adventurous teachers—more than from parents, who feel helpless and unsure in the face of the highly definite viewpoints and brilliant slogans of skill-centric doctrine.

In 2015, a nationwide nonprofit organization called Great Schools posted online its current evaluation of the Rochester, Minnesota, public schools. Great Schools analyzes yearly school-by-school results in cities all over the nation. To set its ratings from 1 to 10, it takes student disadvantage into account by considering both absolute achievement scores and relative growth in the scores from year to year among all demographic groups. We've known since the Coleman Report that a school that induces large yearly gains for all students is a school that is inherently gap-closing in its effects, so the rating system is basically sound. Great Schools' ranking of the sixteen public elementary schools in Rochester gives just one of them a 10: the Core Knowledge Washington School. Four other schools achieve an 8. The other eleven schools fall off badly. The average score of all the fifteen schools remaining after excising the Washington School from the computation is 4.6.

The aim of Great Schools is to inform parents and encourage better performance by schools. In Rochester, the parents were already partially informed, as we know from the long waiting list for the Washington School mentioned on *Rochester Today*. But parents have been unable to change the system. From afar, the American system seems paralyzed, unable to change except under threats of tests, and then in unproductive, test-prep directions. In Rochester, even with a superior model before their eyes, and with parental awareness and radio talk shows, no change is visible. Over the years I have received many frustrated communications from parent groups. It seems a representative situation in the United States. Can anything be done?

My thesis in this book, and my settled belief, is that parents and educators in low-scoring elementary schools like those in Rochester powerfully desire to improve their educational effectiveness, but are prevented from trying out a knowledge-based, communal curriculum because such an approach contradicts the child-centered, skill-centric doctrines that are still an intellectual monopoly in our education world. It is hard to change the received thought of the community to which one belongs, and it is uncomfortable to criticize it. To this psychological barrier must be added two others: an all-too-human resistance to changing one's habitual mode of activity, and an anxiety about teaching unfamiliar subject matters. But we know from decades of experience that these inherent difficulties can be overcome if a new belief system arises within the school under strong leadership. When people see the evidence of success with their own eyes, as in PS 124 and the Washington School, they gain a sense of efficacy. Nor should we underestimate the force of the following consideration: "We've tried everything *except* a detailed knowledge-based curriculum like Core Knowledge, so why don't we give it a try?"

To enable such a change to take hold districtwide, leadership is needed, not just in the schools but also in the community. A districtwide curriculum should be the aim, because the entire district can then cooperate in giving schools the support they need in putting a challenging elementary curriculum into effect. With a good districtwide curriculum, every school in the district can become a good neighborhood school. A further highly important value of districtwide implementation is rarely mentioned: the movement of disadvantaged students from school to school in the middle of the year for economic reasons. This movement of poor students occurs mostly within the district—an inconvenient truth. In most cities, the mobility rate is around 30 percent, sometimes higher, with grave educational consequences. The ill effects of mobility would be much alleviated if students did not have to suffer discontinuities in the subject matters they were studying.

All politics is local; I have no road map for inducing idea change to be followed by political change. One concrete inducement might be this: All district superintendents wish to report good scores on reading tests. After more than a decade of test-prep schooling we know that test-prep has limited utility in raising reading scores. Superintendents and other educators might therefore consider the following logic.

A reading comprehension test is a test of communal knowledge and vocabulary.

To enable all children to possess that knowledge requires a well-delivered, communal elementary curriculum that delivers such knowledge to all.

If all children master such a curriculum, they will be enabled to score well on tests of reading comprehension. QED

That is a long-range view, of course, since communality and language mastery do not manifest themselves overnight. But the syllogism is correct, and the surest and best way to ensure that children in a district master a communal curriculum is for the district to institute a specific districtwide curriculum.

If such a decision were reached openly and democratically, howls of complaint would probably become muted. One obvious advantage of a specific districtwide curriculum is that under it the district could offer logistical and training support to teachers and schools. For instance, while the changeover is under way, an imaginative superintendent could arrange to get a "research exemption" and call a three-year moratorium on skills-based reading comprehension tests. The district could then substitute locally made content tests based on the school curriculum—in full confidence that after the moratorium, students would perform far better than before on the standard reading comprehension tests.[38]

We know from our experience in the field what happens after a good knowledge-based curriculum becomes established in a school. A great improvement in the morale of students and teachers ensues, along with a great improvement in achievement and equity. These favorable outcomes will please everyone, especially the children—who are fascinated by the content they are learning, and proud of their grown-up knowledge. Everybody will be gradually disburdened from the weight of outmoded ideas. If this book can play a small role in that intellectual liberation, it will have achieved its purpose.

Breaking Free

REPLACING INDIVIDUALISTIC IDEAS
WITH COMMUNITARIAN ONES

In the 1940s, American K–12 education still ranked among the best and fairest school systems in the world.[1] Now it ranks below average in both achievement and equity.[2] Our educational decline began when we adopted an early-nineteenth-century Middle European educational ideology whose ideas took root in America beginning in the 1870s. In Central Europe it was called "the new education," and in America it was called "progressive education." Asian nations resisted the philosophy. They have made the fastest progress in the twentieth century, and can now boast the best elementary school systems in the world.[3]

By the 1930s, progressive education had triumphed over the minds of most American educators. By 1960, most twelfth graders in American public schools had experienced twelve years of schooling based on its ideas. The Great American Test Score Decline took place between 1960 and 1980. Scores have never come back. This book has explained the causal connections between the gradual dominance of romantic ideas and our educational decline.

Those romantic ideas still dominate: they hold that education should follow a natural course of individual development; that nothing should be imposed upon the child before the child is naturally ready; that hands-on simulations and projects are better than artificial, "merely verbal," "rote learning"; that the subjects studied are less important than developing critical-thinking skills, since facts can always be looked up. These doctrines have precluded the thing most needed in early education—a definite, well-rounded, elementary curriculum mastered by all students except those who are severely impaired.

Current American resistance to the idea of a local common curriculum is not, then, a reflection of American traditions. It is a post-romantic tradition of the twentieth century. Earlier in the United States, a common curriculum in each locality was a central ideal of the Common School that built the nation. Nation building and nation preserving was a conscious mission of those communal schools. What is needed now is not a change in the basic American tradition but rather a repudiation of the post-romantic deflection toward providential individualism, where nature, not nation, has presided over schooling. Once that outmoded and unsuccessful ideology is dethroned, effective educational reforms can take hold, but not before.

We can start breaking free from that intellectual monopoly when the wider public understands that thinking skills—like "critical and creative thinking" and "problem solving"—are not productive educational aims. Thinking skills are rarely independent of specific expertise. As Anders Ericsson and Robert Poole put it bluntly in their authoritative 2016 book on the subject: "There is no such thing as developing a general skill."[4] The goal of imparting all-purpose skills is a delusion. Once the general-skills idea is exposed as a myth, no persuasive argument is left standing to excuse curricular incoherence. Language competence will then be correctly understood as dependent on subject-matter mastery, gradually built up in a well-rounded school under a specific, grade-by-grade curriculum.

Although no persuasive intellectual argument is left standing to excuse curricular incoherence, an emotional one still remains, and it is powerful. Child-centered education claims to accommodate schooling to the individual child. As I read parental comments about schools, I find low-scoring schools being praised for the individual attention paid to the child, but also, among the comments for that very same school, I read parental complaints of individual neglect. It is not really a contradiction. Both types of comment can be true, since individual attention to some students necessarily means individual neglect of others. The most important *academic* attention that can be paid to the individual child in the elementary grades is to ensure his or her mastery of a communal curriculum that leads to mastery of Standard American English.

The unifying, nation-building function of the schools was paramount in the minds of educators throughout the nineteenth century. Textbook makers contrived to copy one another in a benign conspiracy to foster a positive patriotic sentiment. Noah Webster's project to Americanize the written and spoken language was eagerly accepted by schools in all the states. We now know that Webster's project inherently involved more than common spelling and pronunciation. His *Blue Back Speller* also spread common conventions of knowledge, sentiment, and idiom. We now know that such shared conventions of knowledge and sentiment are part and parcel of language mastery.

Those who would make that shared, taken-for-granted knowledge more multicultural are admirable. They are trying to make communal knowledge more capacious and tolerant. Their efforts have already changed our shared knowledge. But most of the shared knowledge that makes a student expert in the language of print and TV, and commerce and the Internet, is knowledge at the center that changes slowly. To exclude students from that central knowledge is to keep them incompetent communicators—and poor. Multiculturalism helps social justice only if it keeps that larger, central expertise as an aim.

The hopeful motto "out of many one" was the central educational project of American schools in the nineteenth century. It was the urgent aim of the common curriculum in the common school. Commonality and community became understood as the key problem of the American experiment. The success or failure of the experiment depended on preserving national unity as a far-flung community dedicated to common principles. That was Lincoln's theme from the beginning of his career—

from the Lyceum address of 1838, to the address to Wisconsin Farmers in 1859, to the Gettysburg address of 1863, to the second inaugural of 1865. The test of democratic government—determining whether it perishes from the earth—was to be whether it was sustained through "reverence for the laws" and the founding proposition of equality, and through a shared determination that the last best hope of mankind shall not fail through internal disunity. Lincoln saw the Civil War as a crucial part of the experiment: "*testing* whether that nation or any nation so conceived and so dedicated can long endure." Long before that speech, the younger Lincoln back in 1838 invoked the idea that the new kind of democratic nation required shared commitment to ideals gained through education: "Let it be taught in schools, in seminaries, and in colleges; let it be written in Primers, spelling books, and in Almanacs;—let it be preached from the pulpit, proclaimed in legislative halls, and enforced in courts of justice. And, in short, let it become the political religion of the nation; and let the old and the young, the rich and the poor, the grave and the gay, of all sexes and tongues, and colors and conditions, sacrifice unceasingly upon its altars."

The triple theme of American schools should be "think globally; act locally; contribute nationally." The American experiment was not just government of, by, and for the people. It was of, by, and for all kinds of people, as Lincoln put it: "the old and the young, the rich and the poor, the grave and the gay, of all sexes and tongues, and colors and conditions." America was to be a trans-tribal tribe.[5] That paradoxical and noble aim has been an attempt to overcome the deep, divisive tribal instinct, the source of so many human ills. It has been an attempt to create out of many one. That is still the ongoing work of the United States in which the schools have a sacred duty and a central role.

REJECTING THE SKILLS DELUSION

One of the cheering experiences in writing this book was my encounter with Piaget's noble confession that new evidence had caused him to revise his theory of mental development. He concluded that the stages of mental growth did not reflect a purely developmental process but were powerfully influenced by the specific content of education. He concluded that the developmental process could be speeded or delayed by as much as four years. "Maturation," he said, "is not everything." That statement is nothing less than a repudiation of the basic romantic principle of education; Piaget conceded that "training" is, after all, just as potent as "growth" in human development.

Here was a great scientist showing himself more loyal to the evidence than to his own celebrated ideas about child development. Piaget's "return upon himself" is reminiscent of Edmund Burke's change of heart about the French Revolution, so memorably described by Matthew Arnold:

> That return of Burke upon himself has always seemed to me one of the finest things in English literature, or indeed in any literature. That is what I call living by ideas: when one side of a question has long had your earnest support, when all your feelings are engaged, when you hear all round you no language but one, when your party talks this language like a steam-engine and can imagine no other,—still to be able to think, still to be irresistibly carried, if so it be, by the current of thought to the opposite side of the question, and, like Balaam, to be unable to speak anything *but what the Lord has put in your mouth.*[6]

Exactly such a thought revolution, and a willingness to follow the evidence where it leads, is needed far and wide in educational thought in the United States, still dominated by romantic ideas. It is up to those trained in the cognitive sciences to help lead that change. It is up to parents and citizens to encourage them to speak up.

In science one of the most persuasive indications that a finding is correct is that the same result can be derived from multiple separate approaches that are completely independent of one another. Such intellectual triangulation has now occurred in cognitive science with respect to education. We have learned that the growth of expertise in language and other areas is a slow, domain-restricted growth. There are no significant shortcuts to intellectual competence. Domain-specific knowledge and long practice are essential to consolidating a skill in long-term memory. Neither computers nor general critical-thinking techniques can circumvent those arduous requirements.

This conclusion has been triangulated from multiple sources. Scientists need to help educators make that dependable conclusion prevail. School-level educational research, by contrast—with its uncontrolled variables and its constant, breathless reports in the press—is rarely as dependable as is triangulation from the scientific consensus. With or without the "gold standard" of random assignment of students, school-based research into specific programs has proved to be less reliable and generalizable than logically necessary inferences from basic research.[7]

There's a memorable example of such triangulation in physics. In the early years of the twentieth century a positivist like Ernst Mach could still deny the existence of atoms and molecules. This bothered scientists, including young Einstein at the patent office. Some of Einstein's early papers from 1905 to 1910 concerned Avogadro's number N—the number of molecules in a molecular weight of a substance . . . if molecules did exist.[8] Einstein proposed that if the computation of N should turn out the same from independent sources, then a rational person should cease to be a skeptic about the existence of atoms. He set about the task. The young Einstein's feat is beautifully described in the biography by Abraham Pais. In a sequence of papers (most written during his *annus mirabilis* of 1905), Einstein computed N from blackbody radiation, from the viscosity of sugar solutions, from the Brownian motion of small particles in suspension, and (later) from the blueness of the sky. All yielded numbers close to 6.02×10^{23}. After 1905 it had become irrational to disbelieve in atoms.

The foundations of current American schooling—natural development, individualism, and all-purpose skills—have now been disconfirmed from multiple independent perspectives: from large data sets from entire nations (e.g., Sweden, France, Germany, the United States); from developmental psychology, which shows that natural development is no reliable guide to appropriate school content; from psycholinguistics, which shows that communication skills require domain-specific knowledge; from studies of expertise showing that skills depend on specific content knowledge; from Google Translate, which daily shows that algorithms without specific contextual knowledge cannot yield accurate translations.[9] Not even Google Translate is capable of an all-purpose language skill, though gradually it will become somewhat better versed in the communal knowledge of the various national languages. That will not enable the program to disambiguate effectively since the context is not explicitly given. But it will gradually improve from crowdsourcing, thus showing the power of a communal education.

Only a well-rounded, knowledge-specific curriculum can impart needed knowledge to all children and overcome inequality of opportunity. Whether we can summon the will to break the romantic intellectual monopoly that has held us in thrall will be determined by the following concrete test: Will any large American locality be willing to institute a good, content-specific curriculum grade-by-grade throughout all the elementary schools of the district?[10] If one single big district does so, it will be a watershed event in our educational history. The neighborhood school in each area of the district will then become an exciting, interesting, well-rounded school that parents will want their child to attend. Teachers will respond with enthusiasm, as they always do in knowledge-rich schools, by enriching their own educations and becoming intensely interested in the subject matters. The academic results will be significantly better and fairer than current results. Ideas will change throughout the district and beyond. In time, with first-class results, other districts, even states, will adopt the districtwide policy by popular demand. This *will* happen.

The Origins of Natural-Development Theories of Education

FROM HIGH COLUMNS TO A SINGLE STORY

Early twentieth-century school buildings in America are imposing civic structures. Their high flights of steps surmounted by high columns fairly shout: "The school is important to the local and national community." In the morning, in the old massive schools, you can still see the small figures of the children climbing the high steps, the whole scene symbolizing the important place of schooling in the community—and not just in the local community: the design always includes a tall-standing American flag, to which the children pledge allegiance every morning.

Ideas are reflected in architecture. Faith built cathedrals and mosques. Pantheism, the idea that God is nature or suffuses nature, which is the root idea of child-centered education, has built child-level temples to the holiness of childhood. After the Second World War, under the influence of child-centered education, American school architecture changed. The design of the elementary school came to be centered on the child. There were no longer high steps to climb, but direct, child-level paths into bright, low-slung, welcoming buildings, often with gaily colored architectural elements. The new architecture signaled that although the school was devoted to the larger community, and the Pledge of Allegiance was still recited, the main emphasis would be on the children's world, on encouraging their imaginations and developing their individual interests and personalities.

TRAINING VERSUS DEVELOPMENT

Today we hardly know how to separate education from the idea of development. It seems astonishing to us that the idea of the child's natural development was new in American education when it became the central educational theme in the later nineteenth century. One looks in vain for the development idea in eighteenth- and early nineteenth-century writings by the founders of American education—Thomas Jefferson, Benjamin Rush, and Noah Webster—or in their European predecessors like John Locke. The words *growth* and *development*, so essential to educational thought today, are simply not found in their writings on the subject.

Our earlier thinking about schooling stressed correcting nature rather than following her. The first school words for a child who was learning the alphabet from the New England Primer were: "In Adam's fall / We sinned all." Progressive education, by contrast, does not look upon the child as naturally sinful. Quite the contrary: sin is felt to be a result of the imposition of human social customs upon the innocent being who comes straight from God. The romantic poet William Wordsworth, who strongly influenced the feeling and thought of progressive educators in the United States, wrote this in 1802 about the ill effects of socializing the infant babe:[1]

> Full soon thy soul shall have her earthly freight,
> And custom lie upon thee with a weight,
> Heavy as frost, and deep almost as life!

The classical aim of education was to correct nature through civilization. The romantic aim of education is to correct civilization through nature. The influences on education writers who grew up in the eighteenth century (Jefferson, Rush, and Webster) were classical. The influences on those who grew up in the early nineteenth century (Horace Mann and others) were romantic. By the 1840s, Horace Mann would refer to the "development" of the mind seventeen times in his reports to the Massachusetts Board of Education.

Out of the idea that natural is best have come the teaching principles that we immediately think of as key elements of progressive education—some of them, such as "hands-on learning," appearing as early as Mann's *Seventh Annual Report* to the Massachusetts Board of Education in 1844. For instance, Mann praised the German schools for using all the child's five senses in instruction. God gave us five senses, Mann said; hence, education is most natural and effective if we use them all, and we do not limit ourselves to purely bookish, rote-learned activities.[2] By 1945 the natural development idea had become almost universal in our schools, and has been so for the better part of a century—long enough!

Fast-forward from Horace Mann in the 1840s to the founding of the Progressive Education Association in the 1920s. What seemed inherently obvious then to Mrs. Marietta Johnson, the famous progressive educator, and also to her cofounders of the Progressive Education Association—namely that natural growth is far superior to artificial impositions—was far from obvious before her time. By the early twentieth century she was the inheritor of ideas about natural development that seemed intuitively right to her. She stated with great certitude in her memoir: "'Training' and 'growing' are quite different. In training we often dominate or force in order to accomplish certain definite external results. In growing, we provide the right conditions and the end is human and immediate—included in the process—and the moving power is within! If the child is wholesomely, happily, intelligently employed, he *is* being educated!"[3]

By the 1920s and 1930s, when Mrs. Johnson was active as a school head, these ideas no longer needed defense. They had drenched American thinking since the 1880s. To the grandchildren of the romantics like

Mrs. Johnson and ourselves, developmental ideas seem self-evidently right.[4] But they are not right. To know their contingent origins can help make them seem less self-evident, more vulnerable, a consummation devoutly to be wished.

We now understand that these ideas are factually incorrect. "Natural" unfolding is not as natural to the human child as socialization is. "Development" demands from the child what the child does not have. My practical aim in writing this excursus into the intellectual origins of our failed educational ideas is to demythologize them; my secondary impulse is to satisfy my curiosity and perhaps that of others about why we Americans so confidently overthrew our older idea that education is training—the dominant idea from the beginning of human time up to the romantic period. Education is inherently an induction into the adult tribe—and so it has been from the dawn of human social groups. The idea that education is a natural growth has had a relatively recent birth. One hopes it will grow old and die.[5] It is factually and morally wrong. It intensifies inequalities. Here, in a few strokes, is how it captured the minds of educators in the United States.

"THE GRADUAL ADVANCEMENT OF THE HUMAN SPECIES IN DIGNITY AND HAPPINESS"

This title of Horace Mann's valedictory address as a graduating senior from Brown University in 1819 gives the flavor of our post-revolutionary optimism in the early nineteenth century. In Europe, three decades earlier, in 1789, a Paris mob had stormed the Bastille prison where the king kept his political enemies, starting the French Revolution. Coming after the American Revolution of 1776, the two revolutions taken together induced an orgy of historical optimism. With news of the fall of the Bastille, English politician Charles James Fox stated to Parliament: "How much the greatest event it is that ever happened in the world! And how much the best!"

The God-as-nature idea was already in the air in Europe. But it did not become a widespread sentiment until after the fall of the Bastille. Two writers who would greatly influence John Dewey—William Wordsworth and Georg Wilhelm Friedrich Hegel—were both born in 1770, making Wordsworth just twenty and Hegel not quite twenty in July 1789 when the Bastille fell. The French Revolution had a decisive impact on both of them and on their contemporaries.

Hegel, Wordsworth, and other romantics did not call themselves pantheists. That would be an explicit heresy for which authorities in Europe could still jail people, and suppress their writings—especially in Prussia, where Hegel had an instructorship that he could lose. Despite the heretical character of pantheistic feelings, they were intensified in Hegel and others in the post-Bastille enthusiasm. Already in the mid eighteenth century, nonsectarian "natural religion" was a big theme in Europe, with everyone heartily sick of the slaughter caused by the sectarian wars of religion in the seventeenth century. With the two glorious revolutions in America and Europe, human history seemed to be developing forward, as if under a divine plan, as the young Horace Mann proposed in his valedictory address at Brown. Providence was being made manifest in human history.[6] God was immanent in us and in our affairs—and in our natural development from childhood to adulthood.

God was immanent in the natural world, too. Even the natural state of the wild woods began to seem holy. What used to be called "wilderness" now became "Nature." Earlier the woods had been seen as fearsome places to be avoided, as explained in "Hansel and Gretel" and "Little Red Riding Hood." But now Lord Byron—the most famous poet of his day—could begin one of his most famous passages by declaiming: "There is a pleasure in the pathless woods." Pathless? In the older days, paths would have been preferable.

There is a pleasure in the pathless woods,
There is a rapture on the lonely shore,

There is society where none intrudes,
By the deep Sea, and music in its roar:
I love not Man the less, but Nature more,
From these our interviews, in which I steal
From all I may be, or have been before,
To mingle with the Universe, and feel
What I can ne'er express, yet cannot all conceal.[7]

Mountains—formerly dangerous, terrifying, and ugly—became awe-inspiring sources of devout feelings. Wordsworth had a mystic experience in the Swiss Alps. Scholar Marjorie Hope Nicholson wrote a famous book whose title encapsulates the change: *Mountain Gloom and Mountain Glory*. Thus Byron on the sublimity of mountains:

Above me are the Alps,
The palaces of Nature, whose vast walls
Have pinnacled in clouds their snowy scalps,
And throned Eternity in icy halls
Of cold sublimity

But Wordsworth, not Byron, was the romantic poet who exercised the strongest influence in the United States. John Dewey praises his ability to penetrate into "revelations of spirit, of meaning in nature," with:[8]

. . . a sense sublime
Of something far more deeply interfused,
Whose dwelling is the light of setting suns,
And the round ocean, and the living air,
And the blue sky, and in the mind of man.[9]

Wordsworth's most ambitious poem, *The Prelude or Growth of a Poet's Mind; An Autobiographical Poem* (1805), was a production that could only have been conceived under such pantheistic sentiments.[10] It is an account of the growth of his own mind, as it develops naturally in its interchange with the natural world. It is a poem about the benefits and supreme rightness of a natural education. The young boy and then the young poet grow like a plant under nature's divine guidance toward "years that bring the philosophic mind."

Two years later, in 1807, the philosopher Georg Wilhelm Friedrich Hegel published an even more ambitious version of progressive human growth. Entitled *The Phenomenology of Spirit*, it traced the broader historical progress of both individuals and institutions, explaining in detail what Horace Mann in his optimism and enthusiasm would intimate a decade later about the progress of humankind. Hegel's writings became some of the most influential of the nineteenth century. His system was destined to have enormous appeal to thinkers in Europe and America, for whom only a secular religion would do. In post-religious modernity one tended not to speak of "God" but rather of "Spirit," or "The Absolute," or "Nature." M. H. Abrams has given this strand in romanticism the apt label "natural supernaturalism." Hegel fulfilled the imperative of making the religious impulse modern, acceptable, quasi-secular. He also gave substance and authority to the sentiment of progress.

Hegel's choice of secular labels for his ideas helped. His English-language translators were careful to sustain this secular tone. He gave providential meaning to human history in an apparently purely "logical" account of his pantheistic faith in progress. Hegel, of course, resisted the pantheistic *p*-word that so upset the clergy. As a university instructor seeking advancement, he could not afford to be censored or accused of heresy. In the English-speaking world, too, pains were taken to preserve Hegel's respectable secularity. English translations of his *Phänomenologie des Geistes* entitled it *Phenomenology of Mind*, ignoring the overtones of *Heilige Geist*—the Holy Spirit. Similarly, Hegel's verb for the logical progress of *Geist* through time is *aufheben*, a term that means "to cancel" but keeps overtones of its positive root sense "to lift up" (*auf* = "up"; *heben* = "lift"). There's no logical reason beyond divine providence why a purely logical process should go upward. Viruses could take over the world in a downward sweep. Hegel's British translators offered a misleadingly neutral technical term for *aufheben*, rendering it by the technical Latinate term *sublate*. A more accurate flavor of the original would be "supersede." But that sort of translation would reveal the religious, upward-bound, providential impulse. The great twentieth-century scholar Wilhelm Dilthey has written a still-untranslated account of the young Hegel's "mystical pantheism" that states: "Hegel now conceived the workings of Divine power in the world as being a developmental process. The scientific theory of the evolution of the universe was converted into an immanental teleology and a developmental theory. This reached its completion when he could postulate anything and everything as having its ultimate grounding in a Divine teleological goal."[11]

The safe secularity of Hegel's special vocabulary and the brilliance and cogency of his observations helped consolidate his influence on Dewey and many other American and European thinkers. Intellectuals were looking for a world picture to replace organized religion that would, like religion, give larger meaning to history and human experience. What they got in Hegel was a quasi-religion that gave a providential meaning to human history in acceptably secular garb. Hegel, with his more explicitly pantheistic friend, philosopher Friedrich Wilhelm Joseph Schelling, exercised an immense influence on Friedrich Froebel's *Education of Man* (1826), itself the single most influential European book on early education in nineteenth-century America. As late as 1916, Hegel and Froebel still remained key touchstones in Dewey's most ambitious and mature exposition of progressive education: *Democracy and Education* (1916).[12]

In emphasizing Hegel and Froebel and Germany I do not mean to overlook Switzerland, a cradle of progressive education with Rousseau (honored but not much applied by American educators) and Pestalozzi (1746–1827), who had been the early spokesperson for a more child-centered and humane approach to teaching. From Switzerland also came the first significant use of the term *progressive education*, the title of an 1828 book by Swiss writer Albertine Necker de Saussure. *L'Éducation*

Progressive deals with the onward natural stages of the child's development from birth. Necker de Saussure was also the good friend and biographer of Germaine de Staël, the most famous woman of the early nineteenth-century, who, among other achievements, introduced France, England, and the United States to German pantheistic philosophers.[13] The chief intellectual influences on American progressive education were German pantheistic philosophers: Hegel and Froebel.

HEGEL AND FROEBEL

By 1870 Hegel had captured the imagination of our most eminent philosopher, Josiah Royce of Harvard, and also the minds of our most influential educational thinkers. Colonel Francis Parker, known as the founder of American progressive education, was a disciple of Froebel's and very Hegel-savvy.[14] Then there was Parker's friend, the avowed Hegelian W. T. Harris, a St. Louis superintendent of schools after the Civil War, who became the US commissioner of education from 1889 to 1906. There was also Susan Blow, another St. Louis Hegelian like Harris, who started the nation's first public kindergarten in 1873.[15] By the 1860s and 1870s St. Louis equaled Harvard as a center of Hegelian thought. Above all, there was John Dewey, from Vermont and lately from Johns Hopkins, an avowed Hegelian as we will see.

What people now tend to know about Hegel is the formula, thesis-antithesis-synthesis; the synthesis then becomes a new thesis, and the process continues onward and upward in all of nature and human history. While that kind of movement characterizes Hegel's brilliant writings, they are far less mechanical than such a formula would suggest. The more profound sentiment, which Parker, Harris, Blow, and Dewey got from Hegel, was his confident reassurance that the processes of nature, of human history, and of the human mind are infused by "Absolute Spirit" and are thus "necessarily" progressive. Hegel imposed an odd use of the word *necessity*, which his acolytes accepted, no doubt because implicitly everyone knew he was ultimately talking about God.

Colonel Parker (1837–1902), the archetypal American, was named by Dewey as the founder of American progressive education. Parker said that he liked the philosophy of Hegel not because of the details of his metaphysics but because of his "magnificent theory of progress."[16] Parker was a wonderful man who, remarkably, lacks a full-scale intellectual biography. He is important not just as an early romantic educator in the United States, but also as a representative of what child-centered education could have become, if it had continued to combine humane teaching methods with a strong curriculum for children from all social classes.

As a young veteran from the Civil War who had attained the rank of Colonel, Parker first became a school principal in Dayton, Ohio. Then in 1872 he decided to go to Germany to learn the latest theoretical principles of education. He learned German. He studied at Hegel's old university in Berlin, with a tutor who had studied directly with Hegel. He picked up the whole array of romantic pedagogical, psychological, and philosophical doctrines of education that had their center in Germany.

Then he took over as the school superintendent of Quincy, Massachusetts. While Parker wanted a strong, common subject-matter curriculum in the early grades, his emphasis was on pedagogy, on the active, visual, tactile (natural) experience of such a curriculum—the sort of teaching he, like Horace Mann, had admired in Germany. The whole country became fascinated with his child-centered reforms in Quincy. His *Talks on Teaching* became the best-selling education book of the 1880s. These quote Hegel, but mostly they speak of "Froebel's divine intuitions."

Here's a sample of those intuitions from Froebel's *Education of Man* (1826): "The divine effluence that lives in each thing is the essence of each thing. It is the destiny and life-work of all things to unfold their essence, hence their divine being, and, therefore, the Divine Unity itself—to reveal God in their external and transient being. In view of the original soundness and wholeness of man, all arbitrary (active), prescriptive and categorical, interfering education in instruction and training must, of necessity, annihilate, hinder, and destroy."

Parker's own pantheistic pronouncements were not dissimilar. While his lectures to teachers held solid practical advice about hands-on education, they also produced Froebelian utterances like: "One central law controls both man and the universe. The laws of the universe reveal the ego to itself. All law concenters in the law of being, is manifested for the being; all life is for one life."[17]

These pantheistic sentiments aside, if progressive education had followed Parker's demanding view of the curriculum, our educational history would have fared better. Unfortunately, as his many opponents pointed out, Parker's ideas were often self-contradictory. He comes off as a theoretical novice in his debates with his friend W. T. Harris, who wanted to make sure that subject matters were studied and mastered, as did Harris's fellow Hegelian Susan Blow, whose kindergarten was academic as well as naturalistic. Their view of the curriculum did not prevail.

HEGEL AND DEWEY

Honored and influential as Parker was, he did not have the academic credentials to lead the new movement. That fell to John Dewey (1859–1952). Dewey's early writings overtly expressed his underlying optimism and Hegelianism. His first book, *Psychology* (1887), exhibits explicit Hegelian thinking. The book is a remarkable mixture of hard science and Hegel, with doses of Wordsworth, John Keats, and much borrowing from Wordsworth's friend, Samuel Taylor Coleridge, especially regarding the encouragement of creative imagination in the child. He took from Coleridge the distinction between fancy and imagination. It was important to distinguish the two, because the good imaginations of the child had to be distinguished from the bad ones (fancy); only the good ones were sacred and authentic.

Dewey described the development of the child's mind and imagination as an instance of the divine mind realizing itself in the human mind. He wrote: "The knowledge of the finite individual is the process by which the individual reproduces the universal mind, and hence makes real for himself the universe, which is eternally real for the complete, absolutely universal intelligence, since involved in its self-objectifying activity of knowledge."[18] This sentence is perhaps incomprehensible to anyone not immersed in Hegel and his more overtly pantheistic contemporary, Schelling. The key to the sentence is that "the universal mind" and the "universal intelligence" mean the deity. The deity is "self-objectifying" itself in historical time through the "finite individual"—the child growing into maturity. That is the ultimate endorsement for child-centered education. The child's impulses are from God—indeed they are part of God's own self-objectifying activity. To oppose those impulses is to oppose the will of God.

Those divine mental impulses express themselves as "imagination." Dewey quoted the romantic poet John Keats, and hailing the creative imagination as the source of insight into the meaning of things, Dewey says:

> The highest form of imagination, however, is precisely an organ of penetration into the hidden meaning of things—meaning not visible to perception or memory, nor reflectively attained by the processes of thinking. It may be defined as the direct perception of meaning—of ideal worth in sensuous forms . . . In its highest form, imagination is not confined to isolation and combination of experiences already had, even when these processes occur under the influence of sensitive and lively emotion. It is virtually creative. It makes its object new by setting it in a new light. It separates and combines, indeed; but its separations and combinations are not the result of mechanical processes.[19]

That passage is a recasting by Dewey of a famous pantheistic passage in Coleridge's *Biographia Literaria* (1817):

> The IMAGINATION then I consider either as primary, or secondary. The primary IMAGINATION I hold to be the living power and

prime agent of all human perception, and as a repetition in the finite mind of the eternal act of creation in the infinite I AM. The secondary I consider as an echo of the former, co-existing with the conscious will, yet still as identical with the primary in the kind of its agency, and differing only in degree, and in the mode of its operation. It dissolves, diffuses, dissipates, in order to re-create: or where this process is rendered impossible, yet still at all events it struggles to idealize and to unify. It is essentially vital, even as all objects (as objects) are essentially fixed and dead.

Imagination is good and from God. Fancy is not so good and from humans. (Or Satan.) Coleridge and others knew they had to distinguish good human impulses from bad ones. The new age substituted "imagination versus fancy" for "God versus Satan." Dewey's faith in the infallible rightness of the child's imagination came directly from European pantheism.[20]

The educational aim of developing the child's imagination was thus more than just a recognition of childhood in its own right. It also represented a gradual shift from the instructive, molding conception of early education—the classical concept of Noah Webster—to the romantic, pantheistic idea of natural development, in which encouraging the imagination of the child is in effect encouraging the divine spark, the inner light.

Few now believe in this pantheistic theology, but the husk of the inner light tradition has remained in our schooling, even without the explicit theological foundation. In time, it became an unexamined cultural value inherited from the European romantic philosophers and poets. Today, it's obvious to everyone that letting the child develop naturally and encouraging the child's imagination and creativity is much better than didactic training. Or is it?

"Traditionalists" maintained that teaching children substantial knowledge about the world is far more valuable to their future well-being than teaching fanciful, and sometimes not-very-good, stories whose only virtue is that they are "imaginative" and "encourage the imagination."

That is hardly recommendation enough when what passes as imaginative literature in the early grades are rather thoughtless stories like "The Beaver Family Goes to the Beach." The shift from Coleridge on imagination to the current mindless approbation of what Coleridge would have called mere "fancy" marks the decadent empty husk of romanticism.

Dewey said in his later years that Hegel had left a "permanent deposit" in his thought.[21] As Steven Rockefeller has pointed out, there is a Hegelian (pantheistic) undercurrent in Dewey's thought even when his later language is highly modern and secularized. For example, in *Democracy and Education*, which repudiates Hegel and Froebel, Dewey still remains at bottom their disciple.[22] He is departing from them, he says, because *they* conceive development as teleological; they hold that the child is unfolding toward some defined goal, whereas here in modern America we look forward to an unknown, undefined future. Our American educative principle is therefore not "development" but "growth." Yet this change in vocabulary is just Froebel and Hegel in a new key. For if "growth" is a good thing, then it too must be just as progressive for Dewey as "development" was for Hegel and Froebel. Dewey is expressing his faith in progress; he is not celebrating cancerous growth.

FROM DEWEY TO PIAGET AND AFTER

By the time Dewey wrote his more popular pedagogical books and had adopted pragmatism, his expositions had thrown off the metaphysical Frobelian vocabulary—but not the sacredness of the child's natural development. The basic form remained even without the explicit metaphysical underpinnings.

That is the status of progressive education today. The vague underlying metaphysical sentiments remain—without the explicit metaphysical vocabulary. The doctrines of individual "readiness" and "developmental appropriateness" are still guiding ideas in American teacher training, but the naturalistic approach is no longer clothed with the pantheistic authority of Hegel or Froebel. Dewey is still honored as a founding figure, not as a practical guide. Rather, the child-centered principle of individual development is now said to be sanctioned by modern cognitive science, which is said to favor "constructivism" (encouraging children to construct their own learning—on the pattern of the unwinding ball of string), and by stage theory in developmental psychology, both ideas emanating from Jean Piaget (1896–1980). Yet neither interpretation of Piaget is supported by current cognitive and developmental science—nor, as we have seen, by the later Piaget himself. "Training" is making a comeback along with factual knowledge, perseverance, and "grit."[23]

Looking back with a sympathetic view at the progressive movement in American education, we can appreciate that the nineteenth and early twentieth centuries in the United States were a period of tremendous, well-grounded optimism. Child-centered education and faith in natural human progress suited each other. The sense of inevitable progress was reinforced in United States by the clear fact of material progress and greater social fairness. The progressive insistence on childhood as being a time of life with its own value (not as just some way station on the road to goodness and rationality) has added to human happiness, and is an insight we must keep, along with its humane style of teaching.

On the other hand, the deep religious sentiment underpinning the aim of natural development of the innocent young child who comes direct from God, and the sentiment that artificial impositions like "rote learning" are harmful and unnatural, is still powerful in the schools. A vague, quasi-pantheistic Froebelian fundamentalism accounts for our continued resistance to systematic phonics and "the piling up of facts" in early schooling. Such deep-seated metaphysical beliefs in support of natural development are impervious to evidence. That explains the scornful dismissal by New York City Schools Chancellor Carmen Fariña of the superior results achieved by the Core Knowledge reading program in New York City.[24] She had a deeper certitude than mere data could supply about what is best for children. Until we overcome these historically contingent religious certitudes from Middle Europe of the early nineteenth century, progress will continue to elude us.[25]

Many superb teachers here and abroad have exemplified a pedagogy that exhibits empathy with childhood and the child's point of view, yet imparts a strong common curriculum defined by the community. A strong common curriculum is also compatible with ensuring joy and competence for disadvantaged students. We need not relinquish what is admirable about progressive education. We must reject what is unsound, and indeed deeply harmful to social justice and far too individualistic. In following sounder principles of socialization and fairness, we will reduce inequality and recover much-needed civic and communitarian ideals.

Translations of French Reports

METHODOLOGY OF THE FRENCH RESULTS

The following is a translation of the section headed "Methodology" in the original 2008 document *Note d'Information 08-38: Lire, Écrire, Compter: Les Performances des Élèves de CM2 à Vingt Ans d'Intervalle 1987–2007* (Paris: DEPP, 2008), http://www.education.gouv.fr/cid23433/lire-ecrire -compter-les-performances-des-eleves-de-cm2-a-vingt-ans-d-intervalle -1987-2007.html.

METHODOLOGY

Population

The target population in 1987 was that of fifth-grade pupils enrolled in France in the public sector. Comparisons therefore focus on students in the public sector. It should be noted that the percentage of primary school students in the private sector remained stable over the twenty years (about 14 percent). Moreover, in 2007, students in the private sector achieve results equivalent to those of the public sector, whether in literacy, numeracy, or in spelling and grammar.

Samples

At each date of the survey, students were selected according to a sampling plan "by cluster." Around 150 schools were selected at random. All the fifth-grade students in each school participated in the evaluation. In 1987, the selection of schools took place in just five jurisdictions, but the sample was found to be representative of the parent population. In 1987 and 1997 schools were categorized by "rural," "urban," and "disadvantaged zones." In 1999 [math] and 2007, the sample schools were categorized by sector: "public," "disadvantaged zone," and "private."

Tests

The reading test consisted of eight short and varied texts (literary, explanatory, descriptive, etc.). For each text, students had to answer five comprehension questions (literal understanding, overall, grasp of information, etc.). The required answers were usually short, but sometimes required a more elaborate construction. The texts and the questions were identical in the three periods: 1987, 1997, and 2007. The test of calculation concerned the four operations. A page for each, with six or seven operations required, sometimes with blanks to be filled in. The test also featured four small "problems." Some questions in 1987 were excluded from the test in 2007, since a problem concerning the old franc coins could not be adapted, and multiplication and divisions of decimals were excluded as they are not in the present curriculum. To replace those problems, eleven comparable problems were used from a later test of 1999.

Logistics

Instructions for the test were repeated identically in each year. Evaluation in 2007, like 1987, was organized into five sequences (two in reading, two in calculation, one in spelling). It was required not to complete more than one sequence in a half day. The return rate was excellent (95 percent in 2007), and reflected the high degree of involvement by the schools in the survey. Correction instructions were also included in the same. But unlike the assessments of 1987, 1997, and 1999, where the corrections were by the teachers of the students in the sample, in 2007, student responses were centralized and processed via a remote connection. Specifically, more than three hundred thousand student responses were scanned and corrected via a web server by a team of proofreaders recruited by DEPP. This system allowed for more reliable corrections to measure quality. Indeed, one out of ten images was corrected by two different markers. The majority of items had a rate of agreement inter-correcting over 95 percent. The rate was more variable in reading: it dropped to 80 percent for some items, mostly due to hesitation between total and partial success, but had little impact on the final measure of performance.

FURTHER COMMENT ON THE FRENCH DATA

The overall decline in math was more than twice the decline in reading: $-.84$ standard deviation in math, compared to $-.37$ standard deviation in reading. But the decline in equity (the spread between demographic groups) was greater in reading than in math. The increase in spread between the top and bottom groups in math was .1 standard deviation, while the increase in spread in reading was four times as great: .4 standard deviation. Poor schooling has a greater negative effect on equity in reading than in math. This finding is important for schooling as an agency of equal opportunity. Math is primarily a school subject. If the effectiveness of math instruction declines for some, it tends to decline for all.

Reading is both a school and a home subject. It depends upon general knowledge and vocabulary size. The school contribution to knowledge and vocabulary is thus key for the aim of equal opportunity, and needs to be maximized. But a significant increase in vocabulary size cannot be achieved through direct word study and a skills curriculum. The knowledge curriculum can contribute far more to equity than the skills curriculum can. France has now demonstrated this forcefully.

A confounding factor in this reckoning is that the effectiveness of instruction in both knowledge and in decoding declined in France. Indoctrinated in the superiority of whole-language methods, younger teachers spurned the far more effective method of phonics in teaching decoding skill. They also spurned exercises in grammar and spelling in favor of more "natural" approaches. An analysis of the writing errors from ten-year-olds in the two periods showed that the percentage of students who made more than twenty-five errors doubled in the period, from 6 percent to 12 percent!

APPENDIX III

The Japanese Early Science Curriculum

After World War II, when the Americans occupied Japan from 1945 to 1952, they intervened in the school system. They wanted Japanese children to learn democratic values. "Moral training" was abolished, to be replaced by training in democratic ideas. The Americans also introduced the local control idea, taking control of the schools and curriculum away from the central government and putting it into the hands of the municipalities. Fortunately for Japan's schools, the Americans left in 1952. The Japanese public did not support keeping the American reforms. They returned control of the schools to the central government, primarily because decentralization did not work very well, and secondly because they thought both moral training and a common curriculum were sound educational ideas. In recent years Japanese students have ranked at or very near the top across all subjects in the PISA rankings.

I have long been an admirer of Japanese elementary schools, which are very child-centered in the good sense of the term. Details can be found in a book I strongly recommend, *The Learning Gap* by Harold Stevenson and James Stigler.[1] The Department of Psychology at the University of Michigan offers a marvelous video of the joyful and effective Japanese primary school called "The Polished Stones," which is also highly recommended.[2] The schools are caring places, and are also very humane in pedagogy and content. More time is allocated to music and art than to science. Moreover, science study does not even begin until grade 3, and yet Japanese students score at the top of the rankings in science. The delay may be owing to the huge demands of the Japanese writing system.

I will reproduce a translation of Japan's successful science curriculum in this appendix, because it seems to me a model of what is meant by a "curriculum intentionally and coherently structured to develop rich content knowledge within and across grades"—the phrasing in our Common Core State Standards. Noteworthy, too, is the Japanese inclusion of aesthetic and evaluative elements in the study of science, just as they include "morality" as an element in humanistic subjects—an indication of their view that education is socialization. The American concern to avoid "indoctrination" simply places implicit values out of sight and raises suspicions about the schools, because the values are not openly stated in the curriculum. The separation of church and state is not the separation of honesty, diligence, kindness, loyalty, and other civic virtues from the state. It does not mean abandoning the teaching of civics. To teach no values at all is to evade an elemental duty, and lead to rootlessness and incivility. "Open covenants openly arrived at" should be the watchword of the published school curriculum.[3] For every community, what could be more important?

Compare the specificity and coherence of this document with the standards of a state chosen at random—say, Connecticut. Here, from that state, is an excerpt from our typical sort of elementary school science standards:

1. Materials have properties that are directly observable; examples include its state of matter, or its size, shape, color, or texture. Other properties can only be observed by doing something to the material (simple tests). Materials can be sorted and classified based on their testable properties. *[Which properties? What sorts of tests?]*
2. Some materials dissolve (disappear) when mixed in water; others accumulate on the top or the bottom of the container. The temperature of water can affect whether, and at what rate, materials dissolve in it.

3. Some materials, such as sponges, papers, and fabrics, absorb water better.

And so on for fifty pages. Note that this document stays on the non-analytical phenomenal level, which is the antithesis of science. And it makes misstatements: "To dissolve is to 'disappear.'" This sloppiness is characteristic of amateurish state "standards"—amateurish perhaps because the developmental approach to education tries to avoid "premature" concepts. Moreover, the phenomenal observations, which many children already know, do not fit into any larger multiyear, cumulative plan.

THE JAPANESE ELEMENTARY SCIENCE CURRICULUM
Grades 3–6
I. OVERALL OBJECTIVES

To enable pupils to become familiar with nature and to carry out observations and experiments with their own viewpoint, as well as to develop their problem-solving abilities and nurture hearts and minds that are filled with an affection for the natural world, and at the same time, to develop a realistic understanding of natural phenomena, and to foster scientific perspectives and ideas.

II. OBJECTIVES AND CONTENT FOR EACH GRADE
Grade 3

1. Objectives
    (1) To develop perspectives and ideas about the properties and functions of weight, wind, force of rubber, light, and magnets and electricity through investigation comparing phenomena involving these matters, and through probing the identified problem and making interesting learning material.
    (2) To foster an attitude of loving and protecting living things and to develop perspectives and ideas about the relationship between living things and the environment, the relationship between the sun and its effects on conditions on earth, through investigation comparing familiar animals and

plants, and sunny and shady spots, as well as through probing the identified problems with interest.

2. Content

A. Matter/Energy

(1) *Object and weight.* To develop pupils' ideas about properties
of objects by examining weights and volumes, using objects
such as clay: a) the weight of an object remains unchanged
even when the shape changes; b) objects with the same volume may differ in weight.

(2) *Function of wind and force of rubber.* To develop pupils' ideas
about wind and rubber by examining the phenomenon of
wind and rubber in moving objects: a) the power of wind
can move an object; b) the force of rubber can move an
object.

(3) *Properties of light.* To develop pupils' ideas about the nature
of light by using mirrors and other devices and by exploring
the way light travels and its brightness and warmth when it
strikes an object: a) sunlight can be collected and reflected;
b) the brightness and warmth of sunlight changes when it
strikes an object.

(4) *Properties of magnets.* To develop pupils' ideas about the
properties of magnets, by exploring their functions and
the objects that are attracted to them: a) some objects are
attracted to a magnet and others aren't—among those attracted to a magnet, some become magnetic when they are
attached to a magnet; b) opposite poles of a magnet attract
each other, whereas like poles repel each other.

(5) *Pathway of electricity.* To develop pupils' ideas about electric
circuits by connecting a small bulb to a dry battery, and by exploring the connection path and the materials through which
the electricity travels: a) there are patterns of circuit connections that conduct electricity and others that don't; b) there
are materials that conduct electricity and others that don't.

B. Life/the Earth

(1) *Insects and plants.* To develop pupils' ideas about growth patterns and body structures by finding and raising familiar

insects and plants, and by exploring the processes of their growth and body structure: a) insects grow in accordance with a fixed order of growth, and their body parts consist of the head, thorax, and abdomen; b) plants grow in accordance with a fixed order of growth, and their body parts consist of roots, stems, and leaves.

(2) *Observation of familiar environment.* To develop pupils' ideas about the relationship between living things and their surrounding environment through the explorations of the conditions of familiar living things: a) living things are different in appearance, such as color, shape, and size, etc.; b) living things interact with their surrounding environment.

(3) *The sun and the ground.* To develop pupils' ideas about the sun and ground through the exploration of the changes in the position of shady spots and the difference between sunny and shady spot: a) shade is created by blocking sunlight, and the position of shady spots moves as the sun moves; b) the sun warms the ground and there are differences in warmth and dampness between the sunny and shady spots.

3. Handling the Content

(1) In teaching "A. Matter/Energy" in Content, pupils must make at least three kinds of learning materials. (2) With regard to item (1) in "B. Life/the Earth" in Content, special consideration should be made as follows: a) with regard to items a and b pupils must raise insects and grow plants; b) with regard to item b, "Growth of Plants," only summer annual dicotyledonous plants should be used. (3) With regard to item (3a), "movement of the sun," in "B. Life/the Earth," it should be regarded that the sun moves from east to west. In addition, the four directions: east, west, north, and south are dealt with when exploring the movement of the sun.

Grade 4

1. Objectives

(1) To develop perspectives and ideas about the properties and functions of objects, by investigating air, water, changes in

the state of an object, and electrical phenomena, in relation to the functions of power, heat, and electricity, and through probing the identified problem and making learning materials with interest.

(2) To foster an attitude to love and protect living things and to develop perspectives and ideas about the structure of the human body, the activities of animals/growth of plants, meteorology, and movement of the moon and stars, by investigating them in relation to movement, seasons, temperature, and time, through probing the identified problems with interest.

2. Content

A. Matter/Energy

(1) *Properties of air and water.* To develop pupils' ideas about the properties of air and water by exploring the changes in their volume and pressure in compressing air and water in a closed space: a) when air is compressed in a closed space, the volume decreases and the pressure increases; b) air in a closed space can be compressed, but water cannot be compressed.

(2) *Metal, water, air, and temperature.* To develop pupils' ideas about the properties of metals, water, and air, by exploring the changes in warming and cooling metals, water, and air: a) the volume of metals, water, or air changes when heated or cooled; b) the temperature of metals goes up gradually, spreading from the point being heated, but heated air and water move, raising the temperature of the whole; c) the form of water changes into vapor or ice depending on temperature. When water becomes ice, its volume increases.

(3) *Function of electricity.* To develop pupils' ideas about the functions of electricity, by exploring the functions of the dry battery and photocell in attaching them to small bulbs and motors: a) the brightness and the rotation of a motor change as the number or circuit of dry batteries changes; b) a photocell can rotate a motor.

B. Life/the Earth

(1) *Structure and movement of the human body.* To develop pupils' ideas about the relationship between the structure and

movement of the human body, by exploring the movement of bones and muscles and by observing the movement of humans and other animals or by using teaching materials: a) the human body has bones and muscles; b) the human body can move due to the functions of bones and muscles.

(2) *Seasons and living things.* To develop pupils' ideas about the relationship between seasons and animal activities and plant growth by finding and raising familiar animals and plants, and by exploring the activities of animals and the growth of plants in different seasons: a) the activities of animals change depending on the season (warm/cold); b) the growth of plants changes depending on the season (warm/cold).

(3) *Weather conditions.* To develop pupils' ideas about weather conditions and the change of water in natural world, by observing changes in temperature in a day and the process of the change from water to vapor, and by exploring changes in weather and temperature and the relationship between water and vapor: a) the change in temperature in a day is different depending on weather; b) water evaporates from the surface of water or the ground and turns into vapor in the air. In addition, vapor in the air may turn back into water drops (condensation).

(4) *The moon and stars.* To develop pupils' ideas about the characteristics and movement of the moon and stars, by observing the moon and stars, and by exploring the position of the moon and the color, brightness, and position of stars: a) the shape of the moon appears to change day to day, and its position changes throughout the day; b) there are stars in the sky with different levels of brightness and colors; c) the alignment of a cluster of stars does not change, but the position of the cluster changes throughout the day.

3. Handling the Content

   (1) In teaching "A. Matters/Energy" in Content, pupils must make at least two kinds of learning materials. (2) With regard to item (3a) in "A. Matter/Energy" in the Content, both series circuit and parallel circuit should be dealt with.

(3) With regard to item (1b) in "B. Life/the Earth" in Content, the function of joints should be dealt with. (4) With regard to item (2) in "B. Life/the Earth" in Content, the activities of at least two animals and the growth of at least two plants should be observed over the course of one year.

Grade 5

1. Objectives

(1) To develop perspectives and ideas about the regularity of change in objects and substances, by investigating the changes of dissolution of substances, the motion of pendulums, the change and function of electromagnets while focusing on the causes of their changes, and through probing the identified problems and making learning materials in a systematic fashion.

(2) To foster an attitude to respect life and to develop perspectives and ideas about the continuity of life, the function of running water, and the regularity of meteorological phenomena, by investigating the process of plant growth from germination to fruition, the birth and growth of animals, conditions of running water, and weather changes while focusing on the factors such as condition, time, amount of water, and natural disasters, through probing the identified problems in a systematic fashion.

2. Content

A. Matter/Energy

(1) *Dissolution of substances.* To develop pupils' ideas about the regularity of dissolution of substances, by dissolving substances in water, and by exploring the differences in dissolution according to water temperature or volume: a) there is a limit to the amount of solute that can be dissolved in a solvent; b) the solubility limits change according to the temperature and amount of water or solutes, and moreover, using these properties, it is possible to extract solutes; c) the weight of water and a solute remains unchanged when the solute is dissolved in water.

(2) *Movement of pendulums.* To develop pupils' ideas about the regularity of the movement of pendulums, by using weights, and by exploring the movement of pendulums in changing the weight and the length of a thread: a) the time taken for a weight on a string to swing back and forth does not change if the weight changes, but it does change when the length of the string changes.

(3) *Function of electric currents.* To develop pupils' ideas about the functions of electric currents, by passing an electric current through the conductive wire of an electromagnet and by exploring the change in strength of electromagnetic force: a) a coil with an electric current magnetizes an iron core, and when the direction of the electric current changes, the polarity of the electromagnet changes; b) the strength of an electromagnet changes depending on the strength of the electric current or the number of coils.

B. Life/the Earth

(1) *Germination, growth, and fruition of plants.* To develop pupils' ideas about the conditions of germination, growth, and fruition by raising plants, and by exploring their germination, growth, and fruition: a) plants germinate by using the nutrition in seeds; b) it is water, air, and temperature that influence plant germination; c) sunlight and fertilizer affect plant growth; d) some flowers have stamen and pistil—when pollen sticks to the stigma of the pistil, its base develops into the fruit, and the seeds are produced in the fruit.

(2) *Birth of animals.* To develop pupils' ideas about the formation and development of animals by raising fish and by using learning materials about the formation of humans, and by exploring the changes in the states of eggs and small living things in water: a) fish have gender and the state of the inside of the discharged eggs changes as days go by; b) fish live off of small living things in water; c) humans grow inside the mother until they are born.

(3) *Function of running water.* To develop pupils' ideas about the relationship between the function of running water and the

change in ground surface, by observing running water on the ground or rivers, and by exploring the difference in the function of speed and volume of running water: a) running water has functions to cut into the ground, transport, and pile up pebbles and soil; b) the size and shape of pebbles on a riverside differ depending on if they are found upstream or downstream; c) depending on how it rains, the speed and the amount of running water change, and the state of the ground changes drastically due to swelling.

(4) *Weather change*. To enable pupils to develop ideas about weather change, by exploring the movement of clouds by observing the clouds of a day and by using visual information: a) the volume and movement of clouds are related to changes in weather; b) changes in weather can be forecasted using meteorological information such as visual information.

3. Handling the Content

(1) With regard to "A. Matters/Energy" in Content, pupils must make at least two kinds of learning materials. (2) With regard to item (1) in "B. Life/the Earth," special considerations should be made as follows: a) with regard to item (1a), "nutrition within seeds," only starch should be dealt with; b) with regard to item (1d), the coverage of lessons should be limited to stamen, pistil, calyx, and petals. With regard to pollination, wind and insects should be dealt with. (3) With regard to item (2c) in "B. Life/the Earth" in Content, do not deal with the process of fertilization. (4) With regard to item (4b) in "B. Life/the Earth" in Content, weather change along with the pathway of typhoons and the relationship between typhoons and precipitation should be mentioned.

Grade 6

1. Objectives

(1) To develop perspectives and ideas about properties and regularity of materials by examining and reasoning the contributing factors and regularities of the phenomena caused by

combustion, aqueous solution, levers, and electromagnets, and through probing the identified problems in a planned manner and making learning materials.

(2) To foster an attitude of respect for life and to develop perspectives and ideas about the physical functions of living things, interactions between living things and the environment, rules of changes, formations of land, and position and characteristics of the moon, by exploring and reasoning the relationship between physical structures and functions of living things and environment, the formation and the change of land, and the moon and sun, and through probing the identified problems in a planned manner.

2. Content

A. Matter/Energy

(1) *Mechanism of combustion.* To develop pupils' ideas about the mechanism of combustion, by burning objects and by exploring the changes in them: a) when plants burn, oxygen in the air is used and carbon dioxide is produced.

(2) *Properties of aqueous solutions.* To develop pupils' ideas about the properties and functions of aqueous solutions, by using various types of aqueous solutions, and by exploring their properties and how they change metals: a) there are alkaline, acid, and neutral aqueous solutions; b) gas is dissolved in some aqueous solutions; c) some aqueous solutions change the properties of metals.

(3) *Regularity of a lever.* To develop pupils' ideas about the regularity of a lever, by using levers and changing the force points and strength, and by exploring the mechanism and functions of the lever: a) the weight of two objects is the same when the objects are hooked at each end of a pole at an equal distance from a fulcrum and the pole is held level; b) when the force point or strength changes, the power to tilt the lever changes. When the lever is balanced, a certain regularity exists among the force point, the strength, and the power; c) tools using this regularity of a lever can be found in everyday life.

(4) *Use of electricity.* To develop pupils' ideas about the properties and the function of electricity, by using a generator, etc., and by exploring the ways to use electricity: a) electricity can be generated and stored; b) electricity can be transformed into light, sound, heat, etc.; c) the amount of heat generated by a heat wire depends on the thickness of the wire; d) tools using the properties and functions of electricity can be found in everyday life.

B. Life/the Earth

(1) *Structure and functions of the human body.* To develop pupils' ideas about the structure and function of the human body and other animals, by observing human beings and other animals and using learning materials, and by exploring the functions of respiration, digestion, excretion, and circulation: a) oxygen is taken into the body, and carbon dioxide and other gases are excreted from the body; b) food is digested and absorbed while it passes through the mouth, stomach, and intestine and the leftovers are excreted; c) blood travels through the body, is pumped through its course by the heart, and transports nutrition, oxygen, and carbon dioxide.

(2) *Nutrition of plants and pathway of water.* To develop pupils' ideas about the structure and function of plants, by observing plants and by examining the pathway of water in plants and the function of creating nutrition in leaves: a) when sunlight hits leaves, starch is produced in the leaves; b) there are pathways of water in roots, stems, and leaves, and the water taken up by the roots mainly evaporates through the leaves.

(3) *Living things and the environment.* To develop pupils' ideas about the interaction between living things and the environment through exploration, such as observing the lives of animals and plants or using information materials: a) the life of living things is closely related to the surrounding environment, through water and air; b) animals live in an eat-or-be-eaten world.

(4) *Formation and change of land.* To develop pupils' ideas about the formation and change of land, by observing the land and

the matter included in soil, and by exploring the formation and creation of land: a) land is composed of gravels, sands, mud, volcanic ashes, and rocks, and some land has layers; b) geological strata are formed by running water and volcanic eruptions, some of which contain fossil remains; c) volcanic eruptions change land formations.

(5) *The moon and the sun.* To develop pupils' ideas about the moon phases and the conditions of the surface, by observing the moon and the sun and by examining the location and the phases of the moon and the location of the sun: a) the sun is located on the bright side of the moon, and the moon phase changes depending on the positional relationship between the moon and the sun; b) the condition of the moon's surface is different from that of the sun.

3. Handling the Content

(1) In teaching "A. Matter/Energy" in Content, pupils must make at least two kinds of objects. (2) With regard to item (1) in "B. Life/the Earth," special considerations should be made as follows: a) with regard to (1c), it should be mentioned that there is a correlation between heartbeats and pulsations; b) with regard to (1d), lungs, the stomach, small intestines, large intestines, liver, kidneys, and heart should be dealt with as major organs. (3) With regard to item (3a) in "B. Life/the Earth," it should be mentioned that water circulates. (4) With regard to item (4) in "B. Life/the Earth," special considerations should be made as follows: a) with regard to (4a), conglomerates, sandstone, and mudstone should be dealt with as rocks; b) fossils in (4b) should be dealt with as evidence that strata had been piled up by running water. (5) Item (5a) in "B. Life/the Earth" should be dealt with as the positional relationship between the sun and the moon when viewed from the earth.

III. SYLLABUS DESIGN AND HANDLING THE CONTENT

1. In designing the syllabus, consideration should be given to the following: (1) Some considerations should be given to consolidating scientific knowledge and concepts and to developing

scientific perspectives and ideas by enriching observation, experiments, experience in nature, and scientific experience in teaching the Content of each grade listed in Subsection II. (2) Some considerations should be given to enrich activities that pupils can organize and in which they can examine the results of observations and experiments, and can think and explain natural events and phenomena by using scientific terms and concepts. (3) Some considerations should be given to utilize museums and science centers actively by seeking partnership and cooperation with them. (4) Based on the objectives of moral education listed in Subsection I-2 of Chapter 1 "General Provision" and Subsection I of Chapter 3 "Moral Education," instructions concerning the content listed in Subsection II of Chapter 3 "Moral Education" should be given appropriately. The instructions should be in accordance with the characteristics of science and should be related to the period for moral education.

2. In the handling of the content listed in Subsection II, consideration should be given to the following: (1) In giving instructions on observations, experiments, cultivation, raising animals, and making learning materials, appropriate devices should be used, such as computers and audio-visual aids. In addition, special care must be taken to prevent accidents. (2) In giving instructions on living things, weather, rivers, and land, it is necessary to give pupils enough opportunities to go to the field and have experiential activities to familiarize them with nature, and at the same time, to help pupils develop an attitude of cherishing nature and contributing to the conservation of the natural environment. (3) It is necessary to encourage every pupil to take initiatives in solving problems, to make connections between the outcomes of learning and everyday life, and to help them gain realistic understanding about natural events and phenomena.

NOTES

Prologue

1. I have tried to make each of the chapters self-contained, on the assumption that a reader might wish to turn to one of the six "frustrations" as a subject of special interest. To make each of them self-contained has entailed some brief repetitions.

2. See https://en.wikipedia.org/wiki/The_Hedgehog_and_the_Fox.

3. "The Last Word."

4. Planck: "A new scientific truth does not triumph by convincing its opponents and making them see the light, but rather because its opponents eventually die, and a new generation grows up that is familiar with it." Max Planck, *Wissenschaftliche Selbst-biographie. Mit einem Bildnis und der von Max von Laue gehaltenen Traueransprache* (Leipzig: J. A. Barth, 1948), 22, quoted in Max Planck, *Scientific Autobiography and Other Papers*, trans. F. Gaynor (New York: Philosophical Library, 1949), 33–34.

5. http://discours.vie-publique.fr/notices/776000361.html

6. As I explain in chapter 7, this quick account is deliberately overschematized, since the Americanization process had been going on silently in teacher training for more than two decades. Although the structural change was sudden, its intellectual underpinnings had been gradually solidifying since the 1960s, a process that is traced in two key books: Philippe Nemo, *Pourquoi Ont-ils Tué Jules Ferry? La Dérive de l'École Sous la Ve République* (Paris: Grasset, 1991) and Liliane Lurçat, *La Destruction de l'Enseignement* Élémentaire *et Ses Penseurs* (Paris: Guibert, 1998). To these may be added: Jean-Claude Milner, *De l'École* (Paris: Éditions du Seuil, 1984); Jean-Pierre Le Goff, *La Barbarie Douce: La Modernisation Aveugle des Entreprises et de l'École* (Paris: La Découverte, 1999); Marc Le Bris, *Et Vos Enfants ne Sauront Pas Lire . . . Ni Compter: La Faillite Obstinée de l'École Française* (Paris: Stock, 2004).

7. In this book I use the adjective *communal* rather than *acculturative* to emphasize that schooling adds to home culture a communal culture that lends the ability to communicate with strangers. Adding a wider social culture is part of growing up—school or no school. A good school in a modern nation systematically adds knowledge that is highly enabling within a very wide national community. It's something added, not something that necessarily takes over.

8. *Positions du grip sur la crise de l'école et les moyens de s'en sortir,* http://slecc.fr/GRIP/2011_positions_grip.pdf. For a translation of the preamble, see p. 139.

9. Not yet in print, only in emails and conversation, and in original readers' reports on this book.

10. See also Paola Mattei and Andrew S. Aguilar, *Secular Institutions, Islam and Education Policy* (London: Palgrave Macmillan, 2016).

11. The roughly derived confidence interval for French data is .01509 and for the US data it is .01050. The relative standard error for the French data is 1.54 and for the US 1.07. Translation of the French methodology is found in appendix II.

12. The overwhelming evidence of a massive test score decline at all grade levels in all demographic groups between 1960 and 1980 is found in chapter 7.

13. J. P. Keeves, *Learning Science in a Changing World: Cross-National Studies of Science Achievement, 1970 to 1984* (The Hague: IEA, 1992).

14. John Bishop, "Is the Test Score Decline Responsible for the Productivity Growth Decline?" *The American Economic Review* 79, no. 1 (Mar 1989): 178–197.

15. For details from state and national tests at all grade levels, see chapter 7.

16. Ibid.

17. Ibid.

18. The standard deviation of NAEP scores now hovers around 35 points. Before 1996 it was set to around 50, and thereafter to around 35 points. Overall NAEP averages for seventeen-year-olds since 1971 have differed by 2 to 3 points under current scoring.

19. Diane Ravitch, *Left Back: A Century of Failed School Reforms* (New York: Simon and Schuster, 2000).

20. A new advocacy organization (currently called "Knowledge Matters") is being launched by experts from both the left and the right—a welcome sign. Thousands of Core Knowledge parents have voted with their feet—and their willingness to pick up their belongings and move to an area with a Core Knowledge school.

21. Phrased to focus on "locality" though each locality should include both the local public sphere (cultural commons) and the national public sphere. The nation state and the national language have been the chief foci of schooling since modern democracies came into being.

22. One of the most trenchant observations by Richard Hofstadter in his critique of John Dewey was that Dewey's lip service to the wider social benefits of the new education was not backed up with any plausible scenario. Richard Hofstadter, *Anti-Intellectualism in American Life* (New York: Knopf, 1963). See especially chapters 13 and 14.

23. For a discussion of "standard language," see chapter 6.

24. G. H. Mead, *Mind, Self and Society (1934), 135.*

25. www.coreknowledge.org

26. Ibid.

27. In chapter 8 I suggest that in the United States there be at least three different grade-by-grade sequences to choose from, all covering much the same core content.

28. "Before the advent of expanding environments, there was an elementary school curriculum for the early grades in history, geography, and civics. It differed from one school district to the next, but there was a common spirit in its essentials, an intention

to introduce children to exciting stories of important events and significant individuals and to provide them with a basic historical and cultural vocabulary." Diane Ravitch, "Tot Sociology: Or What Happened to History in the Grade Schools," *The American Scholar* 56, no. 3 (Summer 1987): 343–354. See also: Ruth Miller Elson, *Guardians of Tradition: American Schoolbooks of the Nineteenth Century* (Lincoln: University of Nebraska Press, 1964).

29. The most influential and persuasive tracing of the connection between developmentalism and individualism has been A. O. Lovejoy, *The Great Chain of Being* (Cambridge, MA: Harvard University Press, 1936), which is still in print. Systems of ideas, like any other phenomena, can be categorized in multiple useful ways. I claim some privilege for the terms *natural development, individualism,*" and *skill-centrism*, because they reflect the actual categories and concepts used by the adherents themselves from the eighteenth century to the present.

30. The alternative view is that deliberate communality alone will ensure beneficial results. The example is the need for deliberate language normalization by academies and lexicographers. As Joseph Stiglitz memorably said: "the reason that the invisible hand often seems invisible is that it is often not there." Daniel Altman, "Q & Answers with Joseph E. Stiglitz," *Managing Globalization* blog, *International Herald Tribune*, October 11, 2006.

31. From the start of the naturalistic idea, ever since Comenius in the seventeenth century, a parallelism was drawn between human physical development and mental development, and between education and the world of plants and animals. While the physical-mental-development parallelism exists in the first months of infancy, different cultures begin their differential impositions from very early days. See Patricia M. Greenfield et al., "Cultural Pathways Through Universal Development," *Annual Review of Psychology* 54 (2003): 461–490.

32. Elliott A. Medrich, *International Mathematics and Science Assessment: What Have We Learned?*, US Department of Education Office of Educational Research and Improvement NCES 92-011, 1992. Of particular note is the following conclusion: "Use of a differentiated curriculum based on tracking is negatively associated with student performance on the international assessments and also reduces opportunities for some students to be exposed to more advanced curriculum" (p. vii).

33. Robert S. Siegler, Judy S. DeLoache, and Nancy Eisenberg, *How Children Develop* (New York: Worth, 2003).

34. Daniel Willingham, "Ask the Cognitive Scientist: Question: What Does Cognitive Science Tell Us About the Existence of Visual, Auditory, and Kinesthetic Learning?" *American Educator* (Summer 2005), http://www.aft.org/ae/summer2005/willingham#sthash.iSNkW2tW.

35. R. Taconis, M. G. M. Ferguson-Hessler, and H. Broekkamp, "Teaching Science Problem Solving: An Overview of Experimental Work," *Journal of Research in Science Teaching* 38, no. 4 (2001): 442–468.

36. This is mainly true in language arts classes, which now occupy preponderant instructional time in early grades.

37. John Dewey, *How We Think* (Boston: D. C. Heath & Co., 1910), iii.

38. Paul J. Feltovich, Michael J. Prietula, and K. Anders Ericsson, "Studies of Expertise from Psychological Perspectives," in *The Cambridge Handbook of Expertise and Expert Performance*, eds. K. Anders Ericsson et al. (Cambridge, UK: Cambridge University Press, 2006). A forthcoming (2016) book (quoted in the epigraphs to this book) neatly summarizes the issue: "There is no such thing as developing a general skill." Anders Ericsson and Robert Pool, *Peak: Secrets from the New Science of Expertise* (Boston: Houghton Mifflin, 2016), 60.

39. I have therefore used *expertise* at times throughout this book. With young children it's prudent to use the longer phrase *level of expertise*. It is a far more accurate term than *skills* because *expertise* implies an inherent fusion of form and content, knowledge and skill that can't easily be dissociated in the human mind.

40. The most recent PISA scores for the problem-solving abilities of fifteen-year-olds place American students well below Korea, Japan, Canada, and Finland, nations with set, communal curricula in early grades—a fact which lends support to the idea that broad subject-matter knowledge is the basis of problem-solving abilities. *PISA 2012 Results: Creative Problem Solving Students' Skills in Tackling Real-Life Problems* (Paris: OECD, 2014).

Chapter 1

1. Of course math expertise is part of the picture too. For a quick and ready analysis of readiness, a "word knowledge" test" serves well. For conceptual simplicity and convenience, I will focus on vocabulary size throughout this book. Analyses of the Armed Forces Qualification Test (AFQT) showed that the vocabulary size test and the paragraph comprehension test correlate so well that they can be considered to represent the same underlying competence, which was most accurately measured by vocabulary size! (This result anticipated recent work showing that topic familiarity, often indicated by word familiarity, is a stronger predictor of comprehension than formal ability to deal with difficult syntax.) This led AFQT analysts to conclude: "The apparent fact that the two tests [vocabulary and comprehension] measure the same underlying factor suggests an efficient alternative for computing an AFQT is to simply drop the difficult-to-administer paragraph comprehension items and focus on the word-knowledge test." Pamela Ing, Carole A. Lunney, and Randall J. Olsen, *Reanalysis of the 1980 AFQT Data from the NLSY791* (Columbus: Center for Human Resource Research, Ohio State University, 2007). See also: William R. Johnson and Derek Neal, "Basic Skills and the Black-White Earnings Gap," in *The Black-White Test Score Gap*, eds. Christopher Jencks and Meredith Phillips (Washington, DC: Brookings Institution Press, 1998); Christopher Winship and Sanders D. Korenman, "Economic Success and the Evolution of Schooling and Mental Ability," in Susan E. Mayer and Paul E. Peterson, eds. *Earning and Learning: How Schools Matter* (Washington DC, Brookings, 1999).

2. S. T. Coleridge, "Dejection: An Ode."

3. https://www.facebook.com/WhiteHouse/videos/10153858451374238/

4. http://www.ed.gov/news/press-releases/fact-sheet-testing-action-plan

5. http://www.cgcs.org/cms/lib/DC00001581/Centricity/Domain/87/Testing%20 Report.pdf

6. Barak Rosenshine and Carla Meister, "Reciprocal Teaching: A Review of the Research," *Review of Educational Research*, vol. 64 (Winter 1994): 479–530; Daniel T. Willingham and Gail Lovette, "Can Reading Comprehension Be Taught?" *Teachers College Record*, September 26, 2014, http://www.tcrecord.org/content. asp?contentid=17701.

7. Diana J. Arya, Elfrieda H. Hiebert, and P. David Pearson, "The Effects of Syntactic and Lexical Complexity on the Comprehension of Elementary Science Texts," *International Electronic Journal of Elementary Education* 4, no. 1 (2011): 107–125.

8. There is a quick plateau in effectiveness of strategy instruction. Rosenshine and Meister ("Reciprocal Teaching") postulate that children already had to learn comprehension strategies in oral speech, and that the chief accomplishment of strategy instruction is to impart the realization that written speech is also somebody trying to tell you something.

9. Leila Morsy, Michael Kieffer, and Catherine Snow, *Measure for Measure: A Critical Consumers' Guide to Reading Comprehension Assessments for Adolescents* (New York: Carnegie Corporation of New York, 2010).

10. Samuel Messick, *Validity of Test Interpretation and Use* (research report, Educational Testing Service, 1990), http://files.eric.ed.gov/fulltext/ED395031.pdf

11. Similarly, in stressing text complexity, as the Common Core State Standards do, they send the false message that there is a general complexity-managing skill that will enable students to read complex texts.

12. E. D. Hirsch, Jr., "Reading Comprehension Requires Knowledge—of Words and the World," *American Educator* 27, no. 1 (Spring 2003): 10–13, 16–22, 28–29, 48.

13. Elizabeth A. Harris and Ford Fessenden, "'Opt Out' Becomes Anti-Test Rallying Cry in New York State," *New York Times*, May 20, 2015, http://www.nytimes. com/2015/05/21/nyregion/opt-out-movement-against-common-core-testing-grows-in-new-york-state.html?_r=0.

14. Lizette Alvarez, "States Listen as Parents Give Rampant Testing an F," *New York Times*, November 9, 2014, http://www.nytimes.com/2014/11/10/us/states-listen-as-parents-give-rampant-testing-an-f.html

15. I offer examples from Texas and Virginia, since those states did not sign on to the Common Core, and the standards are in force.

16. To keep Texas still in view, these stems were taken from released test questions in Texas for fifth and seventh graders.

17. I don't suggest that this solution to the problem of basing a test on a noncurriculum was cynical. It was simply the best that could be done in the absence of a curriculum.

18. Willingham and Lovette, "Can Reading Comprehension Be Taught?" A further piece of evidence is the simple brute fact that the policy has not improved the reading abilities of our students when they emerge from our schooling.

19. Robert S. Siegler, "Adaptive and Nonadaptive Characteristics of Low-Income Children's Mathematical Strategy Use," in *The Challenge in Mathematics and Science Education*, eds. Louis A. Penner et al. (Washington, DC: American Psychological Association), 619–638.

20. This point is amplified with references to research in chapter 6.

21. The defects of the close-reading standard are discussed in chapter 6, on the Common Core Standards.

22. It's based on the wrong notion that words are univocal and inferences are deductible from that univocal meaning. But words are inherently ambiguous (allowing language use to be flexible), and inferences tend to be of the part-whole situation model, not the deductive-syllogistic model.

23. E. D. Hirsch, Jr., "The Test of the Common Core," *Huffington Post*, August 28, 2013, http://www.huffingtonpost.com/e-d-hirsch-jr/common-core-tests_b_3824859 .html.

Chapter 2

1. "The head of the American Federation of Teachers claimed on Monday that she wanted to see bad teachers removed from classrooms," http://freebeacon.com/issues /head-of-aft-surprises-tv-host-by-calling-for-bad-teachers-to-be-fired/.

2. But there have been laudable triumphs in regular schools too. See chapter 8.

3. Philip Gleason et al., *The Impact of Charter Schools: Final Report* (Washington, DC: Institute of Educational Sciences, US Department of Education, 2010).

4. See, for example, Kate Walsh, Deborah Glaser, and Danielle Dunne Wilcox, *What Education Schools Aren't Teaching About Reading—and What Elementary Teachers Aren't Learning* (Washington, DC: National Council on Teacher Quality, 2006).

5. A large part of human language interpretation is *disambiguation*, the process of choosing appropriate word and clause meanings, and rejecting others. Despite decades of work and billions spent, this problem has not been solved. Yehoshua Bar-Hillel famously argued it could not be solved in his piece "A Demonstration of the Nonfeasibility of Fully Automatic High Quality Translation," *Advances in Computers*, vol. 1 (1960): 91–163. I have not seen a credible refutation of his argument, which is based on the insight that an unstated context is required for disambiguation. So far, no way has been devised even in principle to enable a machine *reliably* to identify which unstated context is the right one. Computers need explicitness; they seem to be very literal minded. So far they are less expert than people in gauging the unsaid that is necessary to grasp the said. Moreover they cannot come up with new meanings for old words—which humans do all the time. Landauer's "Latent Semantic Analyisis" makes a stab by analyzing what other words are and are not present, as does Google Translate (a good stab—but unreliable). T. K. Landauer and S. T. Dumais, "A Solution to Plato's Problem: The Latent Semantic Analysis Theory of the Acquisition, Induction, and Representation of Knowledge," *Psychological Review* 104 (1997): 211–240.

6. Matthew M. Chingos and Grover J. "Russ" Whitehurst, "Choosing Blindly: Instructional Materials, Teacher Effectiveness, and the Common Core," Brown Center

on Educational Policy at Brookings, April 2012, http://www.brookings.edu/~/media /research/files/reports/2012/4/10%20curriculum%20chingos%20whitehurst/0410 _curriculum_chingos_whitehurst.pdf; Grover J. "Russ" Whitehurst, "Don't Forget Curriculum," Brookings.edu, October 2009, http://www.brookings.edu/research /papers/2009/10/14-curriculum-whitehurst.

7. Eric A. Hanushek and Steven G. Rivkin, "Generalizations About Using Value-Added Measures of Teacher Quality," *American Economic Review: Papers & Proceedings* 100 (May 2010): 267–271, http://www.aeaweb.org/articles.php?doi=10.1257/aer .100.2.267.

8. The claim by test makers that their questions are self-contained or made fair by glosses is convenient but erroneous and naive. No text—glossed or not—is self-contained.

9. That is the average intertest correlation between the most reliable tests. Leila Morsy, Michael Kieffer, and Catherine E. Snow, *Measure for Measure: A Critical Consumers' Guide to Reading Comprehension Assessments for Adolescents* (New York: Carnegie Corporation of New York, 2010).

10. "Teacher satisfaction has declined 23 percentage points since 2008, from 62% to 39% very satisfied, including five percentage points since last year, to the lowest level in 25 years." The MetLife Survey of the American Teacher (Feb 2013), https:// www.metlife.com/assets/cao/foundation/MetLife-Teacher-Survey-2012.pdf.

11. Donna R. Euben, *Faculty Termination & Disciplinary Issues*, American Association of University Professors, 2004, http://www.aaup.org/issues/appointments-promotions-discipline%C2%A0/termination-discipline-2004.

Chapter 3

1. IQ tests normally have a vocabulary component.

2. US Department of Health and Human Services, Administration for Children and Families, *Head Start Impact Study: Final Report*, January 2010, http://www.acf .hhs.gov/sites/default/files/opre/hs_impact_study_final.pdf.

3. Sandy Garrett, "Oklahoma Early Childhood Programs: 2007 State Report," Oklahoma State Department of Education, http://sde.state.ok.us/Programs/ECEduc /pdf/Report.pdf; Gary T. Henry et al., *The Georgia Early Childhood Study: 2001–2004* (Atlanta: Georgia State University, Andrew Young School of Policy Studies, 2005); US Department of Health and Human Services, Administration for Children and Families, *Head Start Impact Study: First Year Findings*, June 2005, http://www.acf.hhs .gov/programs/opre/hs/impact_study/reports/first_yr_finds/first_yr_finds.pdf.

4. Data on shining exceptions go back as far as the Coleman Report of 1966, and his later work on Catholic schools. For more recent examples in Core Knowledge schools, see chapter 8.

5. Jean-Pierre Jarousse, Alain Mingat, and Marc Richard, "La Scolarisation Maternelle à Deux Ans: Effets Pédagogiques et Sociaux," Éducation *et Formations* 31 (1992): 3–9; M. Duthoit, "L'Enfant et l'ecole: Aspects Synthetiques du Suivi d'un Echantillon de Vingt Mille Eleves des Écoles," *Education et Formations* 16 (1988): 3–13.

6. Linda Ben Ali, "La Scolarisation à Deux Ans," Éducation & Formations 82 (December 2012).

7. NAEP 2012, *Trends in Academic Progress* (2013). Score gap is least at age nine; greatest at age seventeen.

8. Thomas G. Sticht, "Auding and Reading: A Developmental Model," Catalog of Selected Documents in Psychology 5 (Winter 1975).

9. Jamie M. Quinn et al., "Developmental Relations Between Vocabulary Knowledge and Reading Comprehension: A Latent Change Score Modeling Study," *Child Development* 86, no. 1 (January–February 2015): 159–175; George A. Miller, "On Knowing a Word," *Annual Review of Psychology* 50 (1999): 1–19; Stacy A. Wagovich, Margaret S. Hill, and Gregory F. Petroski, "Semantic–Syntactic Partial Word Knowledge Growth Through Reading," *American Journal of Speech-Language Pathology* 24, no. 1 (February 2015): 60–71.

10. Adrian Staub et al., "The Influence of Cloze Probability and Item Constraint on Cloze Task Response Time," Journal of Memory and Language 82 (July 2015); Nathaniel J. Smith and Roger Levy, "The Effect of Word Predictability on Reading Time Is Logarithmic," *Cognition* 128, no. 3 (September 2013): 302–319.

11. Janice M. Keenan , Rebecca S. Betjemann, and Richard K. Olson "Reading Comprehension Tests Vary in the Skills They Assess: Differential Dependence on Decoding and Oral Comprehension," *Scientific Studies of Reading* 12 (2008): 281–300.

12. The Wikipedia article on "Project Follow Through" is long and accurate; see https://en.wikipedia.org/wiki/Project_Follow_Through.

13. Wesley C. Becker and Russell Gersten, "A Follow-up of Follow Through: The Later Effects of the Direct Instruction Model on Children in Fifth and Sixth Grades," *American Educational Research Journal* 19 (1982): 75–92.

14. Janet Quint et al., *Scaling Up the Success for All Model of School Reform* (final report from the Investing in Innovation (i3) Evaluation), MDRC, September 2015, http://www.mdrc.org/sites/default/files/SFA_2015_FR.pdf.

15. The book will also emphasize (it can hardly be too often repeated) that proper nouns like George Washington, Rosa Parks, and the Taj Mahal are also critical kinds of vocabulary items, and count for a great deal in mature reading ability.

16. William E. Nagy, Patricia A. Herman, and Richard C. Anderson, "Learning Words from Context," *Reading Research Quarterly* 19 (1985): 304–330; William E. Nagy, Richard C. Anderson, and Patricia A. Herman, "Learning Word Meanings from Context During Normal Reading," *American Educational Research Journal* 24 (1987): 237–270; William E. Nagy and Patricia A. Herman, "Breadth and Depth of Vocabulary Knowledge: Implications for Acquisition and Instruction," in Margaret G. McKeown and Mary E. Curtis, eds., *The Nature of Vocabulary Acquisition* (Hillsdale, NJ: Erbaum, 1987).

17. Alessandra Stanley, "French and Italian Preschools: Models for U.S.?", *New York Times*, April 25, 2001, http://www.nytimes.com/2001/04/25/world/25SCHO .html.

18. Diane Ravitch, "Tot Sociology," *The American Scholar* 56, no. 3 (Summer 1987): 343–354.

19. Ibid.

20. Sarane Spence Boocock, "Early Childhood Programs in Other Nations: Goals and Outcomes," *The Future of Children* 5, no. 3 (Winter 1995): 94–114.

21. Ministere de l'Education Nationale, Votre Enfant à l'École Maternelle: Guide Pratique des Parents, Année 2010–2011 (Paris: Futuroscope: Centre National de Documentation Pédagogique, 2010).

22. In the United States over many years this method has been the subject of research by John Guthrie, and its effectiveness has been demonstrated many times over. John Guthrie et al., "Increasing Reading Comprehension and Engagement Through Concept-Oriented Reading Instruction [CORI]," *Journal of Educational Psychology* 96, no. 3 (2004): "Using content goals in a conceptual theme consists of reading instruction with a complex knowledge domain (ecology, solar system, colonial America, westward expansion) sustained for at least several weeks . . . In both studies, class-level analyses showed that students in CORI classrooms were higher than SI [strategy instruction] and/or TI [traditional instruction] students on measures of reading comprehension, reading motivation, and reading strategies."

23. Jarousse, Mingat, and Richard, "La Scolarisation Maternelle." Units are z scores.

24. Ali, "La Scolarisation à Deux Ans."

25. There are now about eight hundred thousand pupils in each primary grade in France. By age four, preschool is universal. See http://www.insee.fr/fr/themes /document.asp?ref_id=ip1429.

26. Ali, "La Scolarisation à Deux Ans."

27. William E. Nagy and Judith A. Scott, "Vocabulary Processes" in Michael Kamil et al., eds., *Handbook of Reading Research*, volume III (Mahwah, NJ: Erlbaum, 2000); Miller, "On Knowing a Word"; George A. Miller and Patricia M. Gildea, "How Children Learn Words," *Scientific American* 257, no. 3 (September 1987): 94–99.

Chapter 4

1. Jennifer McMurrer, *Choices, Changes, and Challenges: Curriculum and Instruction in the NCLB Era* (Washington, DC: Center on Education Policy, 2007). I use the term "reading" as shorthand for "English language arts." The tests involve writing too, which is harder to grade reliably. So reading is the chief high-stakes object of the tests.

2. Tim Walker, "The Testing Obsession and the Disappearing Curriculum," *NEA Today*, September 2, 2014, http://neatoday.org/2014/09/02/the-testing-obsession -and-the-disappearing-curriculum-2/

3. Diane Ravitch, *Left Back: A Century of Failed School Reforms* (New York: Simon and Schuster, 2000), 171–74, 183–88.

4. I remember a charming book by S. H. Fraiberg called *The Magic Years* (i.e., the sensorimotor stage), which described the inability of infants to understand that objects persisted after they disappeared from view.

5. R. J. Siegler, *Children's Thinking* (Upper Saddle River, NJ: Prentice-Hall, 1998).

6. Ashley E. Maynard and Patricia M. Greenfield, "Implicit Cognitive Development in Cultural Tools and Children: Lessons from Maya Mexico," *Cognitive Development* 18, no. 4 (Oct–Dec 2003): 489–510. There's a possibility that the tests for the fourth stage are not suited to the culture, and that if different tests were devised Piaget's categories would prove universal. That's irrelevant to Piaget's own point that the timing of the stages is culturally dependent, which means dependent on externals, not an inner unfolding. Moreover, there is some indication that even in Western cultures people can do formal operations much better when they are tied to concrete experience—another version of the domain specificity of skills. See Paul Sheldon Davies, James H. Fetzer, and Thomas R. Foster, "Logical Reasoning and Domain Specificity," Biology and Philosophy 10, no. 1 (1995): 1–37.

7. Jean Piaget, "Cognitive Development in Children," *Journal of Research in Science Teaching*.2 (1964): 176–186.

8. Pan American Health Organization (PAHO), *Health in the Americas, 2012 Edition: Regional Overview and Country Profiles* (Washington, DC: PAHO, 2012).

9. Jerome Bruner, *The Process of Education* (Cambridge, MA: Harvard University Press, 1960), 33. "We begin with the hypothesis that any subject can be taught effectively in some intellectually honest form to any child at any stage of development."

10. Patricia M. Greenfield et al., "Cultural Pathways Through Universal Development," *Annual Review of Psychology* 54 (2003): 461–490.

11. Chris Berdik, "Is the Common Core Killing Kindergarten?", *Boston Globe*, June 14, 2015, https://www.bostonglobe.com/ideas/2015/06/13/common-core -killing-kindergarten/lydG3pnscVEnTEoELUZWdP/story.html.

12. The developmental appropriateness of Mesopotamia for first grade became a subject for public debate when New York State approved the Core Knowledge Language Arts program. See Paul Riede, "First-Graders and Mesopotamia? New York's Model Lesson Plan Asks Too Much, Critics Say," *Syracuse Post-Standard*, September 5, 2013, http://www.syracuse.com/news/index.ssf/2013/09/new_yorks_model_first -grade_curriculum_slammed_by_critics_ignored_by_central_new.html.

13. Patricia A. Alexander, Jonna M. Kulikowich, and Sharon K. Schulze, "How Subject-Matter Knowledge Affects Recall and Interest," *American Educational Research Journal* 31 (1994): 313–337; Daniel T. Willingham, "How Knowledge Helps: It Speeds and Strengthens Reading Comprehension, Learning—and Thinking," *American Educator* 30, no. 1 (Spring 2006): 30–37. See more at: http://www.aft.org/periodical /american-educator/summer-2014/starting-strong#sthash.NQ2FmpNb.dpuf.

14. The idea that presumably "developmentally inappropriate" topics do actual harm is a myth that was well exploded by developmental psychologists; see Judith J. Carta et al., "Developmentally Appropriate Practice: Appraising Its Usefulness for Young Children with Disabilities," *Topics in Early Childhood Special Education* 11, no. 1 (1991).

15. "Constructivism" in that sense of the word is one of the most astonishing technical mistakes of current educational theory. Ever since the 1930s it's been known

that memory (which is a component of learning) is not a passive, reproductive "faculty," but an active, constructive one. So a semantic leap was taken from the universal meaning of "active construction," which holds for *all* language comprehension and learning, including that gained from books and lectures, to suppose that the 1930s insight was reserved only for "discovery learning," whereby children construct their learning by independently finding things out. Wonderful as those moments are, they aren't the universal model for all constructive learning, especially for children who are behind. All learning is constructed. The general principle does not sponsor any particular pedagogy. To claim so is a fundamental error almost universally promulgated in American education schools.

16. John Dewey, "My Pedagogic Creed," *School Journal* 54 (January 1897): 77–80. Creed: "I believe that the image is the great instrument of instruction."

17. The key text is Friere's *Pedagogy of the Oppressed*.

18. This exploded idea (rejected by Piaget) was a hallmark of the American progressive movement. It was the theme of a highly influential book by Dr. Nathan Oppenheim, who set forth comparative lists showing that the composition and weight of the various internal organs vary between children and adults. Just as their physical organs are different from adults, so, he claimed, are their mental organs. Just as they need child-appropriate food, so do they need child-appropriate mental nutrition that is right for their stage of mental development. Oppenheimer stated: "The child whose sense of sight is wrongly or too early taxed, whose power of food-assimilation is abused, whose order of mental development is ignored, is suffering from poor nutrition. This child who prematurely participates in experiences and ways of living, who is allowed to wander outside of the limits that a conservative idea of growth imposes, who becomes subject to conditions that only the strength of maturity can withstand, is thus subjected to adverse conditions that must surely leave their mark upon his later organic form. Such a child is suffering from a vicious nutrition. The child who assumes responsibilities beyond his years, who undergoes the wear and tear of a wise attending the course of a too rapid development, who lacks the benefits restraint and discipline, is bound to show the effects in a partial and one-sided development that bars him out from the full beauty of finished maturity. Such a child suffers from the effects of a misdirected and vicious nutrition." The main import of Oppenheim's advice is to slow down instruction. His best-selling book *The Development of the Child* (1898) had multiple reprintings, and went through eleven new editions between 1898 and 1924.

19. I hope the reader will share my dazzlement and admiration at how clearly Gramsci saw all this back in 1929. In the same notebook passage where he spoke of progressive education as a church that has paralyzed dissent, he observed that the great error of the idea that education is spontaneous development is that the human baby is from the beginning besieged with socializing forces: "from a few days after birth accumulates sensations and images that multiply and become complex with the learning of a language."

20. A best-selling language arts series stated: "We have chosen what is common, established, almost proverbial; what has become indisputably 'classic,' what, in brief,

every child in the land ought to know, because it is good, and because other people know it. The educational worth of such materials calls for no defense. In an age when the need of socializing and unifying our people is keenly felt, the value of a common stock of knowledge, a common set of ideals is obvious." Franklin T. Baker and Ashley H. Thorndike, "Introduction," *Everyday Classics* (New York: Macmillan, 1917).

21. Lynn Waterhouse, "Inadequate Evidence for Multiple Intelligences Mozart Effect, and Emotional Intelligence Theories," *Educational Psychologist* 41, no. 4 (2006): 247–255.

22. Antonio Gramsci, Notebook 1, 1929, *Quaderni del Carcere*, vol. 1, 2nd ed., ed. Valentino Gerratana (Rome: Einaudi, 1977), 114. My translation.

23. George A. Miller, "Varieties of Intelligence," *New York Times Review of Books*, December 25, 1983.

24. As mentioned in the prologue to this book, an outcome-oriented rather than an innateness view of the matter is supported by new evidence about grit and the importance of resisting the idea of fixed, innate intelligence. See Paul Tough, *How Children Succeed* (New York: Houghton Mifflin Harcourt, 2012); Carol Dweck, *Mindset* (New York: Random House, 2007).

25. Popularized by Paul Tough in *How Children Succeed* (2012).

26. Dweck, *Mindset*.

27. Margaret E. Beier and Phillip L. Ackerman, "Age, Ability and the Role of Prior Knowledge on the Acquisition of New Domain Knowledge: Promising Results in a Real-World Environment," *Psychology and Aging* 20 (2005): 341–355; Fernand Gobet and Herbert A. Simon, "Five Seconds or Sixty? Presentation Time in Expert Memory," Cognitive Science 24 (2000): 651–682; Vernon C. Hall and Beverly Edmondson, "Relative Importance of Aptitude and Prior Domain Knowledge on Immediate and Delayed Post-Tests," Journal of Educational Psychology 84 (1992): 219–223. See more at: http://www.aft.org/periodical/american-educator/spring-2006/how -knowledge-helps#sthash.xHq6HUvp.dpuf.

28. OECD, *Low-Performing Students: Why They Fall Behind and How to Help Them Succeed* (Paris: PISA, OECD Publishing, 2016), http://dx.doi.org/10.1787 /9789264250246-en.

29. Mike Schmoker, "When Pedagogic Fads Trump Priorities," Education Week, September 29, 2010.

30. Some classes continue to use "basal readers" rather than leveled pamphlets. These are also compiled under the Lexile type of readability principle. They are arranged by artificial headings like "Discovery," but the contents are thoroughly heterogeneous, not domain based. In the *Knowledge Deficit* I listed some titles in sequence, from the table of contents of the best-selling first-grade reading program by Houghton Mifflin: A Dragon Gets By, Roly Poly, How Real Pigs Act, It's Easy to Be Polite, Mrs. Brown Went to Town, Rats on the Roof, Cats Can't Fly, Henry and Mudge and the Starry Night, Campfire Games, and Around the Pond, pointing out that making them the cornerstone of a language arts curriculum in the earliest grades has exacted huge opportunity costs.

31. American Library Association, *The State of America's Libraries (Special Issue)* (Chicago: American Libraries Association, 2010).

32. Timothy Shanahan, "Rejecting Instructional Level Theory," http://www .shanahanonliteracy.com/2011/08/rejecting-instructional-level-theory.html.

33. For examples of how to do this, and how well it works, see: John T. Guthrie et al., "Increasing Reading Comprehension and Engagement Through Concept-Oriented Reading Instruction [CORI]," *Journal of Educational Psychology* 96, no. 3 (2004): 403–423.

34. Thomas G. Sticht, "Auding and Reading: A Developmental Model," Catalog of Selected Documents in Psychology 5 (Winter 1975).

35. Diane McGuinness, Early Reading Instruction, What Science Really Tells Us about How to Teach Reading (Cambridge, MA: MIT Press, 2005); Daniel T. Willingham, Raising Kids Who Read: What Parents and Teachers Can Do (San Francisco: Jossey-Bass, 2015).

36. The current formula is secret and proprietary.

37. Shanahan, "Rejecting Instructional Level Theory": "Of course, guided reading and leveled books are so widely used it would make sense that there would be lots of evidence as to their efficacy. Except that there is not. I keep looking and I keep finding studies that suggest that kids can learn from text written at very different levels. How can that be? Well, basically we have put way too much confidence in an unproven theory."

38. Educator's name withheld.

39. http://www.insighteastorlando.com/technology/simulation-can-help-make -the-invisible-visible/

40. Giana Magnoli, "Superintendent Says Culture Will Change in Santa Barbara School District," *Santa Barbara Noozhawk*, August 8, 2013, http://www.noozhawk .com/article/superintendent_says_culture_will_change_santa_barbara_schools _20130806.

41. The date of Dewey's *How We Think* is 1910. See also the 1936 "March of Time" on YouTube (https://www.youtube.com/watch?v=opXKmwg8VQM) where individuality and critical thinking are the focus of "thousands of schools."

42. Paradoxically, that insight was important in the work of Edward Thorndike, the favorite psychologist of early progressive educators in the United States. They liked Thorndike's finding that learning Latin did not "train the mind." It just trained how to read Latin.

43. E. D. Hirsch, Jr., "'You Can Always Look It Up' . . . Or Can You?", *American Educator* (Spring 2000): 1–5.

44. Mike Levy and Caroline Steel, "Language Learner Perspectives on the Functionality and Use of Electronic Language Dictionaries," *ReCALL: Journal of Eurocall* 27, no. 2 (May 2015): 177–196, http://dx.doi.org.proxy.its.virginia.edu/10.1017 /S09583440.

45. George A. Miller and Patricia M. Gildea, "How Children Learn Words," *Scientific American* 257, no. 3 (September 1987): 94–99.

46. Nicholas Carr, "Experiments in Delinkification," *Rough Type* blog, May 31, 2010, http://www.roughtype.com/?p=1378.

47. The problem is exacerbated—especially for young children and Google Translate—by the fact that people make up new meanings for old words as they go along. That's why there's need for so many subdefinitions, with others, not yet listed, getting to be current but not yet recorded.

48. Daniel T. Willingham, "Ask the Cognitive Scientist: What Is Developmentally Appropriate Practice?," *American Educator* 32, no. 2 (Summer 2008): 34–39. See also Daniel T. Willingham, "Do We Underestimate Our Youngest Learners?," *RealClearEducation*, March 11, 2014. See more at: http://www.aft.org/periodical/american -educator/summer-2014/playful-immersion#sthash.hSp3vtTi.dpuf.

49. George A. Miller, "On Knowing a Word," *Annual Review of Psychology* 50 (1999): 1–19.

50. Jill Larkin et al.,"Expert and Novice Performance in Solving Physics Problems," *Science* 208 (1980): 1335–1342.

51. Keith E. Stanovich, "Matthew Effects in Reading: Some Consequences of Individual Differences in the Acquisition of Literacy," *Reading Research Quarterly* 21 (1986): 360–407.

52. The PISA results on problem solving correlate roughly with the results on domain knowledge.

53. K. Duncker, *Zur Psychologie des produktiven Denkens [The Psychology of Productive Thought]* (Oxford, UK: Springer, 1935); M. L. Gick and K. J. Holyoak, "Analogical Problem Solving," *Cognitive Psychology* 12, no. 3 (1980): 306–355.

54. Sacha Helfenstein and Pertti Saariluoma, "Mental Contents in Transfer," *Psychological Research* 70, no. 4 (July 2006): 293–303.

55. Domain specificity is now being detected in elemental brain processers; see Matthias Schurz et al., "Clarifying the Role of Theory of Mind Areas During Visual Perspective Taking: Issues of Spontaneity and Domain-Specificity," *NeuroImage* 117 (August 15, 2015): 386–396.

56. Judith Anderson Koenig, Rapporteur, *Assessing 21st Century Skills: Summary of a Workshop* (Washington, DC: National Academies Press, 2011), 23.

57. Ibid.

58. Private communication, printed with the author's permission.

59. For reasons offered in chapter 1, the focus of this book is on reading and other subjects of the curriculum, including science, that impinge on reading—not math, which has sounder curriculum standards and tests than reading does.

60. Teun A. van Dijk and Walter Kintsch, *Strategies of Discourse Comprehension* (San Diego: Academic Press, 1983).

61. Donna R. Recht and Lauren Leslie, "Effect of Prior Knowledge on Good and Poor Readers' Memory of Text," *Journal of Educational Psychology* 80, no. 1 (March 1988): 16–20.

62. The determination of "good readers" and "poor readers" based on average test scores is reasonable, but also highly unreliable for any individual text. There's a great

deal of variation in reading comprehension in individual elementary school students, making their average scores less informative than educators normally conceive. This small detail turns out to have big importance, as will be explained in subsequent chapters where reading tests are further discussed.

63. Wolfgang Schneider, Joachim Körkel, and Franz E. Weinert, "Domain-Specific Knowledge and Memory Performance: A Comparison of High- and Low-Aptitude Children," *Journal of Educational Psychology* 81, no. 3 (1989): 306–312.

64. Diana J. Arya, Elfrieda H. Hiebert, and P. David Pearson, "The Effects of Syntactic and Lexical Complexity on the Comprehension of Elementary Science Texts," *International Electronic Journal of Elementary Education* 4, no. 1 (2011): 107–125.

65. This has important implications for the text-complexity requirements of the Common Core standards. It means that word rarity and sentence length can increase as a coherent lesson unit progresses over time and students become more familiar with the topic.

Chapter 5

1. Sonia Sotomayor, *My Beloved World* (New York: Random House, 2013).

2. My own guess about this puzzle is that the schools that were being integrated were getting worse. We know this is true from the general nationwide test score decline between 1960 and 1980. As this chapter will show, when schools get worse, it impacts disadvantaged children more than advantaged ones. I have heard from African American colleagues, some from the South and very conscious of the irony, that the segregated schools they attended, with their demanding teachers and no-nonsense, knowledge-based curriculums, were better than the integrated schools blacks attended after Brown v. Board.

3. I hope the reader will forgive the plod of going through a syllogism, but sometimes it's essential to have what M. H. Abrams has called "a keen eye for the obvious."

4. As discussed in chapter 3, the basic principle is this: A good, cumulative curriculum has prepared all the students in the class with the prior knowledge necessary to make probable-meaning hypotheses about the sentences they are hearing and reading. They are all in a position to conjure up a fairly accurate situation model for the discourse, enabling them to make correct-meaning hypotheses about word meanings. So while advantaged students are making gains with, say, ten new words, their disadvantaged classmates are making gains with fifteen. This is the basic structure of gap closing at the molecular level.

5. Described in detail in chapter 8.

6. Christine H. Rossell et al., *School Desegregation in the 21st Century* (Westport, CT: Greenwood, 2002), 301.

7. Ibid.

8. *PISA 2012 Results: Excellence Through Equity Giving Every Student the Chance to Succeed*, Volume II (Paris: Organisation for Economic Co-operation and Development [OECD], 2013).

9. Canada is an interesting and subtle case. Each province issues its own curricular guidelines. The official standards are not as explicit as those of, say, Japan. But there

are ancillary materials that are highly explicit. By this means the Canadians avoid the appearance of arbitrary dictatorial impositions. But ancillary illustrative materials gently induce the reality of arbitrary dictatorial impositions—a subtle approach that might well be tried elsewhere.

10. Its rival in bigness was "Project Follow Through," also dating to the 1960s.

11. Geoffrey Borman and Maritza Dowling, "Schools and Inequality: A Multilevel Analysis of Coleman's Equality of Educational Opportunity Data," *Teachers College Record* 112, no. 5 (2010): 1201–1246.

12. James S. Coleman, Thomas Hoffer, and Sally Kilgore, High School Achievement: Public, Catholic and Private Schools Compared (New York: Basic Books, 1982).

13. James S. Coleman et al., *Equality of Educational Opportunity, Summary Report* (Washington, DC: National Center for Educational Statistics, 1966), 22, http://eric .ed.gov/?id=ED012275.

14. Ibid.

15. There is the positive Coleman Effect, which closes gaps, and the negative Coleman Effect, which increases them. The negative Coleman Effect has long been known as the Matthew Effect, from the Book of Matthew: "For he that hath, to him shall be given: and he that hath not, from him shall be taken even that which he hath." Borman's reanalysis of Coleman's own data showed that good schools made a 40 percent difference in gap closing, not 20 percent as in Coleman's own analysis.

16. As I show in the next chapter, the French data powerfully confirm the Coleman Differential Effect. As French schools got worse between 1987 and 2007, the equity gaps grew bigger.

17. The current reckoning "30 million words behind," based on the path-breaking work of Hart and Risley, could too easily support a sense of educational determinism—just as in the response to the Coleman Report. We can do a much better job of narrowing the gap in the school, without assuming that children's educational fate is permanently determined by the loquacity of parents.

18. John Guthrie et al., "Increasing Reading Comprehension and Engagement Through Concept-Oriented Reading Instruction [CORI]," *Journal of Educational Psychology* 96, no. 3 (2004): 403–423. "Using content goals in a conceptual theme consists of reading instruction with a complex knowledge domain (ecology, solar system, colonial America, westward expansion) sustained for at least several weeks." "In both studies, class-level analyses showed that students in CORI classrooms were higher than SI [strategy instruction] and/or TI [traditional instruction] students on measures of reading comprehension, reading motivation, and reading strategies." The method has long been advocated in second-language learning as the fastest and best way of building vocabulary in a new language. For instance: James Coady, *Second Language Vocabulary Acquisition: A Rationale for Pedagogy* (New York: Cambridge University Press, 1997); A. A. Zevenbergen, G. J. Whitehurst, and J. A. Zevenbergen, "Effects of a Shared-Reading Intervention on the Inclusion of Evaluative Devices in Narratives of Children from Low-Income Families," *Journal of Applied Developmental Psychology* 24, no. 1 (2003).

19. Isabel L. Beck, Margaret G. McKeown, and Linda Kucan, *Bringing Words to Life* (New York: Guilford Press, 2002).

20. It is a plausible hypothesis to be tested whether rare tier-three words should be the only ones singled out for study. If one stays on topic, common tier-two words yield their meaning from context, because the larger meaning is being understood through topic familiarity. The teacher pauses briefly to explain the sense of critical tier-three words like *seismic*. It's those critical tier-three words in the knowledge curriculum that demand brief explicit comment. In a rich textual environment tier-two words will take care of themselves, just as they almost certainly did for the readers of this book when they were growing up.

21. William E. Nagy, Patricia A. Herman, and Richard C. Anderson, "Learning Words from Context," *Reading Research Quarterly* 19 (1985): 304–330; William E. Nagy, Richard C. Anderson, and Patricia A. Herman, "Learning Word Meanings from Context During Normal Reading," *American Educational Research Journal* 24 (1987): 237–270; William E. Nagy and Patricia A. Herman, "Breadth and Depth of Vocabulary Knowledge: Implications for Acquisition and Instruction," in Margaret G. McKeown and Mary E. Curtis, eds., *The Nature of Vocabulary Acquisition* (Hillsdale, NJ: Erbaum, 1987).

22. George A. Miller and Patricia M. Gildea, "How Children Learn Words," *Scientific American* 257, no. 3 (September 1987): 94–99.

23. George A. Miller, "On Knowing a Word," *Annual Review of Psychology* 50 (1999): 1–19.

24. Howard Jackson and Etienne Zé Amvela, *Words, Meaning and Vocabulary: An Introduction to Modern English Lexicology* (London: A & C Black, 2000).

Chapter 6

1. http://www.slate.com/blogs/schooled/2015/09/04/sat_scores_more_diverse _group_of_kids_taking_the_college_board_test_but.html

2. This logical inference standard is defective on two grounds. No text says anything "explicitly" until after it has been interpreted. And, as I pointed out in chapter 1, the inferences one draws in interpretation are not logical, except in a few specialized texts involving syllogisms or other formal principles. Most inferences are part-whole types that do not depend upon logic. They are contextual, and depend upon a set of associations within a constructed situation model. Close reading cannot supply any inference not already stated in a text. If it did, it would not require an inference. Close reading is a metaphor for paying conscious attention to surface features of a text. This can be useful when reading lyric poetry or writing about it. But paying conscious attention to surface features can be a quite cumbersome habit since it distracts conscious attention away from the message to its medium of expression, in instances where the substance is far more challenging and important than the verbal surface. I remember a telling remark on this topic by a guru of close reading, Professor W. K. Wimsatt of Yale. He stressed the importance of genre in whether to apply close reading. The linguistic surface of a long novel may not always be very important, he observed, saying,

speaking of the translator of *Crime and Punishment*, "I just don't believe that Constant Garnett could write that good a novel."

3. http://thefederalist.com/2014/08/05/as-common-core-hits-classrooms-nervous
-teachers-hope-for-the-best/

4. Daniel T. Willingham, *Raising Kids Who Read: What Parents and Teachers Can Do* (San Francisco: Jossey-Bass, 2015).

5. The policy aim of test uniformity was predicated on the widely held but mistaken idea that reading comprehension is a general skill. Would the mistake have been made if the skill were listening comprehension? Probably not, since common sense would urge that listening comprehension is topic-dependent. Mature reading is silent listening. For a recent review, see Hyein Cho et al., "Internally Generated Conscious Contents: Interactions Between Sustained Mental Imagery and Involuntary Subvocalizations," *Frontiers in Psychology* 5 (2014).

6. Of course, there could be good multistate reading tests if several states agreed upon a grade-by-grade sequence of core topics. Perhaps that will happen in the future. It would greatly improve testing and learning.

7. Barak Rosenshine and Carla Meister, "Reciprocal Teaching: A Review of the Research," *Review of Educational Research* 64, no. 4 (1994): 479–530.

8. Rolf A. Zwaan, "Effect of Genre Expectations on Text Comprehension," *Journal of Experimental Psychology: Learning, Memory, and Cognition* 20, no. 4 (July 1994): 920–933; Rolf A. Zwaan, "Situation Models, Mental Simulations, and Abstract Concepts in Discourse Comprehension," *Psychonomic Bulletin & Review* (June 19, 2015).

9. Zwaan, "Effect of Genre Expectations."

10. Oscar Wilde, "The Decay of Lying—An Observation," in *Intentions* (1891).

11. http://parcc.pearson.com/resources/practice-tests/english/grade-5/pba
/PC194821-001_5ELATB_PT.pdfc

12. Kate Taylor and Elizabeth A. Harris, "A New York State Test Questions Tricky for 3rd Graders, and Maybe Some Adults," *New York Times*, August 10, 2015, http://
www.nytimes.com/2015/08/11/nyregion/new-york-state-test-questions-tricky-for
-3rd-graders-and-maybe-some-adults.html.

13. Donald P. Hayes, Loreen T. Wolfer, and Michael F. Wolfe, "Schoolbook Simplification and Its Relation to the Decline in SAT-Verbal Scores," *American Educational Research Journal* 33, no. 2 (Summer 1996): 489–508.

14. http://www.slate.com/blogs/schooled/2015/09/09/common_core_standards_
what_four_teachers_actually_think_about_them.html

15. Diana J. Arya, Elfrieda H. Hiebert, and P. David Pearson, "The Effects of Syntactic and Lexical Complexity on the Comprehension of Elementary Science Texts," *International Electronic Journal of Elementary Education* 4, no. 1 (2011).

16. Daniel T. Willingham, "The Privileged Status of Story," *American Educator* (Summer 2004), http://www.aft.org/periodical/american-educator/summer-2004/ask
-cognitive-scientist.

17. Harper Lee, *To Kill a Mockingbird* (Philadelphia: J. B. Lippincott, 1960).

18. Sally Mitchell, ed., *Victorian Britain: An Encyclopedia* (New York: Routledge, 2011), 145.

19. Susan Ohanian at http://www.schoolsmatter.info/2012/06/ohanian-on-rotted-common-core-and.html.

20. Here are all the uses of *imagine* in the King James Bible (1611), not one of which is positive: Job 6:26: "Do ye imagine to reprove words, and the speeches of one that is desperate, which are as wind?"; Job 21:27: "Behold, I know your thoughts, and the devices which ye wrongfully imagine against me"; Psalms 2:1: "Why do the heathen rage, and the people imagine a vain thing?"; Psalms 38:12: "They also that seek after my life lay snares for me: and they that seek my hurt speak mischievous things, and imagine deceits all the day long"; Psalms 62:3: "How long will ye imagine mischief against a man? ye shall be slain all of you: as a bowing wall shall ye be, and as a tottering fence"; Psalms 140:2: "which imagine mischiefs in their heart; continually are they gathered together for war"; Proverbs 12:20: "Deceit is in the heart of them that imagine evil: but to the counsellors of peace is joy"; Hosea 7:15: "Though I have bound and strengthened their arms, yet do they imagine mischief against me"; Nahum 1:9: "What do ye imagine against the LORD? he will make an utter end: affliction shall not rise up the second time"; Zechariah 7:10: "And oppress not the widow, nor the fatherless, the stranger, nor the poor; and let none of you imagine evil against his brother in your heart"; Zechariah 8:17: "And let none of you imagine evil in your hearts against his neighbour; and love no false oath: for all these are things that I hate, saith the LORD."

21. "Strong Support, Low Awareness: Public Perception of the Common Core State Standards," Achieve Report, October 1, 2011, http://achieve.org/publications/strong-support-low-awareness-public-perception-common-core-state-standards.

22. Samuel S. Randall, *The Common School System of the State of New York . . .* (Troy, NY: Johnson and Davis, Steam Press Printers, 1851).

23. Described in Diane Ravitch, *Left Back: A Century of Failed School Reforms* (New York: Simon and Schuster, 2000).

24. I use this invented term to stress the deliberate, invented character of a shared national culture, well described in Ernest Gellner's excellent *Nations and Nationalism*, 2nd ed. (Oxford, UK: Blackwell, 2006).

25. http://www.merriam-webster.com/dictionary/Standard+English

26. What this means for instructing English language learners, whether through English-only methods or multilingual methods in different proportions is not a question of ideology but of effectiveness—best judged by the expert teacher confronted with a particular group of students. What variations will work best with this group? That is, after all, the ad hoc question every teacher faces with each different group of students in each and every subject matter, whether chemistry or the English language.

27. See the excellent analysis by Nathan Glazer, *We Are All Multicuturalists Now* (Cambridge, MA: Harvard University Press, 1998).

28. My translation from: Ma si è poi formata una specie di chiesa che ha paralizzato gli studi pedagogici e ha dato luogo a delle curiose involuzioni (nelle dottrine

di Gentile e del Lombardo-Radice). La "spontaneità" è una di queste involuzioni: si immagina quasi che nel bambino il cervello sia come un gomitolo che il maestro aiuta a sgomitolare. In realtà ogni generazione educa la nuova generazione, cioè la forma e l'educazione è una lotta contro gli istinti legati alle funzioni biologiche elementari, una lotta contro la natura, per dominarla e creare l'uomo "attuale" alla sua epoca. Quaderno 1, Also *Gli Intellectuali*, p. 138.

29. George Washington, "The Will" (April–December 1799), in *The Papers of George Washington, Retirement Series*, ed. W. W. Abbot, vol. 4 (Charlottesville: University Press of Virginia, 1999), 477–492.

30. "The holiday crossed over from California into the rest of the United States in the 1950s and 1960s but did not gain popularity until the 1980s when marketers, especially beer companies, capitalized on the celebratory nature of the day and began to promote it," https://en.wikipedia.org/wiki/Cinco_de_Mayo.

31. "The fault, dear Brutus, is not in our stars, But in ourselves, that we are underlings." William Shakespeare, *Julius Caesar* (act I, scene II).

Chapter 7

1. Laurent Lafforgue and Liliane Lurçat, eds., *La Débâcle de l'École: Une Tragédie Incomprise* (Paris: Guibert, 2007).

2. http://blogs.lse.ac.uk/europpblog/2012/05/07/france-school/. See also Paola Mattei and Andrew S. Aguilar, *Secular Institutions, Islam and Education Policy* (New York: Palgrave Macmillan, 2016).

3. Elliott A. Medrich, *International Mathematics and Science Assessment: What Have We Learned?* (Washington, DC: US Department of Education Office of Educational Research and Improvement NCES 92-011, 1992). Of particular note is the following conclusion: "Use of a differentiated curriculum based on tracking is negatively associated with student performance on the international assessments and also reduces opportunities for some students to be exposed to more advanced curriculum."

4. Laurent Lafforgue points out (in a private communication) that the French schools began their current decline in the 1960s. The decline did not pick up speed, approaching that of the United States, until after the *loi Jospin* abandoned the national curriculum, and deliberately localized and individualized the topics studied in elementary school. For accounts of this earlier decline, see the following works: Jean-Claude Milner, *De l'École*, (Paris: Éditions du Seuil, 1984); Philippe Nemo, *Pourquoi Ont-Ils Tué Jules Ferry?: La Dérive de l'École Sous la Ve République* (Paris: B. Grasset, 1991); Liliane Lurçat, *La Destruction de l'Enseignement Élémentaire et Ses Penseurs* (Paris: F.-X. de Guibert, 1998); Jean-Pierre Le Goff, *La Barbarie Douce: La Modernisation Aveugle des Entreprises et de l'École* (Paris: La Découverte, 1999); Marc Le Bris, *Et Vos Enfants ne Sauront pas Lire . . . Ni Compter: La Faillite Obstinée de l'École Française* (Paris: Stock, 2004).

5. https://www.youtube.com/watch?v=opXKmwg8VQM. The YouTube video misdates the film as being shot in the 1940s. The correct date is 1936.

6. William W. Turnbull, "Student Change, Program Change: Why the SAT Scores Kept Falling," Educational Testing Service College Board Report No. 85-2, ETS RR

No. 85-28 (New York: College Entrance Examination Board, 1985); Donald P Hayes, Laureen T. Wolfer, and Michael F. Wolfe, "Schoolbook Simplification and Its Relation to the Decline in SAT-Verbal Scores," *American Educational Research Journal* 33, no. 2 (Summer 1996): 489–508; Jeanne S. Chall, *An Analysis of Textbooks in Relation to Declining SAT Scores* (Report of the Advisory Panel on the Scholastic Aptitude Test Score Decline: Appendixes to On Further Examination) (New York: College Board, 1977).

7. Daniel Koretz, "What Happened to Test Scores, and Why?" *Educational Measurement: Issues and Practice* 11, no. 4 (Winter 1992): 7–11. NAEP scores for high school graduates are flat from 1971 to the present. NAEP itself began *after* the decade of decline from 1962 to 1972. Thus it's a basic error for school apologists to point to NAEP as showing that high school verbal scores have improved or stayed stable. The horse was already out of the barn when NAEP began.

8. NAEP, our most reliable nationwide measure, congressionally mandated, issued its first report on verbal proficiency in 1971.

9. For simplicity, I am omitting the term *standard deviation* and its abbreviation, *SD*. To many it is a confusing term in this context. It normally expresses the average variance in a distribution, which is meaningful to experts, but while that is its meaning it is *not* its main function when comparing scores on different tests. There it's used chiefly as a common magnitude like inches or millimeters, to put various test score scales on the same metric. Measures of this kind are also called *z scores*, a term that has the virtue of greater simplicity than *standard deviation*, which is also used in a different context—causing confusion.

10. Robert Franciosi, *The Rise and Fall of American Public Schools* (Westport, CT: Praeger, 2004).

11. L. A. Munday, *Declining Admissions Test Scores: ACT Research Report 71* (Iowa City, IA: American College Testing Program, 1976).

12. Described in appendix I.

13. See the discussion of French methodology in appendix II.

14. Marilyn Binkley, Keith Rust, and Trevor Wiliams, eds., *Reading Literacy in an International Perspective* (Washington DC: US Department of Education, National Center for Educational Statistics, 1997), http://nces.ed.gov/pubs97/97875.pdf.

15. http://discours.vie-publique.fr/notices/776000361.html: *"La definition et l'acquisition d'une même culture pour tous les jeunes francais qui iront tous désormais dans une même école et un collège identique est un élément essentiel d'unité de la société francaise et de reduction de l'inégalité des chances. Ce sera un élément essentiel du changement vers l'unité et la justice."*

16. The committee was presided over by Pierre Bourdieu and François Gros, and consisted of Pierre Baqué, Pierre Bergé, René Blanchet, Jacques Bouveresse, Jean-Claude Chevallier, Hubert Condamines, Didier DaCunha Castelle, Jacques Derrida, Philippe Joutard, Edmond Malinvaud, and François Mathey. See http://www.sauv.net/bourdgros.htm.

17. See http://www.sauv.net/bourdgros.htm for the text of the 1989 Bourdieu-Gros Report upon which the new law was based. "The growth of knowledge renders

vain the ambition of encyclopedism." "L'accroissement de la connaissance rend vaine l'ambition de l'encyclopédisme." In addition, the report defended the progressive idea of teaching general critical thinking skills: "Students are to be taught elementary logic, and, by the acquisition of habits of thought, the techniques and cognitive tools that are indispensable in conducting reasoning that is rigorous and thoughtful—those same general competences are required in the reading of texts." The statement about skills, assumed to be self-evident, is not backed up by any footnotes.

18. See Marc Le Bris, "L'École Primaire: Les Origines de l'Échec Scolaire," in Lafforgue and Lurçat, *La Débâcle de l'École.*

19. Ibid.

20. Jean-Claude Milner, *De l'École* (Paris: Éditions du Seuil, 1984); Nemo, *Jules Ferry.*

21. In the United States these methods are called "whole language" and "balanced literacy." Both are in contrast to "explicit phonics." The fierceness of the debates over these methods in the United States and in France is best explained by the underlying quasi-religious sentiment that naturalistic methods are conducive to happy, healthful development, whereas explicit analytical methods destroy the child's happiness and natural development. The religious origins of these sentiments are described in appendix I.

22. This paradox is discussed in Marc Le Bris's *Et Vos Enfants* and "L'École Primaire."

23. Jeremy Ahearne, *Intellectuals, Culture and Public Policy in France: Approaches from the Left* (Liverpool, UK: Liverpool University Press, 2010).

24. Pierre Bourdieu and Jean-Claude Passeron, *Les Héritiers: Les Étudiants et la Culture* (Paris: Les Éditions de Minuit, 1964).

25. See http://www.sauv.net/bourdgros.htm for the text of the 1989 Bourdieu-Gros Report.

26. Le Bris, "L'École Primaire."

27. Jean Foucambert, *L'École de Jules Ferry* (Paris: Editions Retz, 1986).

28. Besides individualism a complicating aim was "multiculturalism." It was felt to be intellectual imperialism to impose *Le Cid* on children from Portugal and North Africa. So one aim of Bourduieu-Gros was anti–cultural imperialism, placing the home culture on a nearly equal plane with the national public sphere—a suicidal move for national schools. See Francois-Xavier Bellamy, *Les Désherités ou l'Urgence de Transmettre* (Paris: Editions Plon, 2014).

29. This explanation is confirmed by the different demographic pattern for math. In that subject, all groups declined greatly, but in tandem. In language the decline was much greater among the poor than the rich. See page 5 of the report: *Note d'Information 08-38: Lire, Écrire, Compter: Les Performances des Élèves de CM2 à Vingt Ans d'Intervalle 1987–2007* (Paris: DEPP, 2008), http://www.education.gouv.fr/cid23433 /lire-ecrire-compter-les-performances-des-eleves-de-cm2-a-vingt-ans-d-intervale -1987-2007.html.

30. http://www.slecc.fr/GRIP/2011_positions_grip.pdf

31. Several years earlier, the public was informed in a more general and theoretical way by the following powerful books: Lurçat, *La Destruction*; Rachel Bouttonnet, *Journal d'une Institutrice Clandestine* (Paris: Ramsey, 2003).

32. Progressivism introduced its own language police. The word *lesson* (*leçon*) was out because its Latin root was connected with *lecture*—a method forbidden by progressivism whether American or French. As will be seen, well-done lectures are, on the contrary, very effective at all ages.

33. These doctrines contravene years of research going back to Jeanne Chall's seminal 1967 book *Learning to Read: The Great Debate*.

34. Le Bris, *Et Vos Enfants*.

35. http://www.slecc.fr/GRIP/2011_positions_grip.pdf

36. Nico Hirtt, "Pourquoi Sommes-Nous les Champions de l'Inégalité Scolaire? Aped (Appel pour une École Démocratique)," *Journal de l'Alpha*, 167–168, http://communaute-francaise.lire-et-ecrire.be/images/documents/pdf/analyses2009/pourquoi_sommes_nous_les_champions_de_l_inegalite.pdf. See also Le Monde March 12, 2013.

37. Bellamy, *Les Désherités*.

38. The full report (in Swedish) can be found at https://www.riksdagen.se/sv/Dokument-Lagar/Utredningar/Statens-offentliga-utredningar/Staten-far-inte-abdikera---om_H2B35/?html=true.

39. Op. cit. section 2.5.

40. "A change in the national curriculum in 1994 emphasised individualised learning over teacher instruction. A comprehensive study (in Swedish) published in 2010 found that this was among the most plausible explanations for the drop in student performance." S. H., "Education Reform: A Good Choice?" *The Economist*, Democracy in America blog, October 6, 2014, http://www.economist.com/blogs/democracyinamerica/2014/10/education-reform.

41. http://www.oru.se/PageFiles/11905/Towards%20a%20citizenship%20literacy.pdf

42. An English translation of the Swedish law of 1994 can be found at http://www.skolverket.se/publikationer?id=1070.

43. John Dewey, *How We Think* (Boston: D. C. Heath & Co., 1910).

44. http://www.skolverket.se/om-skolverket/andra-sprak-och-lattlast/in-english

45. Amory Burchard and Tilmann Wernecke, "Warum Deutschland sich verbessert hat" *Tagesspigel*, March 12, 2013, http://www.tagesspiegel.de/wissen/die-neue-pisa-studie-warum-deutschland-sich-verbessert-hat/9165012.html.

46. Gabriel H. Sahlgren, *Schooling for Money, IEA Discussion Paper 33* (London: Institute of Economic Affairs, 2010).

47. In 1967, Britain issued the Plowden Report. It encouraged schools to adopt progressivism, and they did, with disastrous results. I decided against discussing Britain, because the British in those days did not keep useful records. An excellent full-scale account from the available evidence is Robert Peal, *Progressively Worse: The Burden of Bad Ideas in British Schools* (London: Civitas, 2014).

48. Derek Gillard, "Education in England: A Brief History," 2011, http://www.educationengland.org.uk/history/chapter06.html.

49. "Doggerel by a Senior Citizen" (1969): "Dare any call Permissiveness / An educational success? / Saner those classrooms which I sat in, / Compelled to study Greek and Latin. / Though I suspect the term is crap, / There is a Generation Gap, / Who is to blame? — Those, old or young, / Who will not learn their Mother Tongue."

50. Neville Bennett, *Teaching Styles and Pupil Progress* (Cambridge, MA: Harvard University Press, 1976).

51. George Counts, "Dare Progressive Education Be Progressive?," *Progressive Education* 9, no 4. (1932).

52. The incoherent view of the currently popular theorist in American education schools, Paolo Friere.

53. *Providential individualism* is a more descriptive term than *romantic individualism* because it captures the naïve faith by the left and the right that things will work out well if they are allowed to follow their natural courses, as if guided by the hand of Providence. Rousseau and Adam Smith were born but eleven years apart. Both conceived that human affairs allowed to develop under proper conditions would work out well, as though by the invisible hand of Providence. A fuller discussion of the theme will be found in appendix I in a discussion of Hegel's influence on the new education.

Chapter 8

1. Joseph J. Ellis, *American Creation: Triumphs and Tragedies at the Founding of the Republic* (New York: Random House, 2007).

2. Ernest Gellner, *Nations and Nationalism* (Ithaca: Cornell University Press, 1983).

3. State and district standards, for example, do not qualify because they deliberately avoid detailed content in every subject except math.

4. I explain in the section on optimal vocabulary gain later in this chapter that vocabulary is a convenient index to knowledge and social competence. Even though knowledge and language are not identical, they are highly correlated.

5. Heather Tooley, "Merriam-Webster Dictionary 2015: New Words Added Include 'Photobomb, 'Jeggings,' 'Meme,' and Tons More," *Inquisitor*, May 27, 2015, http://www.inquisitr.com/2122792/merriam-webster-dictionary-2015-new-words-added-include-photobomb-jeggings-meme-and-tons-more/.

6. Alfred Lord Tennyson, "Morte d'Arthur."

7. Erika Hoff, "The Specificity of Environmental Influence: Socioeconomic Status Affects Early Vocabulary Development Via Maternal Speech," *Child Development* 74, no. 5 (September/October 2003): 1368–1378.

8. Keith E. Stanovich, "Matthew Effects in Reading: Some Consequences of Individual Differences in the Acquisition of Literacy," *Reading Research Quarterly* (Fall 1986): 360–407.

9. The PISA (Program for International Student Assessment) data show that this happens on a large scale in nations that have well-rounded primary schools. In a care-

fully planned two-week unit on, say, the solar system, all students gain key knowledge, but disadvantaged children gain more and learn more words. They were behind at the start of the unit, but rapidly gained knowledge and vocabulary as their topic familiarity grew. This compensatory process can only work if the knowledge differentials are moderate. Later, the gaps grow too wide. Organisation for Economic Co-operation and Development, *Strong Performers and Successful Reformers in Education: Lessons from PISA for the United States* (Paris: OECD, 2011).

10. The civics knowledge of twelfth graders continues to decline, according to the infrequently given NAEP test of civics knowledge. Back in 1987 in *Cultural Literacy*, I noted a sharp decline in civics knowledge, accompanied by a decline in patriotism. Currently, NAEP has indefinitely postponed tests in civics, US history, and geography for fourth and twelfth graders because of budget constraints, but will introduce an expensive test of technology and engineering literacy. Each subsequent test of civics knowledge has shown a decline among twelfth graders. Instead of abandoning the twelfth-grade civics and history tests, NAEP should give it every four years, and in addition should include a history and civics section on the reading tests. The idea that the schools of a nation where the people are supposed to rule themselves should neglect teaching the elemental principles upon which they should rule opens the door to the people being led by the nose.

11. Christopher Winship and Sanders Korenman, "Economic Success and the Evolution of Schooling and Mental Ability," in *Earning and Learning: How Schools Matter*, eds. Susan E. Mayer and Paul E. Peterson (Washington DC: Brookings, 1999).

12. http://coreknowledge.org/mimik/mimik_uploads/documents/33/Abstracts-FromResearch_1999.pdf; http://www.coreknowledge.org/mimik/mimik_uploads /documents/712/CK%20Early%20Literacy%20Pilot%203%2012%2012.pdf. It happens also in Finland and Japan where Core Knowledge–style schools are universal.

13. Thomas G. Sticht and James H. James, "Listening and Reading," in the *Handbook of Research on Reading* vol. 1, ed. P. David Pearson (London: Longman, 1984), 293–317.

14. The most efficient and therefore most pleasurable method of teaching decoding is called "synthetic phonics," now used widely in Great Britain. See Rhona Johnston and Joyce Watson, "The Effects of Synthetic Phonics Teaching on Reading and Spelling Attainment: A Seven-Year Longitudinal Study" (research report), February 11, 2005, http://www.scotland.gov.uk/Resource/Doc/36496/0023582.pdf.

15. These estimates are averages over grades K–6. "Word study" includes phonics in kindergarten and first grade. http://www.ucrl.utah.edu/researchers/pdf/reading _first.pdf; James F. Baumann, "Vocabulary and Reading Comprehension," in *Handbook of Research on Reading Comprehension*, eds. Susan E. Israel and Gerald G. Duffy (New York: Routledge, 2009), 323–346.

16. Thomas K. Landauer and Susan T. Dumais, "A Solution to Plato's Problem: The Latent Semantic Analysis Theory of Acquisition, Induction, and Representation of Knowledge," *Psychological Review* 104, no. 2 (April 1997): 211–240.

17. Isabel L. Beck, Margaret G. McKeown, and Linda Kucan, *Bringing Words to Life: Robust Vocabulary Instruction* (New York: Guilford Press, 2002).

18. William E. Nagy and Patricia A. Herman, "Breadth and Depth of Vocabulary Knowledge: Implications for Acquisition and Instruction," in Margaret G. McKeown and Mary E. Curtis, eds., *The Nature of Vocabulary Acquisition* (Hillsdale, NJ: Erlbaum, 1987), 19–35.

19. Japan is my favorite example, and an excerpt from its curriculum is offered in appendix III.

20. Diana Pulido, "The Effects of Topic Familiarity and Passage Sight Vocabulary on L2 Lexical Inferencing and Retention Through Reading," *Applied Linguistics* 28, no. 1 (2007): 66–86; Jessica S. Horst, Kelly L. Parsons, and Natasha M. Bryan, "Get the Story Straight: Contextual Repetition Promotes Word Learning from Storybooks," *Frontiers in Psychology* 2, no. 17 (2011).

21. John T. Guthrie et al., "Increasing Reading Comprehension and Engagement Through Concept-Oriented Reading Instruction [CORI]," *Journal of Educational Psychology* 96, no. 3 (2004): 403–423: "Using content goals in a conceptual theme consists of reading instruction with a complex knowledge domain (ecology, solar system, colonial America, westward expansion) sustained for at least several weeks." "In both studies, class-level analyses showed that students in CORI classrooms were higher than SI [strategy instruction] and/or TI [traditional instruction] students on measures of reading comprehension, reading motivation, and reading strategies."

22. For a discussion of "tier-one" words, see chapter 5.

23. James Samuel Coleman, Thomas Hoffer, and Sally Kilgore, *High School Achievement: Public, Catholic, and Private Schools Compared* (New York: Basic Books, 1989).

24. Karin Chenoweth, "Piece by Piece, How Schools Solved the Achievement Puzzle and Soared," *American Educator* (Fall 2009): 21. "As one student, who came to PS 124 after being in another school, said, 'I like this school better because you learn more things.'"

25. Karin Chenoweth, "Successful Schools Avoid False Choices," *Education Week*, October 14, 2009, http://www.edweek.org/ew/articles/2009/10/14/07chenoweth.h29.html. Student achievement at PS 124 is "almost indistinguishable from that of wealthy, white schools," Chenoweth notes, "despite the fact that more than 80 percent of its mostly African-American, Latino, and South Asian students qualify for free lunches."

26. George Herbert Mead, *Mind, Self, and Society: From the Standpoint of a Social Behaviorist*, ed. Charles W. Morris (Chicago: University of Chicago Press) 1934), 138. "The individual experiences himself as such, not directly, but only indirectly, from the particular standpoints of other individual members of the same social group."

27. See the reviews of research at coreknowledge.org.

28. Charles Sahm, "The Bronx Is Learning" (provisional title), *Education Next* xvi, no. 4 (August 2016).

29. Karin Chenoweth, *"It's Being Done": Academic Success in Unexpected Schools* (Cambridge, MA: Harvard Education Press, 2007); Karin Chenoweth, *How It's Being Done: Urgent Lessons from Unexpected Schools* (Cambridge, MA: Harvard Education Press, 2009); Karin Chenoweth, *Getting It Done: Leading Academic Success in Unexpected Schools* (Cambridge, MA: Harvard Education Press, 2011).

30. 2012 PISA, Volume III, "Introduction." See also http://www.oecd.org/pisa /keyfindings/pisa-2012-results-overview.pdf, which correlates superior results with applying "more universal policies to raise standards for all students." The first item mentioned: "These policies can involve altering the content and pace of the curriculum."

31. Jeanne S. Chall, *The Academic Achievement Challenge* (New York: Guildford Press, 2000). See also: http://www.aft.org/periodical/american-educator/spring-2001 /jeanne-challs-last-book.

32. As I write, a modest random-assignment, longitudinal study is being conducted in Colorado, under the guidance of the well-regarded researcher David Grissmer.

33. Javier C. Hernandez, "New York Schools Chief Advocates More 'Balanced Literacy'," *New York Times*, June 26, 2014, http://www.nytimes.com/2014/06/27 /nyregion/new-york-schools-chancellor-carmen-farina-advocates-more-balanced -literacy.html.

34. Recently a three-year randomized study, yet unpublished, was undertaken with Core Knowledge charter schools in Colorado with highly enticing positive results, but with too few students to yield high statistical confidence so far. All small comparative studies of Core Knowledge have yielded positive comparative results. For research summaries, consult www.coreknowledge.org. Also valuable are several books by Karin Chenoweth of the Education Trust, including *It's Being Done* (2007). In this chapter, I emphasize that the issue is not whether Core Knowledge as a specific curricular sequence can work well in schools; many examples prove that it can. The issue is whether that *kind* of curricular sequence in elementary school is superior to other proposed curricular schemes. The answer is "Yes, over the world, this has proved to be the most effective curricular scheme both in theory and in fact."

35. See the account of Monbusho (the Japanese Ministry of Education): http:// www.mext.go.jp/b_menu/hakusho/html/others/detail/1317440.htm.

36. For the important concept of "word fields" or semantic fields, see Laurel J. Brinton, *The Structure of Modern English: A Linguistic Introduction* (Amsterdam: John Benjamins Publishing Company, 2000).

37. http://krocam.com/should-the-core-knowledge-curriculum-be-used- throughout-the-school-district/

38. Curriculum-based tests are inherently fair. They possess "face validity." They are also inherently productive educationally. They have special virtues that aid learning: they motivate teachers to teach and students to learn the specific content, because all know that the required content will be the subject of the test. Subsequent test preparation further reinforces content learning, and the actual taking of the test is itself a helpful repetition and review of the content. Un-normed, ad hoc content tests are also

reliable. They exhibit a reliability of about .8, meaning that they are not only valid but also fair. Their educational advantages far outweigh the policy makers' dream of constantly comparing results across the nation. NAEP already does that well enough every four years. See Stephen G. Sireci, "On Validity Theory and Test Validation," *Educational Researcher* (November 2007): 477–481. See also the other articles in that issue devoted to testing.

Epilogue

1. Robert L. Thorndike, *Reading Comprehension Education in Fifteen Countries: An Empirical Study. International Studies in Evaluation III* (Stockholm: International Association for the Evaluation of Educational Achievement, 1973).

2. It scores below the 500 mark in all of the 2012 PISA tests of fifteen-year-olds.

3. According to the PISA results, Japan is a superb example, because right after the American occupiers left, Japanese schools abandoned American-style local control of elementary curricula and returned to a highly specific national curriculum on the grounds that it would work better in all respects. This was in fact the case.

4. Anders Ericsson and Robert Pool, *Peak: Secrets from the New Science of Expertise* (Boston: Houghton Mifflin, 2016), 60.

5. See Randolph Bourne's wonderful essay, "Trans-National America," *Atlantic Monthly* 118 (July 1916), 86–97.

6. Matthew Arnold, "The Function of Criticism at the Present Time," *The National Review*, November 1864.

7. The gold standard of random-assignment research has been the Tennessee STAR study into the effects of class size in the early grades. Despite its elaborate methodological punctiliousness, it has proved to be a poor guide to policy. There were unseen factors at work despite the random assignment of students. Causal insight from basic science is truly generalizable, and is thus a far more reliable guide to policy. Also large-scale epidemiological studies of whole nations and millions of students are more reliable than classroom-level studies.

8. Abraham Pais, *"Subtle Is the Lord": The Science and Life of Albert Einstein* (Oxford, UK: Oxford University Press, 1982), 19.

9. Google Translate understands this perfectly. It is constantly trying to improve the relevant domain knowledge in its vast memory by crowdsourcing—asking users to correct its translations. Bar Hillel argues that this will yield better approximations, but cannot yield uniformly reliable ones (Bar Hillel, "A Demonstration of the Nonfeasibility of Fully Automatic High Quality Translation," *Advances in Computers* 1 [1960]: 91–163). But in any case, if Google Translate over time does greatly improve through crowdsourcing, that will have simply confirmed the thesis of this book: that nothing is more valuable for language skills than a good, broad education.

10. The specific subject-matter topics would need to be published in concrete detail for all to see—the only honest and truly democratic approach, and one that is now carefully avoided.

Appendix I

1. Schiller had about the same time revised the "Ode to Joy," which Beethoven used as the famous finale to his Ninth Symphony. It praised joy for uniting once again "what custom had starkly sundered"—*Was die Mode streng geteilt*.

2. Mann, in his writings, credits the Swiss educator Pestalozzi (1746–1827), not Rousseau, for these ideas.

3. Marietta Johnson, *Thirty Years with an Idea* (Tuscaloosa: University of Alabama Press, 1974). The manuscript was completed just before her death in 1938.

4. Mrs. Johnson's famous school in Fairhope, Alabama, was a school for the well-to-do, for whom basic initiation into communal knowledge was scarcely needed. The dangerous social underside of the "natural development" idea is the unspoken sense that poor children are less able and have slower development. It is unspoken in print, perhaps, but not in actual conversations I have heard and in actual comments to me.

5. For a current account of where developmental psychology stands on the issue of "training" versus "growth," see Patricia M. Greenfield et al., "Cultural Pathways Through Universal Development," *Annual Review of Psychology* 54 (2003): 461–490. The upshot: growth requires external training in humans, according to the culture they are educated into in every human group. That conclusion became inevitable once the unspoken dimension of language use became understood in the 1960s.

6. StateUniversity.com, "Horace Mann (1796–1859)—Education and Training, Career and Contribution," http://education.stateuniversity.com/pages/2197/Mann-Horace-1796-1859.html#ixzz3nhpqvvhD.

7. George Gordon Lord Byron, *Childe Harold's Pilgrimage* (1818).

8. Jo Ann Boydston, ed., *The Early Works of John Dewey, 1882–1898, Volume 2: 1887—Psychology* (Carbondale: Southern Illinois University Press, 1967),174.

9. William Wordsworth, "Lines Composed a Few Miles above Tintern Abbey, On Revisiting the Banks of the Wye during a Tour. July 13, 1798."

10. The publication date was 1850, after Wordsworth's death, and with many subsequent, doctrinally purified revisions. The 1805 version is separately available today, along with an earlier first section from 1799.

11. The 1905 study by Dilthey is found in Dilthey, "Die Jugendgeschichte Hegels; und andere Abhandlungen zur Geschichte des deutschen Idealismus," *Gessamelte Scriften* 4 (Stuttgart, Germany: Teubner, 1961), 238.

12. John Dewey, *Democracy and Education* (New York: Macmillan, 1916).

13. Baroness Stäel Holstein, *Germany* (London: John Murray, 1813).

14. "When asked if his system was based on Hegel's dialectical theory, Froebel responded that he had not studied Hegel's work, but that the whole meaning of his own system rested upon this law alone. It is almost certain that he picked up on Hegel's ideas, which were widely circulated in German universities during Froebel's era." Eugene F. Provenzo, Jr., "Friedrich Froebel's Gifts," *American Journal of Play* (Summer 2009).

15. An excellent short entry on Susan Blow is found in the online Encyclopedia of Education at http://education.stateuniversity.com/pages/1792/Blow-Susan-1843

-1916.html. Both Blow and Harris (and Hegel himself) opposed the child-centered, naturalistic approach to schooling.

16. Jack K. Campbell, *Colonel Francis W. Parker, the Children's Crusader* (New York: Teachers College Press, 1967).

17. Francis W. Parker, *Talks on Pedagogics* (New York and Chicago: E. L. Kellogg & Co., 1894), 384. This sounds like Schelling, who was a big influence on Froebel. So it's possible that, indirectly, Schelling's simpler version of pantheism (which Hegel called "the night in which all cows are black") was the most important indirect influence of all. Certainly Schelling was the chief influence on Coleridge, whose theory of imagination young Dewey adopted without attribution.

18. Boydston, *Early Works of John Dewey*, 157.

19. Ibid., 171.

20. Just as Dewey echoes Coleridge on imagination, so did Coleridge echo Hegel's friend and romantic philosopher, Friedrich Schelling. (Whole passages from Coleridge's book are unacknowledged translations from Schelling.) As an aside: the subject of my doctoral dissertation half a century ago was Schelling and Wordsworth.

21. See Steven Rockefeller, "Neo-Hegelian Idealism and the New Psychology," in *John Dewey: Religious Faith and Democratic Humanism* (New York: Columbia University Press, 1991). This is the best treatment of Dewey's relation to Hegel. Rockefeller concedes the pantheistic tendencies of Dewey's thought. (p. 116.). See also John R. Shook and James A. Good, *John Dewey's Philosophy of Spirit, with the 1897 Lecture on Hegel* (New York: Fordham University Press, 2010); David I. Waddington, "Uncovering Hegelian Connections: A New Look at Dewey's Early Educational Ideas," *Education and Culture* 26, no. 1 (2010): 67–81.

22. *Democracy and Education*, chapter 5: "Froebel and Hegel, the authors of the two philosophic schemes referred to, have different ideas of the path by which the progressive realization or manifestation of the complete principle is effected. According to Hegel, it is worked out through a series of historical institutions which embody the different factors in the Absolute. According to Froebel, the actuating force is the presentation of symbols, largely mathematical, corresponding to the essential traits of the Absolute . . . [Froebel] failed to see that growing is growth, developing is development, and consequently placed the emphasis upon the completed product."

23. Paul Tough, *How Children Succeed* (New York: Houghton Mifflin Harcourt, 2012).

24. http://www.nytimes.com/2014/06/27/nyregion/new-york-schools-chancellor -carmen-farina-advocates-more-balanced-literacy.html

25. Hannah Arendt, "The Crisis in Education," *Partisan Review* 25, no. 4 (1958): 493. "It has first of all made it possible for that complex of modern educational theories which originated in Middle Europe and consists of an astounding hodgepodge of sense and nonsense to accomplish, under the banner of progressive education, a most radical revolution in the whole system of education."

Appendix III

1. Harold W. Stevenson and James W. Stigler, *Learning Gap: Why Our Schools Are Failing and What We Can Learn from Japanese and Chinese Education* (New York: Touchstone, 1992).

2. https://www.youtube.com/watch?v=Tpr6Q2FsJyE

3. "Open covenants" was the first of President Woodrow Wilson's "Fourteen Points" presented to Congress in 1917 regarding the principles for the peace settlement after World War I.

ACKNOWLEDGMENTS

By the ninth decade of life one's intellectual obligations are so numerous and vaguely remembered that many key influences have been forgotten. Between this final book of mine and the one preceding it, *The Making of Americans*, one decisive influencer has died. That was George A. Miller, whose writings about short-term memory and word learning first alerted me in the 1970s to decisive contributions of modern cognitive psychology to verbal comprehension and the achievement gap. His personal encouragement helped me stick to my guns through the culture wars of the '90s.

Then from Robyn Dawes in 1980 I first learned of the path-breaking chess experiments of Adriaan de Groot, later developed by the great Herbert A. Simon. About that same time, Walter Kintsch made clear to me the role of tacit knowledge in verbal communication. My mind had been prepared for the insights of these researchers by the analytical work of Dilthey, de Saussure, and Husserl—decisive thinkers for me in the '60s and '70s. Only gradually have I come to appreciate the full depth and brilliance of Antonio Gramsci's scattered remarks on modern education, which, combined with Ernest Gellner's observations on nations and national cultures, have formed my view of the nature and purposes of modern schooling.

I would never have dared to write about the crucial influence of Hegel on twentieth-century American education without having slogged through Hegel in my youth in George Schrader's wonderful yearlong graduate course at Yale on Hegel's *Phenomenology*. That was followed by Frederick Pottle's oversight of my doctoral dissertation on Wordsworth and Hegel's friend and rival Friedrich Schelling, both big influences on Froebel, all of them thinkers well known and important to the leaders of American educational thought in the late nineteenth and early twentieth centuries. For further insight into that thought my obligations are to Lawrence Cremin and Diane Ravitch, the latter well quoted in the text. For insight into John Dewey's thought I'm especially grateful to Robert Westbrook and Stephen Rockefeller. The latter was especially helpful on John Dewey's early pantheism.

My more immediate gratitude extends to those who have helped form this book. Five knowledgeable colleagues have commented trenchantly on more than one version of the manuscript. They are Chester E. Finn, Jr., Lisa Hansel, John Hirsch, Sol Stern, and Daniel Willingham. To them I offer specially warm and affectionate thanks. This book got helpful organizational ideas from Ann Huebner.

Its final organization only gradually became clear after trenchant criticisms from two anonymous Harvard Education Press readers and, above all, from the penetrating suggestions of its genial and accomplished chief editor, Caroline Chauncey. Her organizational advice was decisive.

My talented son-in-law Pino Trogu has kindly redrawn all of the charts.

Others have helped me greatly in improving the substance: John Ballen, Joseph Buttigieg, John Hirsch, Ted Hirsch, Joel Klein, Nathan Kuncel, Laurent Lafforgue, Valarie Lewis (who kindly contributed an account of PS 124), Peter Meyer, Robert Pondiscio, Charlene Sedgwick, Louisa Spencer, and David Steiner. The infelicities and inaccuracies are my own.

The book is dedicated to the sustaining memory of my dear wife Polly, who was the chief critic of my earlier books, and whose sharp common sense will be missed by readers of this one.

ABOUT THE AUTHOR

E. D. Hirsch, Jr., is the author of numerous books, including the bestsellers *Cultural Literacy* and *The Dictionary of Cultural Literacy* (both Houghton Mifflin). Other books by Hirsch on related subjects are *A First Dictionary of Cultural Literacy* (Mariner); the Core Knowledge Sequence, *What Your [First Through Sixth] Grader Needs to Know* (Doubleday); *The Schools We Need and Why We Don't Have Them* (Anchor); and most recently, *The Making of Americans* (Yale University Press). These works have influenced recent educational thought and practice in the United States and other countries.

Hirsch is a graduate of Cornell University, and holds master's and doctoral degrees from Yale University. He began his teaching career at Yale, specializing in Romantic Poetry and Literary Theory, and in 1966 became Professor of English at the University of Virginia, where he served twice as chairman of his department. Before his retirement in 2000 he held the position of University Professor of Education and Humanities. In 1977, he was elected to the American Academy of Arts and Sciences and in 1997 to the International Academy of Education. He is the recipient of several honorary degrees, has been a Fulbright and a Guggenheim fellow, a fellow of the Center for Advanced Study in the Behavioral Sciences at Stanford University, a Humanities fellow at Princeton University, a fellow at the Australian National University, and an honoree of the Royal Dutch Academy and of the National Academy in Rome. He received the biennial QuEST award of the American Federation of Teachers in 1997, and the Fordham Award for Valor in Education in 2003. In 2012, the Education Commission of the States presented Hirsch with the Conant Award for "Outstanding Contributions to American Education." He has served on many advisory boards, including the National Council on Educational Research.

Hirsch is founder of the nonprofit Core Knowledge Foundation, an organization that continues to advise and help schools, with over one thousand Core Knowledge schools in forty-seven states and abroad.

INDEX